THE
SPECTATOR
ANNUAL

THE SPECTATOR ANNUAL

Edited by Dominic Lawson

HarperCollins*Publishers*

HarperCollins*Publishers*
77–85 Fulham Palace Road
Hammersmith, London W6 8JB

Published by HarperCollins*Publishers* 1992
1 3 5 7 9 8 6 4 2

A catalogue record for this book is
available from the British Library

ISBN 0 00 255160 8

Set in Trump Mediaeval

Printed in Great Britain by
Butler & Tanner Ltd, Frome and London

CONTENTS

FOREWORD

Keith Waterhouse

What gives *The Spectator* its staying power? I happen to be writing these lines in the week that *Punch* ceased publication, aged 150 (but still fourteen years *The Spectator*'s junior). The obituarists were almost at one in diagnosing that, our national taste in humour having changed, *Punch* was seen off by *Private Eye* and *Viz*. My belief is that *Punch* was seen off by itself. It was never really bought for its jokes: it was bought because, like shopping at Harrods and honey still for tea, it jigsawed into the lifestyle of the kind of people who read it. When *Punch* decided to re-vamp itself and go for a younger, brasher readership, it was as if Simpson's in the Strand had gone over to serving Big Macs.

If *The Spectator*, while it has had the odd facelift over the years, has never been tempted towards throwing itself out with the bathwater, it must be because it thoroughly knows its audience – which is the kind of audience you would expect to find reading *The Spectator*. Just as you can spot a *Sun* reader at ten paces, so you can identify a *Spectator* reader one minute into any casual conversation in crush bar or railway carriage or over Sunday morning drinks. Like the *New Yorker* (from which Mr Punch might have learned a few lessons), *The Spectator* has changed with the times, yet it remains its essential, unalterable self. Were an epitaph ever to be required for this estimable organ, and I would not advise any stonemason to waste a good slab of marble in anticipation, it could be contained in the one word 'Civilised'.

One test of a good magazine is how long you want to keep it after you have read it from cover to cover: in my house *The Spectator* gets shelf room until the magazine table begins to creak. Few people seem to bind up their mags any more (ready-made binders with that mandolin arrangement of strings are not the same as binding) and it is an expensive process: I read of a rock star who paid £16,000 to have his complete run of *Rolling Stone* bound in leather. Failing a chunky yearly volume the weight and thickness of a family Bible, the *Annual* is the next best or even the better thing. It contains the essence without the ephemera or the ads, and it is easier to read in bed.

It is also capsule confirmation of my point that *The Spectator* does move on. Here, after his début appearance in last year's *Annual*, is Theodore Dalrymple reflecting (or rather deflecting) the new obsession with health; Mary Killen guiding us through the quagmire of modern manners; and the Unlettered feature reminding us that out there is also a great uncharted bog of illiteracy. All the longer-serving, get-your-knees-brown columnists are here of course, and the Diary is well-represented, as it should be – as fascinating and self-revealing (and I do not say this because a couple of my own paragraphs have survived into the *Annual*) as *Desert Island Discs* without the records. The foreign and political stuff is as strongly offbeat as it ever was, and – but there is an admirable contents list for all this sort of thing. What I do want to mention, as a fuming commuter, is that among the rich social miscellania, and worth the price of admission alone, Joanna Coles's piece will haunt the Little Hitlers of the Permanent Way. Don't read it in bed – read it on the train.

HALFWAY THERE

Jeffrey Bernard

Legal complications are preventing me from moving into the new flat in Soho. I am staying in what could be called the Hotel Limbo. I don't quite know why I called them legal 'complications' for it all seems terribly simple to me – a matter of signing an agreement – but lawyers don't work that way. Witness how long it takes for an injured party to get damages. Thirty years ago I was knocked down by a car travelling on the wrong side of the road. I had to wait two years to collect a lousy £100. Anyway, I am near the end of my ever-shortening tether but at least I am no longer waking up in ghastly West Hampstead and phoning for a mini-cab to come and drive me away from it.

What I fear now is that the management of the Limbo will get sick of the sight of me and ask me to find another halfway house. All I have with me at the moment is the hideous portable Monica, two shirts which drive me back and forth to the laundry every day, half a bottle of vodka and a packet of razors. A chambermaid brings me tea every morning at 7.30 and then if I don't have to assault Monica I go and sit outside the Bar Italia and drink coffee, watch the world go by and listen to *Rigoletto* until the sun is over my adjustable yard-arm. The boss of the Bar Italia, Tony, has a video of *Rigoletto* and he plays it most mornings. How good it is to find somebody addicted to Verdi and not the produce of Colombia.

A strange collection of people passes through Frith Street in the course of a morning. There is Jo-Jo, a Maltese oddjobman who was once seen climbing a steep staircase with an enormous refrigerator on his back. He has been here for donkey's years but, like most of the Cypriots here, can barely speak English. Then we have Ali from somewhere fractionally east of India who drinks whisky all day out of miniatures. He once aimed a righthander at me in the betting shop but was off target. I think he's on the far side of bonkers. Then one day last week I met a man called Alfie who must be the only man in Soho to know about and talk sense about racing.

And sitting at my table outside the Bar Italia yesterday I was approached by a teenager who asked me for a penny. I said, 'What the hell do you want a penny for? You can't buy anything with it.' He said, 'I am saving up for a motorbike,' and I told him, 'If you don't ask people for more than a penny, it will take you a hundred years to get one.' I gave him the wretched coin and he then said, 'You see, I like to do things the hard way,' and he walked away whistling. The hard way? Extraordinary.

So after about three large coffees it is cocktail time and I stagger to the Coach and Horses (I still haven't bought that walking stick) and hope to bump into Roxy Beaujolais, who manages the Soho Brasserie, on the way. A delightful attractive Australian woman – I keep meaning to ask her why and how she came to invent such a marvellous name. It smacks to me of the name of a sexy torch singer in a 1940s Hollywood movie. Anyway, she is aces.

And then it is Norman's. I wonder when they will come to take him away. First it was the book, then it was going on the Terry Wogan show and now, last Sunday, he officially opened the Soho Fair. Will fame go to his head, I hear you ask? It has, it has. He stands or struts behind the bar now like Captain Bligh eyeing a mutinous rabble. Paranoia has set in and he talks to his staff in a way reminiscent of Hitler addressing a Nuremberg rally. And he has achieved it all on Coca-Cola. There's a lesson there somewhere.

20 July 1991

WHAT WOMEN REALLY WANT

Michael Lewis

About a year ago I had a call from an editor at *Glamour* magazine, who was conducting an unscientific poll of the sexual tastes of American men. 'What is it about a woman that makes you want to go to bed with her?' she asked. Until then I had never considered the question. 'The ability to touch her nose with her tongue,' I said, as a guess. But the lady was serious, and refused to accept a flip answer. She became aggressive. She wanted the Truth.

After a moment I said that I was sorry, but that there was no Truth. These were mysterious matters that couldn't be settled so simply. 'Pleeeeease!' she said. 'OK,' I said, recognising the distress of a fellow journalist on deadline, 'just put, "I am attracted to anyone with the good sense not to want to go to bed with me."' Two months later I appeared along with nine other men in a special issue of *Glamour* devoted to 'What men really want in bed'. To the horror of my mother-in-law I was quoted saying that 'nothing turns me on as much as the unobtainable woman who refuses to go to bed with me'.

My mother-in-law and I had nearly overcome the trauma of my first exposure to the bizarre world of women's magazines, when there came a second. While researching an article for *The Spectator*, I visited a London accountancy firm. At first it seemed like any other firm of accountants. Clean-cut men in dark suits bustled boringly in and out of the reception area, wondering how much more they could bill their clients without being sued for fraud. The worried clients soon arrived to fill the seats around me. Not long after the house was full, the seemingly innocuous receptionist raised to her eyes a copy of *Cosmopolitan* magazine. 'THE NEW RULES OF ORAL SEX' it shouted in print bold enough to be read from a moving taxi. We men – who knew nothing of rules – shrivelled in our chairs and tried not to notice, but it was hard.

One recovered. One very nearly returned to a happy, well-adjusted sexual life. Until last week. This time the women's magazine industry struck at my wife's firm on Fenchurch Street, in the heart of the City. Sometime on Thursday yet another seemingly harmless British receptionist made her way to the office photocopy machine with a copy of *Company*, yet another women's magazine. It contains an article called 'Rogues' Gallery: The full frontal picture guide that proves they're not all the same!' The point is illustrated by photographs of 36 different penises, each inscribed in red ink with nicknames: String Bean, Chopper, Love Truncheon, Donger, Blue Veined Piccolo, Joy Stick, Weapon, and so on. The magazine's editors shrunk the hapless organs to fit into 1.5 × 1.5 inch boxes, then laid the boxes neatly in a 6 × 6 grid.

Alas, the photocopied 'joy sticks' came out slightly blurred. Angry and frustrated, the receptionist tossed the blurry copies face up in the dustbin. There they remained, staring forlornly at the ceiling, waiting for the Chairman to spot them. How would he react? wondered some of my wife's colleagues; in a single stroke the receptionist had subverted the office hierarchy. Most likely, he would merely blush and flee to his office until the photocopied penises disappeared of their own accord. Fortunately, he never looked down.

What is it with women's magazines? Is it something in the water? The impression that they cater to a new sexual aggression in their readers is reinforced by a selection of coverlines from the issues currently on British news-stands. SEX AND EXERCISE: IF YOU WANT MORE OF ONE YOU'D BETTER DO MORE OF THE OTHER! (*She* magazine). Why men STILL can't get it right in bed (*Options* magazine). CAN'T GET ENOUGH: CONFESSIONS OF A SEX ADDICT (*New Woman* magazine). The Smart Girl's Guide to Sex. (*More!* magazine, motto: Smart Girls Get *More!*). HIS SEXUAL FANTASIES: how you fit in; MEATY, BEEFY, BIG AND BOUNCY: why every man wishes he was. YES YOU CAN MAKE GOOD SEX BETTER: your hands-on guide to his body, top to bottom (*Company* magazine). Even the putatively high-brow *Marie Claire* carries one piece called SEX IN EUROPE, and another, perhaps even more revealing, called THE WOMAN WHO MURDERED MEN.

With one or two exceptions these magazines make no pretence of being anything but fodder for female sexual fantasies; their male equivalents are *Playboy* and *Penthouse*. This much is clear from the way their editors speak of them. 'Women's magazines are extremely raunchy at the moment,' the editor of *New Woman* recently told the *Independent*, 'we are getting away with stuff we would never have even dared run in the past.' The advice columns, the horoscopes, the features – all are intended for the dedicated man-user. Even the ads for women's clothing tend to depict the pouting model in a come-hither pose, with her clothing falling off.

Of course the obsession with sex is nothing new, even if it has previously tended to manifest itself in women as an obsession with avoiding it rather than with having as much as possible. It is the nature of the sexual obsession found in women's magazines that is so strange. It is almost entirely lacking in old-fashioned romance. One searches the current issues in vain for love-struck men playing lutes on white horses. The magazines assume that their readers reduce matters of the heart to a political science problem: how to manipulate men so they do the things you need. 'Re-organise your priorities so sex is much, much higher on your mental list of things to do,' reads one magazine advice column; another is titled 'Getting your teeth into oral sex'. The troubadour's songs have given way to impersonal tools from jelly-flavoured condoms to Dyna Bands, a miraculous piece of rubber that promises a 'fabulous figure in only ten minutes a day'.

Like many politico-technical advisers (the Foreign Office springs to mind) the women's magazines tend to become so involved in the process that the problem becomes secondary. They contain an astonishing volume of weird, irrelevant information, much of it dubiously sourced, such as *Glamour*'s 'What Men Really Want in Bed'. Sixty-eight per cent of *Company*'s readers say they feel more like having sex on holiday; 61 per cent sunbathe topless. From *Marie Claire* we learn 50 per cent of British women have never performed oral sex, and that 25 per cent of British men have never been on the receiving end; 90 per cent of *New Woman*'s readers say that they 'would try anything once'. *Glamour* offers readers data on the changing annual frequency of men's orgasms over time:

Age 20: 104 per year (49 solo)
Age 30: 121 per year (10 solo)
Age 40: 84 per year (8 solo)
Age 50: 52 per year (2 solo)

Asking why anyone needs to know any of this is like asking why the new maths student carries ten different colour pens in his shirt pocket. Or why the skier snowploughing down the beginners' slope has such expensive, long skis and elegant clothing. The newly aggressive woman is what is known in mechanical circles as a gear freak.

Perhaps that explains why the British receptionist reads so unself-consciously about oral sex. Sex to her is not so much a matter of love, or even secret pleasure, but an urgent quest for self-realisation. The women's magazines are ultimately not about sex so much as the politics of the bedroom. If one didn't know better one might think that the magazines were dreamed up by feminists. But, of course, the conventional feminists are appalled by the importance the magazines attach to men. The British receptionist doesn't mean to terrorise men with her sexual independence. That is why her magazines are so frightening.

27 July 1991

DON'T LET THE TRAIN TAKE THE STRAIN

Joanna Coles

The apology was delivered in the usual British Rail monotone. 'Due to the late arrival of a connecting service from Glasgow this train will be 20 minutes late.' I didn't really mind. I like long train journeys and I was sitting comfortably in first class, having taken advantage of BR's £3 Weekend First Supplement. Edinburgh Waverley to London King's Cross is usually efficient (four and a half hours) and, late to bed the previous evening, I was asleep within ten minutes of leaving the station.

Some 20 minutes later I was woken by a commotion at the other end of the carriage. Various annoyed passengers were being forced by the conductor to move seats, in fact to move coaches. From what I could gather there had been some confusion in the seat bookings and the conductor was evidently in a strop.

Still, having taken the precaution of booking a seat at Waverley, and confident that I was actually sitting in it, I was not unduly perturbed. Until, that is, the conductor arrived at my side, demanded my ticket, and ordered me to move back a carriage. 'I'll have to ask you to move,' he said, 'because I like to keep one coach exclusively for full paying first-class passengers. We can't expect them to pay full first-class fare and then have budget first-class passengers alongside.'

Somewhat taken aback by this reasoning, I pointed out that my seat had been issued by BR that morning and that having also paid to reserve it I was not prepared to move. The conductor, a Mr Baptie, acknowledged that he knew it was BR's error but nevertheless *I* would have to pay for the mistake. I could stay in the seat, he proclaimed, but I would have to give him my home address so that BR could forward a bill for the full first-class fare (£162.00).

At first I had thought he was joking, but his face was beginning to fill with red anger. So I explained politely that on no account would I give him my home address but I gave him my business card. It was a work trip, the *Guardian* had paid for the ticket and I was quite sure it would refuse to make up the difference. At this point he became almost incoherent with rage. 'It's in the Senior Ticket Inspectors' Handbook,' he shouted. 'What is?' I asked. 'The rules, the rules,' he roared, snatching my ticket and throwing down a piece of paper declaring my ticket had been withdrawn. My work address was no use and if I wouldn't give him my home one then he would call the police.

At this point the cellist, Steven Isserlis, who was sitting opposite and who had been giving a BBC broadcast from the Edinburgh Festival that morning, offered me his cello's seat, for which he had a full first-class ticket (ironically issued in compensation for a previous BR mix-up). Mr Baptie became apoplectic. Such an exchange was quite illegal. He was calling the police, who would *deal* with me at Newcastle. 'Fine,'

I said, not really believing him and certainly not believing that any constable would take him seriously. I began to doze off as the man across the aisle, who had also reserved his seat that morning, was giving his home address, a false one verified by an out-of-date driving licence, he later told me.

I awoke 90 minutes later as we were pulling into Newcastle station and there, sure enough, waiting on the platform, were two uniformed members of the British Transport Police. One minute later Mr Baptie bounded down the coach with one of them in tow. 'Here we are, sir, I told you I'd bring the police,' he cried in glee. Mr Isserlis pointed out that I was actually female and would thus be more appropriately addressed as 'miss' or 'madam'. 'I mean madam. This is her, officer.'

I opened my mouth and was just about to explain when the six-foot officer told me in no uncertain terms to hand over my address. Again, I tried to explain but after letting me finish my second sentence he told me it is 'an offence not to give a British Rail employee your address'.

By now I was becoming rather upset. I felt I had been intimidated and told the officer I was sure no policeman would advise any single woman to give her home address in such circumstances.

This time it was his turn to get cross. If I wanted to make a complaint against a BR employee I would have to deal with BR. 'Your work address won't do. And if you give a false one we'll trace you through work and prosecute you.'

Fellow travellers started to remonstrate on my behalf. Mr Isserlis offered me his cello's seat again. 'If you do that you'll both be breaking the law,' warned PC 2068. 'It's an offence to transfer tickets.' Then he added, apropos of nothing, 'Actually, it's an offence for a husband to buy a ticket and give it to his wife.' The man across the aisle snorted with laughter, Mr Baptie and the officer bridled and I had to pinch myself to make sure I was actually on a train rather than still stuck in some piece of fringe performance art.

PC 2068 broke first. 'Right,' he snapped. 'I must ask you to accompany me off the train. If you don't give your address now you will be charged with obstructing the police with their enquiries.'

I gave in. By now the train was around 50 minutes late, I didn't want to hold it up further and I did want to get home. 'How can you tell if I'm giving you a real address?' I enquired. Again, threats of prosecution. 'Why aren't you trying to catch rapists instead of hassling innocent passengers?' someone murmured. No response. Instead the constable pushed a coffee-stained BR napkin across the table. 'Surely I need to write it on something more official than that?' I queried, suddenly feeling contrite. But the napkin was about as official as Mr Baptie got.

He pocketed it with relish. 'I shall complain,' I said, feeling humiliated that I had given in so easily. 'You do that,' sneered PC 2068. 'Why don't you write to your MP?'

We pulled out of Newcastle several minutes later. Fighting the urge to burst into tears I went to buy a sandwich, which proved a fruitless exercise as the buffet car had run out of them, with two and a half hours' worth of journey still to go. It was either chicken Madras or honey and almond flapjack. I settled for a cup of tea. 'I've run out of cutlery,' moaned the steward. 'I've been told to improvise.'

I didn't see Mr Baptie again. At Peterborough, running two hours and ten minutes late, we picked up several hundred passengers from the previous Edinburgh train which had broken down. Had he bothered to come into our carriage Mr Baptie would have found them sitting on the floor – the compartment was so crowded – hardly first-class behaviour. Swapping tales of Japanese passengers who once lynched a driver after a Tokyo train was seven minutes behind schedule, we eventually limped into King's Cross, precisely 50 minutes late.

31 August 1991

DIARY

Jilly Cooper

Oblong bales of straw litter the fields like school trunks on a station platform. One advantage of boarding school is that nothing will ever be as bad again as the going back. I suspect it is less harrowing today: 'Mummy cried so much at the beginning of last term,' a small boy told me, 'that I felt I ought to cry too to make her feel better.' Amy, returning to the Royal School, Bath, seemed so excited that her mother reproachfully asked her if she preferred school to home. To which Amy replied after a long pause, 'Well, that's a difficult one, Mummy.' Today, children seem to get away with anything. I remember a kindly housemaster unsuspectingly helping my son Felix to carry a laundry basket groaning with booze up to his study. That was the same term that Felix smuggled in my long black Sixties wig as a disguise for

'Women, my dear Angela, keep diaries. Men
keep journals.'

when he sloped off to the pub. Private schools are, of course, businesses reluctant to expel any pupil unless really necessary. One of the lines cut out of the recent television programme on Eton was when a friend's son complained bitterly that, 'If one is caught in bed with a girl here, one gets sacked, but if it's a boy, one only gets two hours' gardening.' Returning from Gozo, Felix bemoans the lack of betting shops, but is delighted that the might of communism has been toppled by Boris Yeltsin: 'Rather like Goliath and that little kid he used to hang around with.' So much for private education.

Thanks to the gentle enthusiasm of my instructor, Peter Clarkson from Painswick, I am actually enjoying learning to drive. Together we explore the splendours of the Gloucestershire countryside and get so engrossed discussing Disraeli's *Sybil* or Princess Michael's new Harpo Marx hairstyle, that we fail to notice a half-mile tailback of cars behind us. Peter's pupils range from schoolboys who collapse on the steering wheel moaning they've been tripping all night, to an intrepid Chinese lady who has clocked up 100 lessons. Progress is impeded because she is avidly househunting and keeps rally-driving the car up rockeries of Cheltenham bungalows and sending the latest status-symbol garden gnomes with cordless telephones flying as she jerks across the lawn slap into some kitchen-dinette window. Without the aid of dual control, my own family are less sanguine about taking me driving. Despite having taught Africans to drive lorries during the Mau Mau crisis, Leo is the most nervous, claiming people can only do things by instinct. 'But even Mozart must have had to learn the piano in the beginning,' I say crossly as the car stalls noisily at a crossroads. 'Mozart,' says Leo heavily, 'was not in the business of killing people.' So, irritated, I lose concentration. Next minute the car chassis is propped at 80 degrees against a steep bank, the dog and I are biting the tarmac out of side windows and Leo hangs above us from his seat-belt, purple in the face and furiously mouthing. Mutter that I've always wanted a husband I can look up to. Even the dog joins in the hysterical laughter.

7 September 1991

IF SYMPTOMS PERSIST . . .

Theodore Dalrymple

In the course of my brilliant career I have done a little medical research, and twice I nearly discovered something. Not that discovery is the point of most medical research: publication is. A monkey with a typewriter (according to the theological argument from design) may be expected to type Shakespeare purely by chance after 50 billion years at the keyboard; but his luck with medical papers would be considerably greater. Within a fraction of that time, in fact, he could deluge the world with his scientific observations.

Statistics are at the root of the problem. They are the philosopher's stone which makes publishable the results of any experiment, no matter how trivial. If a correlation between two variables is unlikely to have arisen by chance, it is called *statistically significant*; but unfortunately, statistical significance is no guarantee of significance in any other sense. Indeed, if enough variables are measured, some of them will have statistically significant correlations which are in fact coincidental. That is why scientific observations must be repeated; and why scientific advance is not necessarily proportional to the rate at which scientific papers are published.

Last week, I walked on to our general medical wards to find a young man shouting at a helpless old lady. At first, I wondered whether our society had sunk so low that muggers now entered our hospitals to mug bedridden victims of strokes; but I soon realised that the young man was, in fact, a research assistant.

'Do you feel your situation is hopeless?' he shouted at the old lady through the cotsides of the bed. 'Yes or no?'

Alas, the old lady had lost the power of coherent speech. She could only grunt dysphasically.

'This is terrible,' the research assistant murmured. 'I'll be here all day at this rate, and I've got 15 more to do.'

I asked him what he was doing, and he told me he was administering a questionnaire to patients over the age of 75 to find out whether they grew happier or sadder in the course of their stay in hospital.

He showed me the questionnaire. The only answers allowed were yes or no. People were asked to sum up eight decades of existence with affirmative or negative monosyllables. 'Do you feel your life has been a success?' 'Do you wish you'd done things differently?' 'Does anyone visit you?'

'My last patient,' said the research assistant, 'was sitting in a chair, eating a banana. When I asked him a question, all that happened was a stream of molten banana dribbled out of the corner of his mouth. Is that yes or no?'

What were all these questions for? An ambitious doctor needed publications to further his career, and had hired a research assistant. The answers to the questions would be fed into a computer and correlations generated.

I was reminded of a student nurse I once knew who was anxious to prove her zeal to the ward sister. The sister had ordered her to feed Mr Jones, who was not very well and consequently could not feed himself. I watched her try unsuccessfully to push grapefruit into his mouth, while explaining how good Vitamin C was for him. The grapefruit dribbled down his chin. I went over to the nurse, who was growing quite cross.

'Nurse,' I said. 'I may be mistaken, but I think Mr Jones is dead.'

7 September 1991

LIFE AND LETTERS

SOURCE OF CONSOLATIONS

P. J. Kavanagh

If a writer is asked by a publisher to put together a collection of 'consolations', excerpts from writings of all periods, ones which he considers likely to encourage, or raise the flagging spirits, he knows that the first essential is to avoid sentimentality; one whiff would invalidate the enterprise. When he has put together his selection, reasonably to his own satisfaction, and that of his publishers, should he then discover that those publishers intend to slap onto it a dust-jacket more suitable for the Collected Thoughts of Patience Strong, or the Commonplace Book of an Edwardian Lady, in stark contradiction of its contents; the kind of cover that will make his friends and enemies say, with secret satisfaction, 'Alas, poor P. J. We always suspected he might become the Beverley Nichols *de nos jours*,' the only reaction is to weep, or rage – or go to find the source of the River Wye.

From that walk we are just returned, me to find the proof of the jacket still winking from the kitchen table, but now I am fortified, even consoled.

In truth we probably make a pretty odd couple now, Laurence Whitfield, my old Severn companion, and I. We walked the length of the Severn together, from estuary to source, doing it in short stretches each year. It took us about 10 and now he is getting a little what he calls 'mutt and jeff' and I have to keep on my 'distance' glasses almost permanently, in case I walk into a fence. We reached the source on Plinlimon, a magical place, last year, and there we had such an odd experience it gave us the idea for a further journey.

Then, after a long pull up Plinlimon's bleakness, among the buzzards and the staring sheep, we found we were lost. The source of the Severn was on our map but we were still just off it, so we did not know where we were. We set off to the west, and were saved by the sudden materialisation, it seemed from nowhere in that deserted place, where you can see in every direction for miles, of what we had to presume was a man, who put us in the right, eastern direction, frowned at our not having a compass, muttered sternly that he would always *begin* from the Source, and then vanished as queerly as he had arrived. Shamed, we continued on our corrected way, wondering at this visitation, and concluding that, true to himself, he had disappeared down the hill to the source of the Wye, which is a couple of miles below that of the Severn. Taking his rebuke to heart, enchanted by wild Plinlimon, we resolved to do this ourselves, next year.

So, this year, the day dawned (it was the middle of the coup in Moscow, another reason for being briefly out of earshot of the speculating world) and we drove to Llangurig, to the Blue Bell, booked the taxi-man, 'Merve the Swerve', to take us to the lonely farm at the foot of Plinlimon, and looked forward to renewing our acquaintance with that magic mountain.

He duly drove us there, very fast, as though we were dangerous and he wanted to be rid of us, and we began our climb, over sheep-nibbled whins, incredulous stonechats climbing on fences to have a look at us. It had rained heavily all night, and we were climbing into cloud – again, we had forgotten a compass – but the Wye is easier to find than the Severn, and at the point where our angelic helper had disappeared, the sun breaking through, and what seemed the whole of empty Wales at our shoulders, we climbed down towards it, congratulating ourselves, asking each other why other people seemed never to come to this extraordinary place. We were soon to find out.

Buzzards planed against the wind down the valley and then allowed themselves to be blown back, as though, said Laurie, they had discovered the secret of perpetual motion. We saw a red kite. The young river was joyous, as young rivers are, and sometimes slowed into clear pools, striped with curves of foam like a Bridget Riley painting. After a while the rocks sprouted purple foxgloves.

But young rivers are greedy, they feed from all sides, and here the solid green banks suddenly sprouted marsh-grass, then bright green sphagnum, then, most dangerous of all, a minutely flowering bog plant that gave a rust-coloured effect, and among that you are soon up to your knees in red mud. We were forced to take wider and wider detours to avoid this, away from the river, but even high up we stumbled into unsuspected wet. We had the answer to our question about why more people did not come here. My consolatory sallies were lost on mutt and jeff Laurie and, although I could hear his sighs of despond as he fell into another slough, I could not see him because my distance glasses were mud-splashed and had steamed up. Then came green tussocks whose high plumes concealed the ankle-turning cavities between. And we grew tired of walking the slope, feet at angles of 45 degrees.

At last there was a dust road, and meadow-pipits queuing up to stare at us, as the stonechats had done, flitting just ahead of us and stopping to stare again. Then a footpath marked, along the bank, which turned out to have been closed by the Secretary of State 10 days previously, so the Notice told us, on which the Solicitor of the Council, in Llandridnod Wells, kindly instructed us the way we should now go, but it seemed too complicated so we took no notice and soon we were in bogs again, and green secret glades. Brown to the knees, wet shoes causing unsuspected abrasions, I considered the Russian question, and gave it as my opinion that Gorbachev, whatever happened, was forever discredited. I said this to a grunting sow which had appeared from behind a clump of hazels.

There followed a long trudge along the A44 to Llangurig, lorries blowing our hats off as they passed. No matter, we had made acquaintance with the young Wye, felt we had almost taken possession of it. Nobody but a fool (in waders) would walk that stretch of it, but we had done so, for the world, and felt consoled. At the Blue Bell we learned that Gorbachev had returned, about the time we were wondering at the companionable pipits. 'I knew he would,' said the egg-delivery man, ordering himself a double Bacardi and lemonade. And I had misinformed the sow. Perhaps it was the double Bacardi but the egg-man went out briefly and came back to report that he had dropped the tail-gate of his van on a crate of eggs. The next stretch of the river, to Rhyader, looked bogless and enticing.

7 September 1991

CITY AND SUBURBAN

THE HON ALSO RISES

Christopher Fildes

You would expect to find Mitford girls in the Hons' cupboard, but it is not the first place I would look for a captain of industry. Some field-marshals of industry now disagree; the captains are their sons. The cupboard (Nancy Mitford described it in *The Pursuit of Love*) was full of the giggling daughters of noblemen – the Hon. Linda, the Hon. Jassy, even the Hon. Fanny. Their boardroom equivalents are the Hon. Rocco, the Hon. Robert and the Hon. Simon, whose ennobled fathers run Forte, Hanson and the General Electric Company. These Hons are not gigglers. Rocco Forte, whether as chief executive of Forte or as a director of the Savoy (it was a term of the Forte–Savoy armistice), maintains a lugubrious appearance. Robert Hanson has just graduated to the Hanson board from the corporate finance department of N. M. Rothschild, where you learn how to keep a straight face. Simon Weinstock's public appearances are rare. He too served his time in a merchant bank, S. G. Warburg. He was seen the other day at the annual meeting of GEC, when he was re-elected to the board. He is the commercial director. His father, Lord (Arnold) Weinstock, has been managing director since the early 1960s, and has for much of the time been the most formidable industrialist in this country. He has left the chairmanship to others – as a job for political grandees, or, once, as an incentive in swinging a deal – but no one doubts where, in GEC, power lies. Lord Weinstock is in his later sixties, and it is now apparent that his own choice of successor would be called Weinstock: the Hon. Simon.

Rocco and Robert . . .

I worry about this Honnery. Dynasties have their place in business life – you expect to find Rothschilds at Rothschild and Hambros at Hambros, and there are enough of them to quarrel with their cousins and still staff the banks. In a family business (your own family, or someone else's) you know where you are. Forte, Hanson or GEC are not, though, family businesses. These are major public companies whose ownership is widely dispersed – republics, where the succession to power may still be hereditary. Lord Forte, who remains executive chairman at the age of 82, is king of the company that has borne his name since he had Trust Houses crossed off, and his son is the crown prince. The Hon. Rocco is in his forties, has a degree and an accountancy qualification, and has come up through the company. It seems almost pointless to ask how far he would have got if he had been called Rocco Jones. Hanson as a company still behaves as if succession were a question that has yet to arise. Big, strong and ambitious enough to have set its sights on Imperial Chemical Industries, it is dominated by the two noble bidders, Lord Hanson and Lord White. They have contracts which will keep them going until they are well into their seventies. There is no obvious successor at hand in the group. If the lords stay the course, and if the Hon. Robert trains on, he could in theory be left with a clear run. In practice, life and business are chancier than that.

... and Simon too

GEC, though, has let time go by and left the succession open while the Hon. Simon has been given the chance to train on. That has a touch of the British electrical industry as it used to be run, before Arnold Weinstock turned up to give it the shock of its life. Three big companies dominated the scene 30 years ago: GEC, Associated Electrical Industries and English Electric. At GEC Lord Hirst had laid down that the succession must come from the families. It had reached his 70-year-old son-in-law before GEC took over a promising company called Radio & Allied, and Arnold Weinstock with it. At AEI, the grandee chairman, Lord Chandos, left his management succession

'This is a stuck-up!'

in a muddle which AEI never resolved. At English Electric, the practical chairman, George Nelson, who became Lord Nelson of Stafford, was succeeded by his son, 'Young George' or 'Half-Nelson'. Within a decade the young Weinstock had forced his way to the top of GEC and taken the other two companies over. He cleared out whole boardrooms, scrapped rule by committee, and sold the palatial head offices. He made his managers take personal responsibility – for better or worse. He watched their performance beadily, and kept the closest of grips on their cash. Staff numbers fell, financial numbers rose. No one ever thought that working for him would be cosy, but a new generation in business modelled its style on his. Style alone, though, cannot deliver the goods, and in the 1980s GEC's results and its share price began to move sideways. The decade of privatisation found GEC too dependent on the public sector. Doubts over the succession dragged on. Big investors began to grumble, though none of them had the nerve to do more. In financial markets Lord Weinstock remains a fearsome opponent. His clash with Plessey, which threatened to challenge his own position, ended with Plessey in GEC's grasp and its ruling family, the Clarks, knocked out. 'The City', Sir John Clark told a House of Lords committee, 'took my company away.' It was not his company. It was a major public company whose ownership was widely dispersed. He was the chairman, like his father before him. It is dangerous for a steward to mistake himself for an owner. He may be tempted to look for the next steward in the Hons' cupboard. At Forte, barring a bid, the succession seems to be cut and dried. At Hanson, we shall have to see whether the two lords will carry on, jaunty as ever, running the group in their eighth decades, or whether ICI's counter-attacks on their style – that subsidiary which owned racehorses to race in Lord White's name – will leave their mark. All is still to play for. At GEC, I suspect that the cycle has come round, and that it now needs, as it needed when Lord Weinstock first arrived, not Hons but rebels.

14 September 1991

LOW LIFE

RICE WITH EVERYTHING

Jeffrey Bernard

At long last the Westminster Hospital has fixed me up with some home help. The said help is a very pleasant woman, originally from Granada, who comes in every morning at 9.30 to wash me, dress me and clear up whatever is lying about. She is very valuable, as are my nieces and the bombshell from the Soho Brasserie, Roxy Beaujolais. Try putting on a pair of trousers, tucking a shirt in at the same time, with one hand. You can't. When Josey finally zips me up I find it depressingly symbolic of the age I have reached. There was a time . . . Oh well.

Anyway, the minor inconveniences that go with a broken arm and elbow are getting me down. I can't peel a potato, although Josey would if I could carry some home, so it is rice with everything. Also I got stuck in Wandsworth last Monday when I should have been meeting David Gower for a drink in the Groucho Club. What a glorious batsman he is. I was choked that we didn't meet up. Apparently he sent me his regards and told them that he hopes I recover soon, although he doesn't know me. He reads *The Spectator*, however. I wonder what Ian Botham reads. The *Sun*? Perhaps that conjecture isn't fair but he sometimes bats as though he does.

But, apart from providing home help, the Westminster Hospital is driving me mad. Everything they do takes two hours, right down to the trivial business of getting a prescription for pain-killing tablets. I am afraid that vodka doesn't work for pains worse than the petty ones of divorce, bereavement or moving house. And the tablets don't go with vodka although I am trying to teach them to do so.

The last time I wrote here I forgot to tell you about the strange chat I overheard in the West Suffolk Hospital in Bury St Edmunds. In the next cubicle a small boy was having his ears syringed out and being quizzed by a doctor. It transpired that while he had been fast asleep the night before, his brother had crept into his room and filled his ears with peanut butter. I knew there must be some use for the stuff. But it is rather extraordinary how our various orifices fascinate children and I thank God that I am not a banana.

Meanwhile, Norman's mother – the poor old thing is 93 – is in hospital with a broken hip caused by a fall. That can be a serious business at her age but she seems to be coming along okay. What tickles the number one son is the fact that she thinks she is in an hotel. She swears she will never come back to it and that it is not as good as the Miami Hilton. He has offered to look after her rings but dementia stops there and she will not let go of the £50,000 job that we have all had our eyes on for some time now.

Norman is a kind but sometimes embarrassing hospital visitor, paying calls as he does to every bed in the ward and then announcing in a loud voice gloomy prognoses on the doomed inmates. 'He hasn't got long,' is his usual verdict. He should wear a black cap on his hospital rounds.

And now Josey has just left, telling me that I am very brave. She should hear me moaning in the night. I am just a baby in long trousers with what she takes to be a glass of water in one hand. I wish I could take her on full-time.

14 September 1991

DIARY

Jilly Cooper

I sat next to a delightful caterer at a polo match who told me he used to do state dinners at Downing Street and that Mrs Thatcher's passionate involvement at all levels inspired his staff. The emphasis was on plain food perfectly cooked. Mrs Thatcher's secret was to refuse second helpings of this wonderful grub, but press them on her guests. Then, when their mouths were full, she could belabour whatever point she wanted to make uninterrupted. She only appeared fazed once, when President Reagan stirred his coffee with a gold fountain pen. But as a waitress shot forward with a teaspoon on a tray, Reagan foxily revealed the pen was a container for sweeteners.

When I first interviewed Mrs Thatcher in 1976, a photograph had just appeared in the papers of Denis's first wife. 'My dear,' Mrs Thatcher told me, 'I was amazed how like me she was.' Not only had she never before seen a photo of the first wife, but, not wanting to hurt Denis, had never questioned him about her, which shows staggering self-restraint. Today, ripped untimely from the seat of power, Mrs Thatcher is behaving exactly like a first wife who cannot stop telling the second wife and everyone else how the electorate like creases in the front of their boxer-shorts and their broccoli *al dente*. But in Mrs Thatcher's case, the electorate didn't have a chance to 'stand by her', as the *Sun* would call it, before a second marriage had been arranged.

14 September 1991

ACID REIGN

Stephen Anderton

I motored homeward with the crowd
That sits on tails and queues up hills
When all at once, – I cried aloud –
Another slab of daffodils;
Despite the salt, beneath the trees,
Where'er I looked, this bright disease.

Continuous as the cars that grind
and rumble all the working day,
They stretched their never-blending kinds
Along the urban motorway:
Ten thousand saw I at a glance
Nodding their heads, St Vitus' dance.

The sun above them flamed; but they
Upstaged the sun chromatically;
My eyes could not be dragged away,
From this naive and trite display.
I gazed – and gazed – but little thought
What loss to me the show had brought.

For oft, when on my couch I lie
In what should be a pensive mood,
They flash upon that inward eye,
That vegetable platitude!
And then my heart with horror fills
and winces at the daffodils.

14 September 1991

NASTY, BRITISH AND SHORT

Theodore Dalrymple

I live in a wasteland. In the council estates, the glass of many of the windows has been replaced by plywood; such gardens as there are have reverted to grey-green scrub, with empty beer and soft drink cans, used condoms and loose sheets of tabloid newspaper in place of flowers; and the people trudge through the desolation as disconsolately as in any communist (or formerly communist) land.

When I visit such an estate, my first problem is to find the street in which my patient lives. The road signs have generally been removed or defaced beyond recognition, and the residents do not know the names of the streets next to theirs; to ask the way is pointless. In any case, councils up and down the country have devised a method of naming and numbering streets which is incomprehensible to anyone but a thought-disordered schizophrenic. Streets change their names halfway along for no reason whatever, and runs of even-numbered houses are replaced by runs of odd-numbered ones. The woman who lives in No 129 does not know where No 129A is, which is where the patient lives. 129A turns out to be on another street altogether (but mysteriously of the same name). Everything is disorientatingly arbitrary, just as bureaucrats like it: compared with the average British public housing estate, the Cretan Labyrinth was a model of classical regularity.

Here, if anywhere, is where the rioting underclass lives and takes its being. Women shuffle along in jumble sale clothes and fly-paper curlers, prematurely undergoing the physical shrinkage of old age, a cigarette attached by dried saliva to their lower lip; young men, bodily mature but with the mind and inclinations of juvenile barbarians, eye the world with sullen hostility, which the tattoos on their knuckles, necks and forearms not infrequently express in words. They are unemployed and often profoundly unemployable: they are intolerant of any external restraint on their behaviour, and cannot fix their minds upon anything for more than a few moments. What job could one give them?

This is a world in which schools not merely fail to educate, but are actually anti-educational establishments. I ask my young patients about their experiences at school, and they are depressingly uniform: violence, boredom, indiscipline, insolence, intimidation, truancy and a determination to bring everyone down to the same abysmal level. Any effort to achieve is treated as treachery, and if persisted in leads itself to violence. I meet many teachers also, and essentially they tell the same story.

Teachers soon come to have the same outlook as prison governors: to survive a day without serious incident is a success or even a triumph. There is no question of imparting knowledge: schooling is a form of remand in custody. A teacher told me of a recent circular from the headmaster of his school reminding staff that physical force was not to be used on pupils, *except in self-defence*. The same teacher told me about a recent parent–teacher meeting at his school: the parents of five out of 110 pupils found time away from their videos to attend. He telephoned the father of one of his pupils whose progress had been particularly poor (or whose regression to barbarity was particularly marked).

'I'm your son's class teacher,' he said.

'Are you?' came the reply. 'Well you can fuck off then.' And the father slammed the receiver down.

Stories such as this (which I hear almost every day) render the recently broadcast suggestion by Baroness Blackstone that more training was required for the underclass, not merely inadequate but laughable, the modern liberal equivalent of holding a religious procession to halt the progress of the plague. (In similar vein, Baroness Blackstone, Chairman of the Institute for Public Policy Research, remarked that one of the reasons why she 'could not condone' the recent riots was that they took place in the deprived areas where the rioters themselves lived, as if to say that it would have been more acceptable if the rioters had vented their spleen on more prosperous areas.)

Yet it is far too comforting to suppose that the moral collapse I have described is confined to a small underclass of 5 or 10 per cent of the population, the mirror-image, perhaps, of a small and highly educated elite. In the first place, the underclass is extensive and not readily distinguishable from the rest of the population; in the second place, more alarmingly still, the pauperisation of the minds and spirit of our people extends well beyond the confines of any such underclass.

Whenever my foreign friends come to this country, they are struck – even if they come from countries much poorer than Britain – by two things about the British: the first is their crushed and defeated demeanour, the second the extreme ugliness of their lives. Just as my foreign friends confirm my judgment that British food resolutely remains the least appetising in the civilised world, so they confirm my observation from clinical practice that, taken all in all, the British are spiritually, culturally and emotionally the most impoverished people in the world, compared with whom the slum dwellers of Mexico City or the tribesmen of the Congo (both of whom I have observed at first hand) lead fulfilling lives.

The problem is both philosophical and psychological, and is to be cured neither by pills nor by public spending.

The corrosive ideal of social justice has been etched on to the psyche of the British so that it has become the good that is the *sine qua non* of all other goods. If society is unjust, anything goes. The assumption of personal responsibility can be postponed until social justice (always defined by its absence, for defining it positively is rather difficult) has been attained. In the meantime, one can behave abominably, yet feel aggrieved.

I meet a combination of aggressive irresponsibility and self-righteous resentment among patients almost every day. Mothers with four children by three different fathers complain accusingly that their lives are difficult, as though something else were to be expected. The deficiency is not a cognitive one: they know where babies come from and they know about contraception. Our hospital serves a quarter of the city, and 70 per cent of the children born here are illegitimate. Either bastardy is not confined to the underclass, or the underclass is much larger than commonly supposed.

But surely, I hear liberals sigh, you don't want to bring back *stigma*? After all, there is no intrinsic reason why unmarried parents should not look after their children perfectly well: to which I reply that many surgical operations can be performed on the kitchen table, but that is no reason why they should not be performed in hospital. I live in a world so liberal that no stigma attaches to anything (with the exception of constructive effort at school). But a world without penalties, where anything and everything is both understood and forgiven, and where everyone expects rewards irrespective of his or her own behaviour, is a nightmare world without meaning.

Last week I was consulted by a woman whose husband had left her. He said he wanted a divorce, but that if the court ordered him to pay maintenance for his three children, he would cease working rather than comply. At the same time, he would demand access to his children, *as of right*. I have no doubt he will get away with it. In the wasteland, rights multiply, but duties wither away.

In the absence of a system of values, adolescent revolt has become a permanent state of mind. The lack of belief in anything is compensated for by shrillness, as if mere noise could fill the inner void. The malaise is not confined to an underclass: every week I meet members of the middle classes who consider themselves victims of some injustice or other in order to lend significance to their lives. But they are only victims in the sense that Marie Antoinette was a shepherdess.

The attempt to find transcendent meaning in social justice has strange consequences. It destroys or perverts aesthetic appreciation: for how, it is asked, can beauty and injustice subsist in the same world? The aggressive ugliness (not mere lack of taste) of the mode of dress of many of my younger patients, especially those with intellectual pretensions, is intended to provoke the very rejection that will then be used to justify the resentment that gives meaning to otherwise meaningless life.

I recently treated the daughter of a quite senior diplomat who complained that society was too intolerant to see beyond her appearance. As this consisted of hair dyed red and done into spikes, a steel ring through her nose, black boxing boots and black culottes, and a multi-coloured serpent tattooed on her forearm, I remarked – mildly, in the circumstances – that she seemed rather reluctant to compromise with society in this regard. She flared up and said that so intolerant a society was rotten. By what historical standard, I asked, or by comparison with what ideal?

There was no social justice, she said: some were rich while many were poor.

It took only a short Socratic dialogue to discover that her indignation was not strictly proportional to her knowledge of history or the coherence of her moral standpoint. One did not have to be Freud, either, to discover that her essentially personal dissatisfactions (of the kind attendant upon life) were projected on to society as a whole. This projection, of course, has its advantages: it absolves one of the often painful necessity of self-examination. But it breeds the angry passivity that is now almost a national characteristic.

It is an ill wind that blows nobody any good. A passive population that considers itself victimised by society is distinctly advantageous to certain groups, among them politicians who promise salvation

'It's just me: the man you love to hate.'

and professional humanitarians who regard self-reliance as a petty bourgeois vice. When Mr Hattersley thunders that something must be done for the underclass, he reinforces the mindset that makes it the underclass in the first place. (The Chinese in Britain are not a racial minority precisely because they refuse to play the role of victim that the humanitarians would like to cast for them.) When Mr Des Wilson fulminates at the Liberal Democrat party conference against the terrible corruption of the British political system – as if Britain were Peru or North Korea – he reinforces the notion that political power in a liberal democracy is all-important, when it is precisely the glory of liberal democracy that politics are *not* all-important. When Baroness Blackstone calls for job creation, she implies that the number of jobs (unless the Government intervenes) is a fixed quantity, independent of the quality, inclinations and proclivities of the people seeking them. Meanwhile, millions of people are waiting for Godot.

There appears to me to have been a terrible deterioration in the character of the British people over the last few decades. I know that people have been saying this kind of thing for centuries, but this does not prevent it from being true at some time in history, and we live in such a time. The sullenness of many of my young patients is not mere adolescent rebellion, it is a permanent condition: they will not grow to courtesy. They do not have the dignity or self-respect of previous generations which have known suffering that is not self-inflicted. Persuaded of their rights, they think that authority is continually cheating them.

No doubt Thatcherism will be held responsible, but the deterioration was evident many years before her advent to power – which changed nothing. Mrs Thatcher was an epiphenomenon in the life of the British people. The mother-in-law of the nation spoke much, but achieved little. She was unable to defeat what has become the essential British addiction: blaming others.

No complex phenomenon has simple causes. The decline of religious belief in Britain, which provided a basis for personal responsibility, occurred at the same time as a decline in our world power. Intellectuals, impotently enraged by this, mocked at every value and belief, without providing alternatives. Unlike France, which remained the standard-bearer of a language and a culture, Britain was turned into a province, a deep humiliation for a country which had been metropolitan for two centuries. Our young people have been deliberately deprived of any knowledge of British achievement: they know nothing (I have asked them) of Shakespeare and Dickens, Newton and Darwin, Brunel and

Lister. They know of nothing of which they can feel proud. They have been left with a culture that is not a culture, but a form of ruminant grazing. They believe life is, or should be, a video film.

A nurse from one of my wards recently returned from a holiday in Hong Kong. It opened her eyes. 'The trouble with this country,' she said, 'is not the Government. It's the people.'

21 September 1991

AND ANOTHER THING

LEND ME YOUR MOISTURISER, OLD GIRL

Paul Johnson

'Perfume for men has arrived', states an ad in the current issue of *Tatler*. A poll taken by Fabergé suggests that men are spending longer in the bathroom each morning and making increasing use of cosmetics to improve their appearance. Hair-gel, mousse, moisturiser, hand and cold cream, even scent – often borrowed from their wives – are being furtively but daily applied to male skins. No doubt the poll is self-serving but it confirms the evidence of my own nose and eyes. At a lunch party not long ago, I noticed at least two men who had been using make-up. Like most trends, it started in America. If, in a big city like Chicago or San Francisco, you travel down in a hotel lift around 7.30 in the morning with a phalanx of male executives heading for key breakfast appointments, the stench of toiletries is overpowering.

Are we witnessing the start of one of those great historical shifts in relations between the sexes? Until the 1820s, in most Western societies, men and women competed shamelessly to spend time, money and trouble on their personal appearance. They made equal use of glittering fabrics, strong or delicate colours, jewellery and gilt, wigs, creams and powders, and both whalebone and padding. If you look at the paintings of, say, Nicholas Hilliard or Van Dyck, it is, on the whole, the men who dazzle. Puritan interludes, as during the Commonwealth of the 1650s, affected women no less than men, thus keeping the battle of the sexes equal, and they did not last long. By 1663, that old curmudgeon Anthony Wood was complaining that men were spending more on their appearance than women, and making use of scent and cosmetics, including face-patches. He said that the officers of Charles II's Life Guards were among the worst offenders. The attempts of the sexes to outdazzle each other continued throughout the 18th century.

Jane Austen, as always, was quick to scent the wind of change. In *Persuasion* (written 1815–16), she contrasted the plain, masculine naval officers she admired (two of her brothers rose to be admirals) with the silly, scented Regency buck, Sir Walter Elliot. Sir Walter regarded himself as an authority on beauty, male and female, and the means to enhance it. He was devoted to Mrs Vincent Gowland's skin-creams. When his daughter Anne arrives in Bath, he compliments her on her improved appearance. 'Had she been using anything in particular?' 'No, nothing.' 'Merely Gowland,' he supposed. 'No, nothing at all.' 'Ha! He was surprised at that', adding that he recommended 'the constant use of Gowland during the spring months'. Sir Walter, who liked to lounge around Bath, on the lookout for handsome men as well as women, arm-in-arm with his friend Colonel Wallis ('Fine military figure, though sandy-haired'), was particularly hard on the appearance of naval officers. There was poor Admiral Baldwin, only 40, but 'his face the colour of mahogany, rough and rugged to the last degree, all lines and wrinkles, nine grey hairs of a side, and nothing but a dab of powder at top'. By contrast, Admiral Croft, who rents Sir Walter's house, complains to Anne that her father seemed 'rather a dressy sort of fellow for his time of life'. He had to get his wife Sophy to help him shift all 'the large looking-glasses' from his dressing-room.

But, *pace* Sir Walter, even admirals took a lot of trouble with their appearance. The daughter of Sir Edward Codrington, victor of Navarino, left a description of watching her father put on his powder, while she would sit 'reading to him one of Miss Edgeworth's charming little stories', her father correcting her punctuation as she did so: 'There was the white powdering cloth spread out on the carpet, the powder-puff which seemed to me to be a fairy's work, the matter-of-fact powder-knife which cleared off the fairy's work from forehead and temples.' This was the last period during which men could scrutinise the physical beauty of their own sex without being accused of homosexuality. The artist-diarist Farrington records a large, all-male breakfast at which 'Gregson the Pugilist' was displayed in the front drawing-room, stripped naked, to be admired 'on account of the fineness of his form'. Farrington also went with Sir Thomas

Lawrence, the portrait-painter, to inspect a 'handsome black man' who turned out to have 'the finest figure they had ever seen'. Ladies could comment on a man's shoulders, waist and legs without seeming bold. Legs, particularly calves, were much scrutinised at dances. The Wordsworths were mortally offended when Thomas de Quincey, whom they had befriended, wrote a magazine article criticising the poet's legs, and said he ought to have two pairs, one for walking and 'another for evening dress parties, when no boots lend their friendly aid to mask our imperfections from female rigorists'.

All this began to go when the revolution in male dress introduced by Brummel got a grip. True, he introduced the strap over the instep which stretched trousers tight (and caused Pope Pius VII to ban them as obscene), but in general he hated colours, favoured black, white and grey for men, and stressed the importance of cleanliness, daily baths, frequent changes of linen, and diet. He vetoed scents, unguents, grease and hair-oil, and thus prepared the way for the ultra-masculine male who took over in Victorian times. When I was a young man, only homosexuals used cosmetics. Once, up in London from Oxford for a dance, I found myself having to share a room with a queen of 25 or so. He behaved impeccably but I was fascinated to watch him make up in the morning: it took him half an hour, about par for a girl-model today. This phase in human history, when ordinary males put up with presenting their beauty unaided, has lasted about 150 years and was bound to end. Television has played a potent part in the change. Since politicians and other celebrities discovered the improvement make-up could bring to their appearance, they have been tempted to make discreet use of it even off the box. It is spreading rapidly, in my observation, along with the more obvious use of bright colours, glitter and jewellery among young males. It is only a matter of time before traditional male evening dress goes for good, and we are back among the silks and satins. And, when mousse and moisturiser march for men, can wigs be far behind?

21 September 1991

A CONUNDRUM SOLVED

A. L. Rowse

When James Joyce died in 1941 T. S. Eliot wrote a letter to *The Times* to protest against the inadequacy of its obituary notice. Courteous as always, he proposed 'one or two cautious qualifications'. The letter was not published, so a fortnight later he wrote to the paper to say that he felt free to publish his letter elsewhere. Thereupon the Obituaries Department returned his original letter with the usual excuse that restrictions of space had made publication impossible.

Eliot then composed a much stronger letter which he saw fit not to send. He had toned down his original letter to something bland which *The Times* would print, hoping that 'it might get by as an "Appreciation"'. Now he took up his pen to say what he really thought. 'I have read with stupefaction your obituary notice on the greatest man of letters of my generation.'

This time he did not pull his punches but read *The Times* a lesson. If they wanted to save space they could have done so by omitting the trivialities they had descended to. Such 'notices should be written by the right persons in the beginning', and he proceeded to give them several useful points of advice as to how it should be done. He ended with a reproof lest people should 'believe that England has lost respect for that one of the arts for which it has been chiefly renowned'. One sees Eliot expressing his feeling of responsibility for the well-being of literature in his time.

When he published these two letters together in *Horizon*, he did so under the curious title, 'A Message to the Fish'. What did he mean by this? Eliot was fond of crossword puzzles, and the answer to the conundrum is to be found in a poem of Lewis Carroll, in *Through the Looking Glass*:

> I sent a message to the fish:
> I told them 'This is what I wish.'
> The little fishes of the sea,
> They sent an answer back to me.
> The little fishes' answer was
> 'We cannot do it, Sir, because –'
> I sent to them again to say

'It will be better to obey.'
I told them once, I told them twice:
They would not listen to advice.

I do not know if this little piece of mystification has been explained before; but it is worth recording as the kind of esoteric joke that Eliot liked.

21 September 1991

HIGH LIFE

WHERE CHARITY BEGINS

Taki

Mykonos

I was not surprised to read that John Latsis has given £2 million to the Conservative Party to help smooth its cash crisis. Here's a man who bought the old Aspinall's Curzon mansion and offered it to the Saudi government (it was accepted), who regularly gives large amounts of money to various royals and who earlier this year made Bridgewater House (his London headquarters) available to the G7 summit leaders in exchange for having his picture taken while he stood between President Bush and the Queen.

In view of the fact that the Tory Party is far more important than money-grubbing royals and oil-rich towelheads, in my not so humble opinion the oily Greek has done a very good thing. After all, he's been accused of many things, but being dumb is not one of them. Mind you, it could all be a false alarm, although his past record makes me believe the story.

He pulled his first stunt on his elementary school teacher. Having been told that he was not about to pass his final exams, he approached the school principal with a large turkey and told him that this was all the Latsis family possessed in the world and they were giving it to the principal in order to show him how important it was for young John to go on to a higher school. The principal told the teacher to pass him despite the fact that Latsis never attended classes. A turkey back then was worth much more than, say, a cow is today. Once the results were published the principal was visited by a tearful Latsis who admitted having given the turkey away without his father's permission. He said he feared for his life if the old man discovered the theft. The result of the story was that Latsis not only passed his exams, he also got to keep the turkey.

Latsis has dined out on this one in the past, but was more reluctant to discuss the reasons his sister married the village policeman some 50 years ago. The *mauvaises langues* have it that the fuzz caught the future tycoon messing about with a caique. Latsis offered the cop his sister, and they lived happily ever after.

'Couldn't you wait until our guests have gone
before you revert to your normal self?'

True or false, it has all been published in the Greek press and it's fodder for sidewalk café gossip, which believes that Latsis always comes out on top, but it is a long way from, say, Athens in 461 BC. That is when the ancient city was run by Pericles, the champion of a universally accepted moral law, the promoter and sustainer of *sophrosyne*, moderation. Moderate Latsis is not. Nor is he all that moral in his philanthropy. Giving to the rich in order to become even richer in return is not what charity should be all about. When Latsis bought the Niarchos yacht for the then unheard-of price of 35 million greenbacks and gave it to King Fahd, it was not because the fat one was in need of a boat. In Arabic it's called *baksheesh*.

Still, he's a generous man whose contribution to the Conservative Party I thoroughly approve of. By now he's so rich he probably wants nothing in return, except perhaps an honorary knighthood, like Getty's. And speaking of honorary knighthoods, I wonder what my chances might have been had I not landed in Pentonville. After all, I've been wining and dining the needy at Annabel's for more than a quarter of a century, and that's a lot longer than Latsis has been dining the needy royals.

21 September 1991

YOUR PROBLEMS SOLVED

DEAR MARY . . .

Mary Killen

Q. I am a 34-year-old bachelor. Because I am supposed to be eligible, I am always being asked by women I meet at dinner and drinks parties if I am married and if not why not. I do not know the answer to this, nor am I that keen on being drawn into discussion of the subject with someone I have just met – though I realise the question is often posed flirtatiously. How can I swiftly close the subject without seeming rude?

N. S., W11

A. In the more casual and ephemeral atmosphere of a drinks party you could answer the question 'Are you married?' with an enigmatic but conclusive 'Not exactly.' At a dinner party it would be safer to allow an emotional rigour to come over your face before you whisper the answer, 'Ask me that question again in four weeks' time.' You can continue giving this reply *ad nauseam* should you happen to run into the same questioner again.

Q. What is the correct way to ring a gong? I have just inherited one and would rather like to put it to use, but it has been so long since I stayed in a house where such an instrument was used to summon guests to dress or to dinner that I have forgotten the rhythm with which the blows should be struck, though I seem to remember that three is the correct *number* of blows.

S. B., Essex

A. Three gong blows are no longer suitable as they bring the unconscious association with the tension which is introduced nightly around Britain by the opening moments of the *News at Ten* television programme. Far better to strike one single resounding blow, such as one sees at the start of the J. Arthur Rank advertising sequences in a cinema. Occasionally you might even perform this in a loin-cloth to amuse your guests.

Q. This year I opened our garden to the public in aid of our local church roof. Various ladies were asked to bake cakes to be sold on the day and they did so. Unfortunately I have since heard that some of the cakes we sold as 'Fresh Home-baked Cakes' were, in fact, shop-bought and past their sell-by-dates with the wrappers taken off. How can I prevent this from happening again next year? Obviously we cannot taste the cakes before offering them for sale.

Name and address withheld

A. Would it be possible for you to write to all the ladies involved instead of asking them verbally if they might be persuaded to provide cakes? This would afford you

the opportunity to include in your letter the following
piece of Euroese: 'I am obliged by law to mention that
due to new EC regulations all cakes to be sold as fresh
and home-baked must legally fulfil these requirements,
or their supplier will stand liable to prosecution and a
term of imprisonment.'

21 September 1991

DIARY

Dominic Lawson

The obituarist's art has been enjoying a period of high fashion. Now, not just *The Times* but also the *Telegraph* and the *Independent* offer a whole page of notices every day. But sometimes I wonder if the struggle to fill such an expanse of space has not resulted in a lowering of standards. Here, for example, is the heart of an obituary which appeared the other day in the *Independent*: 'He was educated at Millfield and Southampton University and went on to serve in the Merchant Navy for five years, an experience which he once said made it difficult for him to settle down. He then stumbled into the public relations business. He was an assistant public relations officer for British Rail's Southern Region at Waterloo from 1970 to 1976 and was upset when he was made redundant. After losing his job he worked as a jewellery salesman but was not very successful. He later ran his own public relations business. He had an inventive mind and unsuccessfully tried to market an idea to prevent paint solidifying when the tin had been opened. In 1988 he tried to get elected to the European Parliament without success.' And then, three years later, obiit. It is the sort of obituary which one might read in a particularly desperate parish magazine, and which, for some reason, would give one uncontrollable giggles. But what was all this doing across two columns in a national newspaper? Was it because the dead man was an earl? But such a fact could surely never weigh with the intensely meritocratic and republican *Independent*.

It seems that an inquiry will be held into how Lambeth council permitted a 14-year-old called Norbert McCootie to stay in an insecure children's home, even though he had a long list of serious convictions and was on bail, accused of rape. On his fifth escape from the children's home, McCootie raped, at the point of a knife, a 53-year-old grandmother. Only a month after that did Lambeth social services put the young man into secure accommodation. One might think from this that Lambeth council does not adequately protect its residents from the danger of violence; but a document has come into my possession which suggests that the council cares desperately, and I feel it should be made available to the forthcoming inquiry into *l'affaire* McCootie. It is in fact a letter from a Mr Strong, the 'Principal Librarian (Adult and Specialist Services)' in the borough, to Barbara Powrie, who happens to be a reader of *The Spectator*. Miss Powrie wanted to take out a copy of the best-selling book by Thomas Harris, *The Silence of the Lambs*. 'Dear Miss Lowrie,' wrote Mr Strong, slightly inaccurately, 'I am writing to you about your reservation for this title. As you may know, *Silence of the Lambs* concerns the investigation of the brutal murder of a number of women. The librarians who assessed the book were concerned at the general use of graphic and horrific violence by the author, including scenes in which the injuries of female and male victims of the killer are described in detail. In addition, the murderer, Gumb, is portrayed in a very stereotyped way as a homosexual who is also a transsexual, and whose obsession with his mother is used to explain his disturbed fantasy of flaying his women victims and wearing their skins. This negative use of a gay character for shocking effect would certainly be offensive to many readers. For this reason, the book will not be purchased for stock in Lambeth's libraries.' One suspects that if Thomas Harris had portrayed Gumb as a rampant heterosexual the book would have passed the Lambeth Board of Censors. Somehow I don't believe that Mr Strong would then have written to Miss Powrie that 'This negative use of a straight character for shocking effect would certainly be offensive to many readers.' But the message is clear. The streets of Lambeth may not be safe, but its library shelves certainly are.

In the little village where we spend the weekends, a large number of the most prominent and elegant trees have, almost overnight, been disfigured by a new blight. These are shiny yellow 'Neighbourhood Watch' signs. The placards show a helmeted policeman having a discussion with a black man, something which I don't think is seen very often in Gloucestershire. The idea of these signs, some nationwide job lot from the Department of the Environment, is presumably to encourage everyone to keep a careful eye on what is going on. This is faintly insulting. The whole point of village life is that everyone knows what everyone else is up to. When nosiness is second nature, there is absolutely no need for official encouragement. And the signs have had another bad effect, apart from defiling the trees. They have so terrified one of the three townee households in the village (yes, I admit, we are one) that they have installed a searchlight which automatically and dazzlingly comes on whenever anyone passes their house. Oh well, there goes the neighbourhood.

28 September 1991

IF SYMPTOMS PERSIST . . .

Theodore Dalrymple

The world is so full of great tragedies that it might seem almost self-indulgent to draw attention to a small one. Doctors, however, deal with individuals rather than with statistical aggregates, which explains why their conceptions are narrow and their outlook pessimistic. Too close or inescapable an acquaintance with human folly takes its toll, and youthful *joie de vivre* declines into middle-aged *taedium vitae*.

Last week, I met a patient whom life had treated as a 50-ton truck treats a cabbage leaf in the road. Her father was a production-line worker, and it is tempting to suppose that his domestic tyranny was a reaction to his impotence at work. At any rate, his daughter was permitted neither to visit friends nor to have them home; and all the normal enjoyments of childhood were strenuously denied her.

The rule of her father was as arbitrary as that of any oriental despot. He was sultan and janissary rolled into one, and his wife was as complaisant as the inmate of any harem.

Eventually, however, she grew tired of her subordination and fled into madness, from whose refuge she never returned. In her case, the local asylum offered asylum indeed.

At about the same time, my patient's father lost his job, and concluded that the world was against him. He began to hear voices, mocking and tormenting him. He searched for them in the street, challenging them to come out and fight like men. He became a local character and, as is so often the case, life imitated psychosis: before long, the children and youths of the neighbourhood *were* mocking and tormenting him.

His daughter, my patient, thenceforth devoted her life to looking after him, though without his gratitude for her sacrifice, rather the reverse. One day the youths gathered outside the house and pelted it with stones, in mockery of its inhabitants: it was more than my patient could bear.

Soon afterwards, she met an older man in the street who appeared sympathetic. She told him her troubles, and he invited her to his home. Every day for a month she visited him; then he raped her.

'Before he did it,' she said, 'I didn't know nothing about that kind of thing.'

Nevertheless, she returned to him: he was the only person who had spoken to her kindly in adult life. He continued to demand sexual favours, and I imagined in my mind's eye and ear counsel for the defence remarking, with sarcasm issuing from every pore, 'You say you were unwilling, Miss X, yet you repeatedly returned to the scene of the rape.'

Soon her lover-assailant brought his friends to have intercourse with her while he watched: he derived great excitement from this. Still she returned to him, but finally refused to do so when he asked her to go on to the streets. He needed a holiday, he said, but had no money to pay for one. It was then that my patient resorted to illness to evade his attentions. She trembled like an autumn leaf.

A small tragedy, as I have said, unaffected by the great historical events of the last months.

28 September 1991

THE NEW FETISHISTS

Henry Porter

The jeep, a big square Mercedes, drove down the shingle beach and turned round to reverse its trailer into the Solent. On the trailer were two jet skis – double-seaters painted in different liveries: one white, turquoise and navy blue; the other yellow, red and white. Four people got out of the car – two couples in their thirties – and began preparing the jet skis for launch. And, oh, what preparation it was!

The two men slipped into a practised figure of activity. They unbuckled straps, checked gauges, filled fuel tanks, tapped and prodded and knocked and jiggled bits of their machines, urging the engines into throaty splutters. It was all done with the earnest speed of a Formula One pit-stop team or a flight-deck crew of an aircraft carrier. This was serious business; man and machine were about to elide in a perilous celerity. Everything had to be checked and double checked and checked again.

The girls were putting on their wetsuits, matching their partners who had already changed. These suits were memorable. One couple wore a grey outfit with flashes of lime and mauve – the colour of blackcurrant mousse. The other wore grey, yellow and red.

They had life jackets, too, which they strapped up and buckled, occasionally patting the little gas cylinder that inflates the jacket in emergency. One girl wore an oversized waterproof watch, the other carried a yellow waterproof camera. She walked to the front of the jeep and bobbed up and down by the wing mirror to check her appearance.

Then they were all set. The jet skis were launched. The men revved the engines, the girls climbed on board and the two machines moved off in formation, their passengers looking very serious. They sped up and down the shoreline, made circles with the wash, and in no time at all had returned to the beach to fiddle with their equipment.

Anyone who has used a jet ski will testify that it's dull as hell, and predictably these people had got bored. What they took their pleasure from was the equipment, the gear, the kit, the specialised sporty-coloured trappings that joined them to the bright noisy machines.

There is a lot of this equipment fetishism about. Take the New Cyclist and his sturdily-built mountain bike, with its thick tyres and its no-nonsense horizontal handlebars. Is this bike much better than the drop handlebars and light-as-a-feather frame of the racing bike? Probably not, although the New Cyclist will not hear a word against the mountain bike, whose name somehow suggests a gruelling traversal of the Snowdonia National Park.

The other day I found a New Cyclist wheeling his mountain bike along the pavement in London and this is what he was wearing: light, perforated trainers, lurex cycling shorts which came down to just above the knee, a racing vest, chamois leather gloves, a watch that told him the time in Tokyo, a face mask to protect him from carbon monoxide fumes, a crash helmet and a pair of sunglasses which stretched round to his ears and looked more like a visor. All this to ride a push-bike in London.

Cycling has been transformed from a perfectly ordinary form of transport into a rather glamorous activity which now with its protective accessories implies a level of danger and manliness that is very difficult to take seriously. The same happened to sailing about 20 years ago when a young man playing about on a Midlands canal attached a small mast and sail to a surfboard by means of a universal joint and invented the windsurfer. He cannot have imagined the sort of garish kit that would follow in his wake, the sleek wetsuits, the extra-grip rubber boots, straps and buckles, harnesses and in some cases rubber balaclavas which are designed to help the air flow past the dashing mariner. The windsurfer in all his trappings looks like some sort of bound-up pervert. Windsurfers do it tied up.

Where did all this come from? Jean-Claude Killy has much to answer for. After his success in the 1968 Winter Olympics, the downhill skiing champion toured the world endorsing all sorts of products, but particularly gloves, boots, skis, ski suits, headbands. The gear of the

slopes became *de rigueur* and has developed into an enormous industry which does not actually help people to ski better but may afford them more protection.

Then came the more extravagant winter sports that only a few lunatics would consider: they surfboarded down slopes of more than 45 degrees, jumped from planes to ride the ice-crystal sea above the alps, ski-dived from mountain tops, leapt from helicopters to take on the groaning summer glaciers. And the equipment that came with these new dangerous sports! How they loved the buckles and straps and suits and goggles and the fluorescent face-paint that is worn in stripes along the nose, around the mouth and beneath the eyes and protects them against wind and sun.

The New Cyclist is just as serious about his equipment as the high mountain snow-surfer or the hang-glider – another common gear fetishist. It is entirely acceptable now to pedal along the Gray's Inn Road looking like a warrior from a sci-fi comic strip, ostentatiously protected from unimaginable dangers and, incidentally, from recognition.

To a degree, this is about fashion. Since the 19th century sporting clothes have been absorbed into everyday wardrobe: tail coats, sports jackets, golfing trousers, shooting tweeds, anoraks, track-suits and now shell-suits all have their origins in various sports. They lend the wearer an athletic and outdoor look when he is in town.

But equipment fetishism is more than the desire to look sporty. It thrives where people imagine themselves, or may even be actually engaged in, taking on the elements – the wind, the mountains, the sea. The kit expresses the danger to which these hardy souls expose themselves and it also carries an extravagant trust that is the mark of all fetishism. These straps and buckles and suits and clips and goggles are revered for their satisfying snap action, their purpose-designed ability to aid and protect the user. The hill tribes of Borneo would understand all about the New Cyclist in the Gray's Inn Road and his totemic equipment.

28 September 1991

BOOKS

THE RETURN OF DR DEATH

James Buchan

TIME'S ARROW
by Martin Amis
Cape, £13.99, pp. 176

Towards Auschwitz, an artist can take one or more of several positions: ignorance, horror, pity, curiosity, rage and silence, which can be the silence of indifference or the silence some people observe at the sides of graves. You can also do what Martin Amis does, which is fabricate an Auschwitz out of literary sources and use it as a setting for an elegant and trivial fiction.

The product can be, and is in this case, striking, but in the way of one of those magazine photographs of models wearing couture in bomb sites or slums. The problem is one of taste (and by taste I don't mean liking Victorian telephone boxes but the faculty that every artist must possess for matching his method and material to his intention). Martin Amis may have had misgivings on the taste front because he adds to the end of this short book a statement in which he thanks many people, not all of them celebrities, for talking to him about the Holocaust; makes a reference to tennis and to Primo Levi, about whose suicide he has a theory; and says that the offence of Auschwitz

> was unique, not in its cruelty, nor in its cowardice, but
> in its style – in its combination of the atavistic and the
> modern.

Against the larger offence of the book, this shallow solemnity is neither here nor there. But it reveals a twitch of conscience and I'd advise Martin Amis to drop it from the paperback – the tennis thing can, if it is important, be used elsewhere. Time, on which Martin Amis speculates fitfully in the novel, is on his side. The murmur of the dead of Auschwitz, muffled by its passage across nearly half a century, doesn't have a chance over the chatter of books such as this one. Already, some people will find my review ludicrously stiff and pompous.

In *Time's Arrow*, Martin Amis reverses the narrative flow usual in novels: narrative time runs backwards. The book opens with the soul of Tod Friendly bursting out of darkness into an operating theatre full of frantic American doctors. A page or two later, Tod is bundled roughly out by paramedics, given the kiss of life and dumped in his garden.

This method produces quite startling effects. As you might expect, Amis begins by having a lot of fun with eating, wanking, going to the lav and the supermarket; but his descriptive ambitions grow as the book progresses. Tod is himself a doctor, making people ill. Just one passage will show how witty and striking the writing can be:

> Where would the poor girls be without their pimps, who shower money on them and ask for nothing in return? Not like Tod and his tender mercies. He just goes around there to rub dirt in their wounds. And backs off quick, before the long-suffering pimp shows up, and knocks the girl into shape with his jewelled fists. As he works, the baby in the cot beside the bed will hush its weeping, and sleep angelically, secure in the knowledge that the pimp is come.

Once you put the book down, the world seems differently organised, as after a weekend of chess or cards.

Tod's life moves in jolts: one-night-stands, changed identities, countries and jobs. As his soul says somewhere, creation is quick and easy, destruction is slow. Love affairs begin with a fight and end with the brush of knees under a restaurant table. The book is written in short sections – borrowed, like the interest in time and the winsome and portentous proper names, from Kurt Vonnegut, I imagine – and each ends in a lovely cadence to which Amis applies all the metrical care of a Latin prose writer of the Silver Age (e.g. to his thrilled fingertips/ and all its gruesome crap/ earth's exiled or demoted soul/ knowledge that the pimp is come/ and shit for the dogs/ in strange apartments/ like a garden path etc.). Through it all runs a dreadful foreboding. As in tragedy, Tod is rushing towards his fate, which we know from his dreams (and Amis's career record) has to be pretty appalling. It is years since I read a book where the dramatic pull was so strong.

This is what Amis's method can do. What it can't do is any of the interplay of character, cause and effect which is what makes novels worth reading. Even in the very best passages in *Time's Arrow*, where you think Amis might just be about to stumble on something, you see you are just reading a book back to front:

> There is a nurse called Nurse Elliott who is always sneering at me without meeting my eye. In the elevator yesterday, under her breath, she called me an asshole. I know the signs – when a woman is leading me on. She's just slipped into the Laundry Room. After a minute or two I follow her through the door. She stands by the window, checking her face in the silver compact. I walk towards her with my knees trembling.

The only character drawn is the soul, who tells the story in forwards or biological time and has the opportunity to appear innocent, quizzical and streetwise. For Tod under his various names, Amis is restricted by his method. Dialogue is obviously out, as too hard to follow: in practice, Amis largely confines himself to two or three palindromic lines of quoted speech at a time. Any complexity of character would, in any case, be incomprehensible. One pushes on through the book, thankfully identifying types of character and setting – suburban American codger, stressed-out big city doctor, gent with a past in Portugal, a doctor in white coat and black boots at Auschwitz, a rollicking and Jew-baiting *Bursch*. Let me repeat: things happen because they have happened, not from cause or motive. Towards the end, Amis does at last make a stab at asking why Tod acted as he did and the book crashes. Tod is by now called Unverdorben, a name from *The Truce* in another transparent effort to get Primo Levi on side:

> I've come to the conclusion that Odilo Unverdorben, as a moral being, is absolutely unexceptional, liable to do what everybody else does, good or bad, with no limit, once under the cover of numbers. He could never be an exception; he is dependent on the health of his society, needing the sandy smiles of Rolf and Rudolph, of Ruediger, of Reinhard.

This is amazingly uninformative, and embarrassing as well.

It is an almost overpowering relief to see the crimes of Auschwitz undone in a book. The optimism makes Amis sometimes sound like Dame Juliana: all shall be well. But the notion that a crime can be reversed by reversing time is banal in the extreme, tautologous or nonsensical (I wonder if Martin Amis possesses a VCR). The backwards-time method merely allows Amis to exploit the horror and glamour of Auschwitz without the bother of confronting the conundrum of the place, which is the why of it. I know the Derrida mob will gasp and clap their hands but I find it creepy to see Primo Levi – his suffering, his calm – rearranged for literary fun and profit. Even old Kurt Vonnegut: the speculations about time in *Slaughterhouse 5* are no less nonsensical than in *Time's Arrow*, but at least he was writing from an actual, unmediated experience of war.

I feel as perplexed by *Time's Arrow* as by Ian McEwan's *The Innocent*. Who are these guys? Why do they mug up the recent history of Germany to commit acts of literary sadism? What do they do with their time except read and, I suppose, do sports? Listen: Auschwitz is not just about style. It is about aberrant behaviour by people in mass which is hard to understand even with great thought and study. Martin Amis is just about style.

28 September 1991

LETTER

CREEPIER THAN THOU

Sir: Nothing in my book can compare with the blasphemous cuteness, and robust vulgarity, of your front-page headline (28 September): 'Designer gas ovens'. As for your reviewer, James Buchan: I couldn't shock him as much as he shocks me. His vision is, indeed, forbiddingly bleak. 'I find it creepy', he writes, 'to see Primo Levi – his suffering, his calm – rearranged for literary fun and profit.' What could be creepier, and more callowly ungenerous, than such an imputation? All books, by the way, including *If This Is a Man*, are written 'for profit'. All reviews are too – however exalted, however eagerly cynical.

Martin Amis
London W11

5 October 1991

THE BICKERSTETH WAR DIARIES, 1914–18

July 5, 1917

I was distressed to hear from our Colonel that the man who came to us under arrest as a deserter six months ago and who had deserted again *four times* since, had been condemned to death. The previous sentence of death passed on him had been commuted and then suspended to give him another chance, but he deserted again during the Battle of Arras and so lost his only chance.

'*Yours disgusting, Tunbridge Wells.*'

A wire shortly came from the Brigade HQ telling me that I should be expected to attend him from the moment of the promulgation to his death.

Monday July 2nd I left our HQ in the Line fairly early and went straight down to see the Senior Chaplain, who himself had intended to take on this sad business, but as I have been seeing the man practically every day for three or four months I asked him to let me see it through. I felt it was my duty. So after some lunch with him I went to our Transport Lines and saw the firing party, picked by military requirements from our own men. These men had been sent down specially from the trenches. I made several arrangements about the digging of the grave and then went on to the spot where the promulgation was to take place. This consisted of the prisoner being marched under escort to a spot just outside the village. Here he was placed in the centre of a hollow square formed by representatives drawn from each battalion in the Brigade. At a given signal the prisoner is ordered to take two paces to the front, which he does, and his cap is taken off, and then the officer in charge of the parade read the sentence which concluded a recital of the crime for which the prisoner had been found guilty. I stood close behind the prisoner to support him by my presence all I could. There was a terrible silence when the promulgation concluded with the sentence of death. The man seemed a bit dazed, but stepped back to between his guards fairly smartly. I walked off the ground with him. He was taken to a little back room on the second storey of a two-storeyed semi-detached villa in the village.

Let me try to describe to you the man before I tell you more. Heavily built, rather vacant-eyed, low forehead, very dirty in appearance in spite of all the efforts of the military police to make him clean himself, his utterance was indistinct and his mastery of the English language somewhat limited. His previous history was typical, I suppose, of many others, but not without its sadness. Our modern civilisation had done but little for him. His father, a 'cabby' in East London, had died when the boy was 13. His mother, reduced in her circumstances, lived afterwards in one room. The boy was sent out to 'do what he could for himself'. He lived from hand to mouth. He soon learnt enough to avoid the police, to get enough to eat, but his home ties soon began to mean less and less to him. Occasionally he brought his mother home a few pence to add to the limited family exchequer. On this effort he dwelt in his reminiscences to me with pride. And who knows it may stand before the Judgment Seat for much. It meant at least a spark of filial duty. But with no one to help him much he soon drifted into bad company and before he was 20 found himself in prison. On coming out the first time he still kept in touch with his mother, but a second conviction soon after meant a longer time in prison and when at last he was free again his mother had moved from the single room she occupied before he went to prison and from that day to this he had never seen her again. He never found out, or troubled to find out, where she had gone. His two sisters had several years before gone into service and disappeared from the family circle. The Military Service Act caught him in its meshes and he became a soldier. During his training in the East End he found one good woman, who lived next to the Military Depot or guard room, who used to give him meals on credit. The address of this woman he remembered, but not her name. Accustomed always to do as he pleased, he had deserted twice before he left England and was brought across under arrest. Escaping soon after, he was caught and sent up to the Line, only to escape on the way, and when he was apprehended, we had to send our battalion military police to fetch him – not a very propitious entry into the regiment. He had belonged to another regiment of the 'London Regiment' and was only attached to us at the Base.

This was six months ago, and from that day to this he has almost the whole time been in our Guardroom.

This was the man I had to tackle with only 12 hours more to live. There were not a few who said he was mad, or at least something wrong with his brain, but our Doctor had been unable to certify that he was in any way not responsible for his actions and certainly he was quite intelligent in a good many ways. He could read and write well.

He sat down heavily on a chair. The room was furnished with a small round table, three chairs, and a wire bed raised six inches from the ground. I took a chair and sat next to him. 'I am going to stay with you and do anything I can for you. If you'd like to talk, we will, but if you would rather not, we'll sit quiet.' Two fully armed sentries with fixed bayonets stand one by the door and the other by the window. The room is only 9 feet by 10 feet. Anything in the nature of a private talk seems likely to be difficult. An appeal that the sentries may be removed is not accepted. There are no bars to the windows and the prisoner might seek to make an end of himself. So I sit on silently. Suddenly I hear great heaving sobs and the prisoner breaks down and cries. In a second I lean over close to him, as he hides his face in his hands, and in a low voice I talk to him. He seems still a little doubtful about his fate and I have to explain to him what is going to happen tomorrow morning. I tell him about Morris and of how many splendid men have 'passed on'. What fine company he will find on the other side. After a time he quiets down and his tea comes up – two large pieces of bread and butter, a mess tin half full of tea and some jam in a tin. One of the sentries lends me his clasp knife, so that I may put jam on his bread, for the prisoner of course is not allowed to handle a knife. After his tea is over, I hand him a pipe and tobacco. These comforts, strictly forbidden to all prisoners, are not withheld now. He loved a pipe and soon he is contentedly puffing away. Time goes on. I know that he must sleep, if possible, during the hours of darkness, so my time is short. How can I reach his soul? I get out my Bible and read to him something from the Gospel. It leaves him unmoved. He is obviously uninterested and my attempt to talk a little about what I have read leaves him cold. Where is my point of contact? I make him move his chair as far away from the sentry as possible, and speaking in a low voice close to him, I am not overheard, but of what to speak? There is no point of contact through his home, which means nothing to him. I get out an army prayerbook, which contains at the end about 130 hymns, and handing him the book, ask him to read through the part at the end, so that, if he can find a hymn he knows, I can read it to him. He hits on *Rock of Ages* and asks, not if I will read it to him, but if we can sing it. The idea of our solemnly singing hymns together, while the two sentries eye us coldly from the other side of the room, seems to me so incongruous that I put him off with the promise of a hymn to be sung before he goes to sleep, but he is not satisfied and he returns to the suggestion again. This time I had enough sense, thank goodness, to seize on 'the straw', *and we sat there and sang hymns together for three hours or more.*

And the curious thing about this extraordinary man is that he takes command of the proceedings. He chooses the hymns. He will not sing any one over twice. He starts the hymn on the right note, knows the tunes and pitches them all perfectly right. Music has evidently not been denied him. The words mean nothing to him, or else he is so little gifted with imagination that the pathos of such lines as 'Hold Thou Thy cross before my closing eyes' and many similar lines, which in view of the morrow should cut deep, leave the prisoner unmoved.

Oh! how we sang – hymn after hymn. He knew more tunes than I did. Girdlestone came and fetched me away for half an hour's dinner and then I returned to the little room and in the rapidly fading light went on with the hymn-singing. I brought him a YMCA hymn-book, which contained several hymns not in the other. He was delighted and we sang 'Throw out the Life-line', 'What a Friend we have in Jesus' and others. When 10.30 p.m. came I was anxious to see the prisoner sleeping, for his own sake, though I was willing to go on singing hymns if he wanted to. His stock, however, was nearly exhausted, as he would never sing the same hymn twice over. So we agreed to close the singing, but we would sing one of the hymns he had already sung, a second time as a last effort. So he chose 'God be with us till we meet again.' He sang it utterly unmoved. *While I was ruminating over how to make use of the hymns for getting a little further on, he said 'We haven't finished yet – we must have "God save the King"' and we then and there rose to our feet, and the two Divisional Military Police, who had replaced the ordinary guard and been accommodated with two chairs, had to get up and stand rigidly to attention, while the prisoner and I sang lustily three verses of the National Anthem! A few seconds later the prisoner was asleep.*

I felt that the hymns, even if the words had not meant much to him, had been a prayer – or rather many prayers – and seeing him inclined to sleep, I did not try to get his attention to pray more with him. I have never spent a stranger evening. I think it was a distinct effort on his part to give Religion full play. To him, hymn-singing meant Religion. Probably no other aspect or side of Religion had ever touched him and now that he was 'up against it' he found real consolation in singing hymns learnt in childhood – he had been to Sunday School up till 12 or 13. Anyhow, that was the point of contact I had been seeking for. *All night I sat by his side.* One sentry played patience – the other read a book. Once or twice the prisoner woke up, but he soon slept again. At 3.0 a.m. I watched the first beginnings of dawn through the window. At 3.30 a.m. I heard the tramp tramp of the Firing Party marching down the road. A few minutes later the police Sergeant-Major brought me up a cup of tea and I had a whispered consultation with him as to how long I could let the prisoner sleep. A minute or two later I was called down to see the APM, the divisional officer in charge of the police, and he gave me some rum to give the prisoner if he wanted it. It was a dark morning, so he did not want the prisoner awakened for another ten minutes. I went up again and at the right time wakened him. While his breakfast was being brought up, we knelt together in prayer. I commended him to God and we said together the Lord's Prayer, which he knew quite well and was proud of knowing. Then he sat down and ate a really good breakfast – bread and butter, ham, and tea. When he had finished it was just four o'clock and I poured into his empty mug a tablespoonful of rum, but when he had tasted it, he wouldn't drink any of it. 'Is it time to go?', he said. *'Yes, it is time. I will stay close to you.'* Down the narrow stairs we went and through the silent streets of the village our weird little procession tramped. First a burly military policeman, then the prisoner, unbound, and myself, followed close on our heels by two more policemen, the APM, the Doctor, and one other officer. We had about 300 yards to go to a deserted and ruined house just outside the village. I held the prisoner's arm tight for sympathy's sake. Reaching the house, the police immediately hand-cuffed the man and the Doctor blindfolded him. He was breathing heavily and his heart going very quickly, but outwardly he was unmoved. I said a short prayer and led him the 10 or 12 paces out into the yard, where he was at once bound to a stake. I whispered in his ear 'Safe in the arms of Jesus', and he repeated quite clearly 'Safe in the arms of Jesus'. The APM motioned me away. In three or four seconds the Firing Party had done their work. Poor lads – I was sorry for them. They felt it a good deal and I followed them out of the yard at once and spoke to them and handed them cigarettes.

Girdlestone turned up and together we took the body in a motor ambulance to the nearest cemetery, where I had a burial party waiting, and *we gave his body Christian burial.*

I went back to the Transport Lines and tried to get some sleep.

This is an extract from a letter to his mother from the Reverend Julian Bickersteth, MC, Royal Army Chaplains Department with the 56th London Division. It forms part of 11 volumes of the family's unpublished diaries, mostly consisting of letters to their mother from five serving sons, kept between 1914 and 1918. The same recipient began again in 1939 and put together a further seven volumes of correspondence from her by then extended family.

28 September 1991

FOOD

IMPERATIVE COOKING: UNHEALTHY MEDITERRANEAN FOOD

Digby Anderson

Healthy-eating loonies divide into two sorts. There are those who would eat cardboard if told it would extend their miserable lives by an hour. They have no interest in food. Then there are those whose even more implausible message is that eating cardboard is not only good for you, but that good quality cardboard, carefully prepared and thinly sliced, can be quite as delicious as roast pork.

They have found a cover for their deceitful and evil propaganda, the Mediterranean. The Med peoples, they claim, eat wonderful food which is also very healthy. For health and pleasure, just switch to the diets of Languedoc, Catalonia, Puglia, Calabria, Crete and Andalucía.

The claim is fraudulent and a slur on the Mediterranean which has some splendidly, indeed several uniquely, 'unhealthy' dishes and characteristics. Or at least, they are 'unhealthy' as defined by the loonies. Loonies disapprove of animal fats, eggs and dairy products (except low-fat yoghurt), sugar, salt, alcohol, tobacco, and like fish, vegetables and anything brown.

It is true that along some of the actual coasts of the Mediterranean a lot of fish is eaten. I remember wonderful dishes of mussels near Sete steamed open and stuffed with so much sausage meat they had to be tied in cotton before cooking; from the same region, mussels and grey mullet, baked in a buttery, creamy béchamel. Nearby, and a little inland, is the famous brandade of salted cod mashed with oil and milk and served with fried bread. Both inland and on the coast, these are the lands of charcuterie, salami, mortadella, chorizo, pancetta, all with lashings of fat and salt, not to mention pâtés with at least 50 per cent fat. Proper households in southern France certainly eat fish but as often as not follow it with meat daubes, lamb with garlic, ducks or tripes.

Olive oil does not banish other fats. Nowhere is more duck or goose fat eaten than in south-west France. Countless recipes call for oil and the French and Spanish equivalents of bacon. Much of northern

'Do I detect a Gallic influence in the casserole,
Vanessa?'

Mediterranean Italy uses butter copiously. The pasta and rice are next
to never brown. The cheeses of France are full of dairy fats.

In Andalucía, as I keep reminding *Spectator* readers, breakfast may
well be toasted white bread covered in pork fat preceded by full cream
milk (with chocolate) accompanied by very unhealthy strong coffee,
sent down by a triple brandy or anise and aided by a cigarette or
even a cigar. Late at night, before retiring, the Almerians visit the
Bar S. Rita for quails' eggs fried with white bread, more brandy
and a thin piece of chorizo which awaits them lying submerged
in three inches of melted fat in a square dish on the *plancha*.
And everywhere, from Spain back to southern Sicily, there is salt,
in anchovies, in semi-preserved cheese, in charcuterie, in all cooked
dishes, with handfuls thrown on salads. Southern Spain and Italy are
also the lands of sweet syrups and sticky Arab-influenced dishes and
cakes and biscuits, while southern France has its pastry tarts, and all
put away with gallons of ice-cream. This wonderful culture of sugar,
salt, meats, dairy products and tobacco is lubricated by wine, pastis,
brandy, grappa and strong espresso coffee. What good news that it is
statistically associated with health.

Anyway, it all means there is fun to be had. If you know a healthy-
eating loony, invite him to a 'Mediterranean dinner'. I suggest: Pastis

(three); assorted salami, the bloodiest morcilla, the fattiest pancetta and pâté with lots of butter; then, either lasagne 'stuffed' with pork, béchamel and butter, or eggs fried in goose fat with potato; for fish, mixed fried fishes but it must include salt-cod puréed with oil and milk, breadcrumbed and deep-fried; then Elizabeth David's 'Mediterranean' cassoulet with belly of pork, breast of mutton, pork rind, gammon, preserved goose, goose dripping or pig's lard plus beans and herbs. Cassoulet can be heavy, so chaps will want a smoke after and it will need lots of strong red wine (at least 13 per cent). Then on to a full cheese board with some Italian and Spanish 'dried' cheeses – to keep the salt up – and Frog ones for fat; a Mediterranean extravaganza of pastries and sweets; cigars, espresso coffee and brandy. Bread is white and there is optional ice-cream.

Just before your loony guests leave, offer them a S. Rita for the journey home – the driver will need a napkin so that he can eat his chorizo as he drives without it oozing red pork fat on to his trousers.

28 September 1991

FIGHTING TALK

Frank Keating

Joe Bugner was derided by the panatella fancy at ringside as a big stiff who couldn't punch his way out of a paper bag, the original Joe Palooka. But Bugner was a survivor all right. In two fights he went 27 rounds with Muhammad Ali without being knocked down, and Muhammad Ali was not far out of his prime. Bugner stayed the full dirty dozen on his feet against Joe Frazier too. In over 70 fights Bugner lost only 12. His one trouble, an important one for a prizefighter, was that he did not actually like hitting people. Not after his 15th fight.

Bugner lost his first pro fight, freezing with a debutante's nerves, but the next 13 victories took him only 33 rounds as he laid about a string of opponents with meaty venom. His 15th fight was against a nice boxer called Ulric Regis. Bugner won. Young Ulric never regained consciousness. Joe Bugner never liked hitting people any more.

Then there was Angelo Jacopucci, who fought Alan Minter for the European middleweight title 13 years ago. Another 12th-round knockout. Afterwards Minter talked us through it: 'It was the left hooks. When the count reached 5, he waved his right hand feebly. He collapsed backwards with his knees bent under him. His shoulders rested on the bottom rope and his neck twisted horribly over the second rope.' Angelo Jacopucci died next day.

I saw Johnny Owen, a pale waif of a flyweight with soulful Pinnochio eyes and a Scaramouche nose, wind up his training at the Tredegar Miners' Institute and then excitedly pack his bags and go off to California to fight for the world title. Weeks later his body came back to Wales, after doctors at a Los Angeles hospital had turned off his life-support machine. I was only feet away, at the Albert Hall, when Willie Classen, a no-hope middleweight, lay pole-axed by Tony Sibson in the second. He should not have been fighting anyway. Classen's boxing licence had expired, and he was under medical suspension by the New York boxing commission after a knockout he sustained five months before.

When he had recovered that night at the Albert Hall, we asked him 'How d'you feel, kid?' He said he had double vision. But it didn't stop him collecting his pay packet and getting a minicab to Heathrow. Only 40 days later, his licence renewed, poor, pale Willie faced an up-and-coming headhunter called Willie Scypion at Madison Square Garden. Classen was knocked out in the 10th . . . and buried a week later at St Raymond's cemetery in the Bronx.

One lucky thing for beleaguered boxing this week was that the antis' chief, living, Exhibit A – A for Ali (and also for alas), who is now a shuffling, mumbling wreck – failed to turn up to help launch his gripping, no-holds-barred biography by Thomas Hauser. His condition would only have fuelled the furore. The same publishers, Robson, have also brought out a biog of Primo Carnera, the Ambling Alp, the Leaning Tower of Tagliatelli. Ernie Schaaf died after being kayoed by Primo, in New York in 1933. Everyone said the real damage had been done to Schaaf in his previous fight with Max Baer in Chicago. Carnera was interviewed afterwards by the homicide squad, but it came to nothing for the test case had been three years earlier after Baer himself knocked out Frankie Campbell, who died next day. Baer spent two days in San Francisco jail before manslaughter charges were dropped.

Sixty years on, if they were really serious about banning boxing, the law shouldn't go for the fighters – who are, in Brian London's immortal phrase, 'only innocent prawns in this game' – but for the promoters or, for incitement, the men who make the pre-fight TV trailers.

That would hurry them back to snooker, and pronto.

28 September 1991

DIARY

Julie Burchill

It has always been my dream to write *The Spectator* diary. Why? I hear you ask. I've turned down *Wogan* three times. Told Andrew Neil twice that he couldn't afford me. Been publicly denounced by Salman Rushdie, peace be upon him. There's no serious spondulicks to be had here; no fame, no glamour. What there is, is the best platform going to offend the maximum number of constipated, change-counting Anglo-Catholic creeps at once. But I don't only do it to annoy. I really think I can make a difference to your drab lives. You see, the organs for which I usually kick-start the circulation – the *Face*, the *Modern Review*, the *Mail On Sunday* – are notorious for their unimpeachably hip readership. But here, at last, is the chance to bring some colour and excitement into the life of the nerd in the herd, the schmooze in the mews.

Someone sends me a horrible book called *The Change*. I'm only 32, for God's sake. Then I see it's by Germaine Greer. I muse over how the Government's laughably-named policy of Community Care has had many unfortunate side effects, perhaps the worst of which has been the distressing spectacle of many of our more senior citizens – who would be far happier locked up snugly in a soothing sort of *eau-de-nil* room dribbling Farley's rusks all over themselves and weaving raffia table-mats – left unattended to wander around Medialand. When challenged, they tend to babble obscenely and show their drawers. Hence, in the late Eighties, Dr Greer's break-out from her commune in Catatonia and her incessant chattering ever since about motherhood, menstruation and Colonel Mengistu, for all the world like some Left-dressing version of Victoria Gillick. A seminal Green Cow, who seriously posited the notion that the Western habit of wearing high-heeled shoes was a mutilation of women comparable with the Eastern habit of clitorectomy (and the Muslim habit of amputating thieves' hands is pretty much like having a manicure, no doubt), Greer has now come out with the notion that the menopause is a blessing in disguise which frees women to express themselves creatively. For some reason – probably because she was sponging Farley's off her twinset at the time – Miss Greer seems to have overlooked the glaringly obvious fact that those women who have created great art have done so at the peak of their fertility – whether or not they chose to take up Mme Nature on her kind offer. This includes Miss Greer herself, who wrote her masterpiece in her thirties and has been slowly turning into a bag of nutty slack ever since.

5 October 1991

TELEVISION

NATURAL INGREDIENTS

Martyn Harris

I have a theory about TV food shows, a sub-clause of Murphy's Law probably, which states that the higher the quality of the cookery programme, the worse the quality of the cooking.

The BBC's *Food and Drink Programme*, for instance, is a very slick production: all fast cutting between news items, and quizzes, and consumer scares, with jolly patter from the wheezing fat men in patterned sweaters, and that extraordinary Jilly Goolden, who sounds as if she is gargling an oyster. The recipes are always fairly dreadful – the sort which tell you if you can't get truffles, a tin of Chesswood mushrooms will be absolutely fine.

At the other extreme is *Anton Mosimann – Naturally* (Channel 4, 8.30 p.m., Friday) which is risibly incompetent as a TV programme, but which has me scribbling down recipes all the way. *Time Out* said 'the appeal of this series lies in its simplicity', by which they must have meant the simple way the camera keeps sawing off the head of Mr Mosimann's assistant, or the simple manner in which programmes go crashing between Switzerland and Bedford, and from Caesar salad to soufflé without the smallest pretext of continuity.

A story about Anton Mosimann that I have always liked relates that when he was 12 years old, in his home town of Twann in Switzerland, he decided he wanted to own a Triumph Spitfire sports car. Accordingly he set up a business selling old newspapers and medals to schoolfriends. At 16 he established another business selling live rabbits to housewives and restaurants. At 18 he owned the Spitfire.

He is a serious man, in other words, but also an extremely boring one, and has had to work very hard to turn himself into a television personality. Where your average TV weirdo, for instance, is content with a single trademark, whether it be funny hat, or funny moustache, or silly bow-tie, or comical accent, M. Mosimann has acquired all of them, all at the same time, and is still mildly tedious.

It is to do with his being German-Swiss, I suppose, which debars him from doing anything really engaging or outrageous, such as getting drunk like Graham Kerr and Keith Floyd, or getting fat like

Philip Harben and Tom Vernon, or wearing false eyelashes like Fanny Cradock.

He made his name as a chef at the Dorchester with what he was pleased to call his 'cuisine naturelle', a development of nouvelle cuisine, which avoids 'unhealthy' ingredients such as butter, cream, flour and alcohol. Mosimann concentrated instead on fresh, lightly cooked food, with an emphasis on fish, vegetables and exotic fruit – all in very small portions. It was a quintessential Eighties concept in fact: greed without fat; ostentation with austerity; hunger at £100 a head.

It was also largely a sham, as any of the current series of programmes illustrates. Mosimann will make great play with the fact that he uses low-fat fromage blanc in the dressing for a Caesar salad, but entirely abandons dietary principles for the next dish, which is a four-egg soufflé with a half pound of hard cheese, or a smoked salmon pizza smothered in sour cream and olive oil. Nouvelle cuisine or cuisine naturelle was a marketing gimmick, designed to flatter rich fatties into thinking that they were dieting as they spent, and was often only a precursor to the surreptitious midnight swig from the custard jug.

But that is enough sniping. Mosimann is the most astonishing cook, endlessly creative and deeply committed to the integrity of ingredients. Perhaps the only thing he needs to do to work on television is to fade away behind the chopping board like Johnny Cradock, and to front his act with Madame Mosimann – with or without the false eyelashes.

5 October 1991

DIARY

Dominic Lawson

Last week our car was snatched by the police. Actually it was not our car. The week before the roof of *our* car, a convertible, was slashed by a thief. It was a rented car that the police grabbed. We had parked the car legally, but four days later, when we next wanted to use it, we found that some utility had started to dig up the road, in particular under the tarmac which supported our hire car. The police, called to remove the vehicle, made no attempt to tell us, or the owners of the car, that it had been impounded. Economically this was rational of them, because they charge incrementally for every day a car is impounded. We were required to hand over £109 at the Kensington car pound in Warwick Road before we were allowed to drive our borrowed car through the automatic gates of the pound and back on to the mean streets. A girl ahead of us in the queue to pay the police for their services found things less easy. Unlike us she did not possess a credit card. Her fee was over £50, the limit of her cheque guarantee card. She was an attractive, very well spoken woman, somewhat weighed down by many shopping bags. She had obviously had a very tiring day. She needed the car badly because she wanted to drive to the airport the next day, she explained. Couldn't she write two cheques? Not without giving more evidence of her identity, said the police employee behind a glass screen. She said she had some airline tickets with her name on ('the same as on my cheque book') and some envelopes addressed to her, which might be in the car. She went off to the car and returned with these items. The police employee, all the more sinister for being very softly spoken, said no, that was not enough, although our identity was accepted by his colleague on the strength of an addressed envelope. At this point the woman burst into tears. The man looked on, unblinking. We cracked before he did, and asked the girl how much more money she needed to pay the fine. 'Fifteen pounds,' she said, in a shaky voice. We handed her this sum, and she wrote a cheque to us for the same amount. I don't know whether the police employee had enjoyed humiliating his elegant, but now mascara-stained victim. I don't even know his name, since when I asked him for it, he refused to answer. I suppose I should have asked him what proof he had of his lack of identity, but instead I reflected that it was difficult to make a complaint against someone employed by the police if he refused to give his name or number. And I further reflected that if the police are seriously worried about the diminishing esteem in which they are held by the British public, the remedy lies in their own hands.

The result of the escapade in the car pound was that we were an hour late for dinner with John Simpson and his girlfriend, Tira. When we told them of the reasons for our late arrival, John instantly responded with a story which returned the smile to our faces. A friend of his, whom he described mysteriously as 'one of the heroes of the Gulf war', came back to London from an assignment overseas, to find that his car had been impounded. But his heroic friend was determined not to pay. He skirted the car pound on foot, and observed that the fence around it could be scaled, unaided. He scaled it. He found his car, and drove it very quietly towards the automatic gates. When another car began to leave, he followed, speedily getting out before the gate fell. The staff at the pound didn't notice, and the driver in front didn't care. Some weeks later just back from another foreign mission our hero was sitting at home when his door bell rang. It was the police. Two of them. One of them then told him that something very embarrassing had happened. They had impounded his car, but it had unaccountably disappeared while it was in their charge. They were very sorry, and would gladly be prepared to reimburse him for the cost of replacement. The Gulf hero said that this was all very surprising. For while it was true his car had disappeared one day, a few days later it had most mysteriously reappeared. Wasn't that strange? The two policemen looked at each other. Suddenly they knew. But there are some cases in which it is too embarrassing for the police to prosecute. So they left the Gulf war hero with his urban victory.

26 October 1991

'THE NOVEL AS AN ALTERNATIVE TO KNITTING'

Charles Moore

We sat and digested in the Guildhall last week and listened to the chairman of the judges, Jeremy Treglown, as he explained why his team had just awarded the Booker Prize to Ben Okri, for his novel, *The Famished Road*.

We sniggered as Mr Treglown told us of 'a man writing from Windlesham Manor, Windlesham, in Surrey' who had asked, in a letter to *The Times*, whether 'there was an inference to be drawn from the fact that none of the novels . . . is set in the United Kingdom'. Mr Treglown made short work of that poor simpleton, and of everyone else who lacked his own cultural boldness:

'Some literary people seem to inhabit a Heritage theme-park, in houses with no television, where, after the family has spent the evening around the piano, or at their Latin grammar, Father reads aloud to them from Mrs Humphry Ward.' A hit, Jeremy, a palpable hit!

'No one even half-conscious,' he went on, 'who had recently looked around a British city could suppose that Bombay or a Nigerian village are settings less immediate to the imaginations of readers here than, say, Barchester.'

Half-conscious as I was my attention wandered from Mr Treglown's daring denunciation of dim-witted squires and Tory education ministers, and the first sentences of a novel floated into my mind:

> An ancient English Cathedral Tower? How can the ancient English cathedral tower be here? The well known massive grey square tower of its old cathedral? How can that be here? There is no spike of rusty iron in the air, between the eye and it, from any point of the real prospect. What is the spike that intervenes, and who has set it up? Maybe it is set up by the Sultan's orders for the impaling of a horde of Turkish robbers one by one. It is so, for cymbals clash, and the Sultan goes by to his palace in long procession. Ten thousand scimitars flash in the sun-light, and thrice ten thousand dancing girls strew flowers. Then, follow white elephants caparisoned in countless gorgeous colours, and infinite in number and attendants. Still the Cathedral Tower rises in the background, where it cannot be, and still no writhing figure is on the grim spike. Stay! Is the spike so low a thing as the rusty spike on the top of a post of an old bedstead that has tumbled all awry?

That is how Dickens starts *Edwin Drood*. Within the first paragraph, he has conjured up for us Barchester (as it were) and Bombay (as it were) and put us in an opium den in east London. And he did all this at a time when there was no television and the family was sitting round the piano in the evening and Father was incapable of reading Mrs Humphry Ward aloud because she had not yet published her first novel. (By the way, I know Mrs Humphry Ward's name makes her irresistibly amusing, but I wonder whether Mr Treglown thinks that a novel like *Helbeck of Bannisdale*, with its fierce portrayal of the conflict between religion and human love, would make cosy reading for his imaginary literary family, or is inferior in power to any winner of the Booker Prize.)

As I write, I have in front of me the first edition of *Edwin Drood*. It was produced as a monthly magazine, the first instalment appearing in April 1870. The text is supported by advertisements for other books and for Borwick's Baking Powder and Jay's London General Mourning Warehouse and the Vowel Washing Machine (not an early invention of reactionary grammarians, but a washing machine) and, of course, the despised 'Twenty Guinea Pianoforte with check action'.

'. . . this is yet another formula "body-in-the-library" whodunit and hopelessly out of date with today's mystery readers . . .'

Only if one understands that context will one see why Dickens got so much into the first paragraph. He was writing fast for a popular market. He had to grab the attention and hold it. There was no *Guardian* whom he could inform, as Ben Okri did last week, that 'My road is a way, a road that is meant to take you from one place to another, on a journey towards a destination. The novel moves towards infinity. The novel as a form, if it is not going to be artificial, can only move towards infinity.' He had to write a book that people would actually want to read, and he was determined to do so, even if it killed him, which, before he had finished *Edwin Drood*, it did.

Another Booker judge, Jonathan Keates, writing in last Saturday's *Independent*, praised Mr Okri's book thus '. . . a passionate, daring visionary creation which will torment those who think of the novel as an alternative to knitting.' What have such people done that Mr Keates wants them to be tormented?

The novel obviously *is* an alternative to knitting. It does not exist *in vacuo*. It is there for readers, and readers are people with a choice about how to spend their time who, unlike Booker Prize judges, are not paid to read novels.

If a novel has the manners to try to please and move them, they will read it. If not, they will knit, or whatever, and it is not them we should blame if they become the *tricoteuses* at the scaffold of literature, but the arrogant complacency of people who think they have achieved something by promoting the unreadable, 'exploding conventional ideas of naturalistic reality' (that is what Mr Okri's novel does, according to his blurb), or offending whoever lives in Windlesham Manor, Windlesham.

I am not trying to argue that the public is always right, but that an artistic establishment that measures its courage and originality by its defiance of the public is always wrong. The effect is to debase public taste. The ordinary reader picks up the message that 'good books' are not for him, and so turns to Jeffrey Archer. 'It's crucial for any culture that those with power and influence in it should be open to what is new,' said Mr Treglown. Yes, but not half as crucial as that they should be open to what is old. People can find out for themselves what is new, simply by observing what is around them. They need to be taught about what is old.

There are now people who come up to read English at Cambridge who have hardly read any poetry or fiction written before this century. In a recent exam answered by 63 Cambridge applicants and marked by a friend of mine, they were invited to comment on the phrase 'through a glass darkly'. Only one of them identified it. At my village primary school in the mid-Sixties, mainly attended by the children of gypsum miners, 90 per cent would have recognised it.

Yes, yes, Jeremy Treglown is right that grammar is not static, and our culture has changed, and we must all welcome innovation and not be nostalgic, but that is not the problem facing the writing and the teaching and reading of literature. The problem is that virtually no one knows anything any more. Mr Treglown told us 'just how hard-working, imaginative, sensitive, resourceful and – yes – expert most of the people are who are teaching English in our struggling state schools'. Judging by the knowledge of the pupils emerging – and what else is there to judge by? – this is blatantly, pitifully untrue.

2 November 1991

NOBODY TALKS LIKE THAT

Robin Simon

I write as one of only three people known to have played table football with Anthony Blunt. You probably know the game – it is still a familiar sight in French cafés, although I confess that I prefer the lighter weight of the English version (made by the Brighouse Company) to that with the heavy pottery men you find in France. It enjoyed a great vogue among the more discerning Courtauld Institute postgraduates around 1970, and Blunt was apparently delighted to be invited to join in. We were not entirely surprised to see that he was unable to resist placing an exploratory arm of congratulation around the shoulders of his partner, an attractive young man who is now a happily married Inspector of Ancient Monuments. For my part, I had a more wily ally in the form of the deputy director.

The occasion was one of the excellent annual garden parties which took place on the lawn behind the great Adam house in Portman Square. The Courtauld has now moved to Somerset House but the Portman Square building was used, quite correctly, as the setting for the appropriate scenes in the recent television adaptation of Alan Bennett's stage play *A Question of Attribution*. This choice was itself evidence of the usual television search for authenticity, something stressed in the preceding publicity, and so it is worth recording that in almost every other respect the portrayal of Blunt was grotesque.

Perhaps I am in a good position to judge, for the reason that it is chiefly on outward appearances that I am able to do so. My acquaintance with Blunt was not in any sense an intimate one. He admitted me to the Courtauld; I heard him lecture; but apart from the table football encounter my only insight into anything other than the public persona came as the result of my attempting to operate the Institute's 1930s switchboard at weekends. In fact, despite being paid to do so, I was never able to work this anthropomorphic monster, which was made up of an intestinal tangle below and numbered porcelain discs above which flicked up and down like eyelids. As a result, for anything but the most direct communication between operator and the director's flat at the top of the house, Blunt had to come down four floors in order to receive any incoming calls.

Remarkably, he remained unfailingly tolerant and courteous, amused rather than annoyed, and, more astonishingly, I retained my occasional post in its strategic position just inside the front door. The comings and goings were intriguing to witness and the 'goings-on', as my colleague the Irish cleaning-woman called them, even more so. On these lonely mornings she was the only other person in the main part of the building. She had some sort of lair in the crepuscular basement from which she would emerge at intervals to mutter furiously about naked youths – 'wearing just an earring' – who scampered up and down the main staircase in the early hours. The rest was silence, for Blunt was discreet, and to me the sole give-away about the 'goings-on', apart from the irregular stream of gentleman callers, was the gin.

Every Saturday morning Blunt would sidle out – and a key point missed by the television was his lop-sidedness, in face, mouth, body and hands – soon after opening time, shortly to struggle back laden with carrier-bags stuffed to bursting with gin. When I finally saw inside Blunt's flat after his departure I was baffled to work out how it had contained so many for so long, especially as Blunt's regular partner, a nice former soldier, was in residence throughout. Hints of orgies apart, those inept hours of mine at the switchboard principally revealed a humorous and gentle aspect of Blunt to add to his consistent kindness to myself and to other students. Conflicting reports suggest that he could be both a bully and a bitch in private and a cynic might say that he had nothing to lose by being so nice to insignificant students. Yet I still cannot see that he had anything to gain. Certainly, any suggestion that he possessed such amiable qualities was missing from the television impersonation, but here we are in deep waters, and the programme was full enough of problems on the surface.

The most glaring and unpleasant inaccuracy in the television portrayal of Blunt was the voice. It was one of his most attractive and well-deployed features, 'ever soft and low', an upper-class accent of genuine refinement. In its place we were treated to an extravagantly affected kind of Queen's English as if uttered through a mouthful of Toffo. I was at first reminded of Jack Lemmon's response in *Some Like It Hot* to Tony Curtis's devastating take-off of Cary Grant – 'Nobody talks like that'. But then I realised that somebody does, and that the strangulated vowels we could hear were those of none other than the ubiquitous Mr Brian Sewell.

The actor playing Blunt was James Fox, who had been reported in the advance hype as having turned to Mr Sewell in the course of his 'research' for the part. He had evidently taken the fatal decision to mimic Mr Sewell as a reasonable substitute for the real thing and his ear is, alas, perfect. If one turned away from the screen, as too often one felt impelled to do, the effect was unbearable. In addition to the weird accent, it was painful to hear 'Blunt' talk of a painter by the name of Joe Varney Bellini – and then there was the crass lecture, littered with further solecisms. Blunt, although amusing and possessed of a ready wit, was far too fastidious, intellectually at least, to crack jokes in a lecture and was quite incapable of the relentless puns and trite innuendoes that this script assigned to him.

The extraordinary wardrobe that Fox had to wear must have been as much an embarrassment to the actor as it would have been to the living Blunt. Those jackets! Blunt was indeed much given to sports jackets, but here we were offered bookies' checks and a cardboard fit in place of the exquisitely well-cut and well-worn style of the genuine article. It was as if an image of a well-bred Englishman had been devised by an urchin with his nose pressed against the window of Burton Tailoring. The hair was apparently courtesy of Mr Whippy via the *Spitting Image* puppet of Douglas Hurd. In life it was a wispy affair surmounting an aesthetically cadaverous face and figure. On all counts, James Fox was simply far too well fed.

There were other howlers which would have been obvious to those who had no direct knowledge of Blunt, although more so to those with even so slight a knowledge as my own. In a crucial scene he was shown enjoying a drink in the National Gallery – backed by paintings from the Berggruen Collection which only arrived there this year. Other pictures in shot at the same location could not have been seen in Blunt's time for the very good reason that they were not then on view. Dramatic licence, perhaps, must be the excuse for this prolonged parody, and a play, of course, is a play is a play and not history, but after watching this one I was reminded of a troubled voice I heard on emerging from the stage performance of Shaffer's scatalogical *Amadeus* – 'I never knew Mozart was like that'. He wasn't, and nor was Blunt.

In respect purely of outward appearances, in the matter of which the television production strove so hard to be accurate – this representation of Blunt got it all wrong. And yet . . . Blunt himself appears to have been a master of deception, not least amongst those who thought they knew him best. In its bizarre way this misleading film may be as apt an epitaph as any.

2 November 1991

FULLER'S EARTH

P. J. Kavanagh

We should say goodbye to poets gratefully, if they were any good. Out of the muddle of their lives they may have put together some words which could clarify ours. Such a one was, is, Roy Fuller, who died a few weeks ago; and the remarkable thing about him is, that as his focus grew tighter, his range of experience more limited by illness and age, so did his poems get better. His messages from slippered and suburban retirement – he had been by profession a solicitor, Director of the Woolwich – his wry accounts of the evening highball, of putting out the garden chairs on his modest terrace in SE3, became one of the delights, and in an odd way one of the most original recordings, of our times. It was garden chairs that first suggested to me that something interesting was going on. In a 15-line poem, 'Great Events' (to be found in *Consolations*, 1987), he interrupts an observation of his own ageing: 'Damn it, I'll not/ Enshed the garden chairs: thus engineer/ Tomorrow's great event – the shock of meeting/ Light-fleeing earwigs when I come to unfold/ The blue or scarlet in yet another noon.' A man who can make something of earwigs hiding in a garden chair deserves watching.

The problem for a writer is always to catch and hold the material in hand; Roy Fuller was doing this, and knew it. 'I try my best with poetry to match/ Everybody's marvellous and varied prose.' It is poetry about being an elderly man, not an old man's poetry – he would be in his mid-seventies when he was writing that – and what clarity and humility it contains is the outcome of a lifetime's writing. Surprisingly, for he was a defiant secularist, he uses as an epigraph to *Consolations* a quotation from John Donne's *Essays in Divinity*; but it is apt.

> Let no smalnesse retard thee; if thou beest not a Cedar to help towards a palace, if thou beest not Amber, Bezoar, nor liquid gold to restore Princes; yet thou art a shrub to shelter a lambe, or to feed a bird; or thou art a plantane, to ease a child's smart; or a grasse to cure a sick dog.

There is much feeding of birds in these late poems, such tits and robins as Blackheath afforded. He even feeds 'Good Boy' vitaminised chocolate drops to dogs tied up outside the supermarket:

> Reason: unclear. It's surely not the sense,
> Retained from indoctrination when a child,
> Of the approach, near death, of Judgment Day.
> Besides in almost every other way
> Old age is famous for its selfishness;
> And it may well be, having lost one's looks,
> One tries to get in even dogs' good books.

I first came across him in the Fifties, in back numbers of *Penguin New Writing* and, though 'he had been heard to babble/ "Poets should be intelligible" ', he was not always so. But what made him stand out then was what became so attractive 30 years later; his ability suddenly to earth himself in a poem, describing where he is sitting, what he is looking at, why he is thinking what he is.

Such a method has its drawbacks. He later wrote some autobiographies which, though lively in places, sometimes went into such detail about how sailors tied the tiddly-bow round their caps or folded their bell-bottoms that one suspected the mickey was being taken. His poems, too, could bore. He had begun far to the Left, 'fond of Uncle Joe'; slowly he found he could no longer believe in all of that, or in anything else, and he went on about this. It seems that only when he admitted to himself that he really had no faith in mankind, or even affection for it, that he began to appreciate what was under his nose. There is no paradox in this. He had relieved himself of a strain. Nevertheless, he would have no truck with higher consolations. He asks how could he

> Respect those priestly leaders, arguing
> Whether the Second Person of the Three
> Is equal or subordinate to the First . . .
> I suppose their creed must conquer in the end
> Because it gives the simplest and most complete
> Answer to all men ask in these bad years.

(He concludes, 'Disgusting questions, horrible reply.') You cannot help liking him, nor could you when you met him. Neat moustache, thick wavy hair as tidy as his suit, the picture of the Man from the Woolwich, with attractive Lancashire vowels. I once sat in on a meeting of the

Arts Council Literature panel, of which he was the chairman, and his exasperation was a joy to watch. It was a time of experiment, and money was going to all sorts of things he disliked – concrete poetry, 'happenings', and so on. At last he burst out: 'And how the hell can we make sensible decisions when we have to look at that bloody picture!' Facing us was an over-excited abstract expressionist in puce and orange and pea-green, perhaps the pride of the Arts Council, certainly one of its 'investments'. I was shocked; I thought we artists ought to stick together, but afterwards I found his outburst refreshing. I too had thought the picture a mess, but he had dared to say so. We needed Roy Fuller.

This made greater the pleasure in the success of his last lap. It is time to give a late and representative example. His last book, *Available for Dreams*, 1989, is not all success; there are some obscurities, but also there are clarities. His wife is ill, he fears her death and his own, also fears his bladder trouble. He has to dive into the Gents of a pub and out again. 'The marvellous relief was all/ Too quickly cancelled out by feeling like/ A sparrow flying through a feasting hall.' He feeds the birds and still defies the gods. 'I turn to get some bread to throw: a god/ Typically unreliable, even mad.' His wife has an operation (we infer this, the biography is of his mind), and returns home; his relief and preoccupations are those of

The Elderly Husband

> Once more a lenient December: is
> It really the case that I am spared to try
> To burn what fell when she was at death's door?
> I hear the usual robin as I rake;
> I have to quit the smouldering when the dusk
> Announces strangely that it's time for tea;
> A quince of summer crunches underfoot;
> Below the rot a gold or even green
> Sprouting prognosticates the still-far Spring.
> I bear a cup to her, then guiltily

Over my own hear Gerald Finzi's work
For cello that illegally I've changed
From air to tape. What gods can possibly
Exist to whom thanks must be breathed for this?

2 November 1991

DIARY

P. D. James

I was sitting in a first-class carriage at Paddington (first-class travel
being an occasional extravagance) when a distraught young man burst
into the otherwise empty compartment. His story was that he and his
wife and three children had just returned from visiting his brother in
Australia. He had enough money to buy all the family's tickets to
Newport but not his own. Could I lend him £30? His father-in-law
was meeting the party at Newport and would repay me then. He
offered to hand over the family passports as a guarantee of honesty,
or even produce the children themselves who, he said, were sitting
with their mother in standard-class further up the train. 'I hate doing
this,' he said in evident distress, 'it makes me feel like a beggar.' My
suspicious nature, of which I'm not particularly proud, saved me from
handing over the £30. I said that he should explain the situation to
the ticket collector, and tell him that I would pay his fare and where
I was sitting. When the collector came round, I told him the story and
undertook to pay the fare when he returned. He received the proposal
with a marked lack of enthusiasm and went on his way, leaving me a
prey to guilt. If only I had had the generosity to hand over the £30 I
could have saved the young man the humiliation of publicly telling his
story. Three quarters of an hour later the collector returned. Neither
the young man nor his family were, of course, on the train. I told this
tale to my grand-daughter who, by an extraordinary coincidence, had
met the young man, or one of his ilk, in a local pub. He had described
the con to her. Apparently he calls it 'working the terminus', and
reckons that with careful selection of his victim he can get £30 for
each alternate departing Intercity train. He is, of course, helped by the

fact that there is no longer any need to buy a platform ticket. The whole thing was certainly extraordinarily convincing and a fellow writer on the train, more generously minded than I, told me that she had been perfectly willing to hand over the £30 but was unable to as she hadn't sufficient cash on her. I have always somewhat despised the credulous victims of conmen but after this display of virtuoso acting I shall be more sympathetic.

9 November 1991

DIARY

P. D. James

A surprising number of life's minor pleasures are being destroyed, including riding in a London taxi. The new seat-belts at the back are the most uncomfortable I have ever attempted to clip on, effectively preventing me from leaning forward to speak to the driver or from opening the window. Being fiercely strapped to the seat in a locked cab while one's ears are assaulted with continual pop music is hardly a pleasure for someone mildly claustrophobic and allergic to noise. A more important pleasure I miss is visiting churches, particularly in the country. Invariably, because of vandals, they are now locked. I have been told of a country vicar who has placed a notice on his church door in French explaining where the key can be found and asking visitors to replace it after re-locking the church. He will no doubt be criticised for élitism, and the assumption that no one who can understand French can possibly be a vandal is open to question. However, I understand that it works.

16 November 1991

ENGLISH, OUR ENGLISH

John Simpson

The trouble with viewers and listeners is that although they do not watch or listen with much care, they are absolutely certain that they have seen and heard correctly. A week or so ago, a group known as Tin Machine appeared on *Top of the Pops*. Its drummer was a man called Hunt who, for some reason, had had his name tattooed on his knuckles. Twenty-nine prurient prudes, mistaking the H for a C and assuming it was one of those words which Lord Rees-Mogg tells us are now used by professors in private, rang in to complain about the BBC's use of bad language, campaign to subvert the morals of the young, left-wing bias, etc.

Britain is a country where people apologise if someone else barges into them; they are far less forbearing towards the people who broadcast to them. Bad language, whether misread on people's knuckles or spoken, upsets some viewers greatly, though fewer now than in the past. Politics, by contrast, seems to bother people less. Rank-and-file Conservatives were asked recently by their party chairman to complain to the BBC if they believed it was dealing unfairly with the Government, yet there have been far more calls complaining about the recent postponement of *Star Trek*.

The greatest passions are probably stirred up by the use of English on the BBC. Some people – judging by their letters to the BBC – are goaded beyond endurance by what they hear:

'I can't stand it any longer! Over a period of years I have suffered under BBC mispronunciation of this Gulf State [Qatar], which has varied from "Catter", "Quater" (to rhyme with crater) and other hopeless variations, but you now appear to have settled for "Catarrh".'

'Could you do something about financial experts who talk about "Wawn thay-ousand pay-ounds"? It grates so.'

'When will you stop employing idiots who cannot distinguish between "disinterested" and "uninterested"?'

'Can you please do something to prevent the demise of the sibilant "s" from the English language? In just the last week on BBC Radio 4 and BBC TV I have heard Dezember, dezolate, dizgrace, perzist, dezision and Loz Angeles.'

Most of us have our King Charles's heads: 'REsearch' as opposed to 'reSEARCH', perhaps, or misbegotten grammatical imports like the American subjunctive ('she asked that she not be identified'), or the home-produced anti-toff tendency which is killing off the gerund ('I had no objection to him leaving'). Indeed, almost everything seems to be disliked by someone, even the standard English which the BBC is usually accused of abandoning:

'I propose your announcers etc. give us a widely used diet of words instead of what is often known as "affected speech" suitable to "clever" people in West London.'

Yet, however loony, however spluttering, however reactionary, every such letter receives a polite, carefully reasoned response from the small group of people whose task it is to make sure that the BBC uses the language correctly. The Pronunciation Unit works in a quiet room at the back of Broadcasting House in London. It feels like the library of a Cambridge college: there is the same air of research being done for its own sake and people who visit it instinctively talk in whispers. Books of reference line the room, and the drawers in the old-fashioned cabinets (the BBC has not yet computerised the Unit) contain reference cards which record meticulously the correct pronunciation of a quarter of a million words and names.

There are only four of them: the Pronunciation Adviser, two other linguists trained in the use of phonetics, and a clerk. The Pronunciation Adviser is a pleasant, donnish man with a beard, who specialises in Spanish, French and Norwegian but has an encyclopaedic knowledge of pronunciation worldwide. Graham Pointon's task is not an easy one: 36 hours of news and current affairs broadcasting per week on network television, 66 hours on network radio, and all the other programmes and services including World Service radio and television, represent a great deal of pronunciation, and some of it is bound to be wrong.

I once encountered him the day after I announced the news of the murder of Anwar Sadat of Egypt in 1981 and the assumption of power by Hosni Mubarak. Graham shook his head and clicked his tongue at me. 'MuBArak,' he said, accentuating the second syllable; 'you said MOObarak.' He walked on, a disappointed man. I long ago gave up trying to use travelmanship as a counter to the Unit's edicts: claiming to have been to the place or to have met the person in question has no effect. The Pronunciation Adviser and his staff, like cricket umpires, are never wrong.

Yet they appreciate that rightness is something to be re-examined at frequent intervals. And there is, of course, no single rule which applies. With some names the Unit accentuates the foreignness ('GorbaCHEV', when every instinct makes one want to say 'GORbachev'). With others

it favours the familiar; the Unit recommends 'Peking' rather than
'Beijing', has returned to 'Cambodia' from 'Kampuchea' and never left
'Burma'. Until a month or so ago, Maastricht was just a town in the least
attractive part of the Netherlands, and the few people who mentioned
it on the BBC tended to call it MAAstricht, because the first syllable
usually catches the stress in British English. Now newsreaders and
correspondents seem to be saying it all the time; and since the Dutch
are a second-syllable people, accuracy demanded that the instruction
should go out: MaaSTRICHT. Soon, no doubt, the place will slip back
into pronunciation limbo and the unnatural-sounding stress will lapse.
Going native has its limits; the Unit prefers 'Félipe Gonthaleth', but
that sounds too much like Violet Elizabeth Bott and the broadcasters

'It's a lot smaller than it used to be.'

rebelled. Ultra-authenticity has been out of fashion at the BBC since the days when Angela Rippon read the *Nine O'Clock News*, and would speak of 'guerrEEyas', or pronounce 'Joshua Nkomo' Ndebele-fashion.

The legacy of Empire died slowly. The BBC was asked by the Kenyan government to change from the colonial 'Keenya', so it did. It clung on to 'Sy-nee-eye' until the BBC correspondents in the Middle East pointed out that 'Sinai' hadn't been pronounced like that since biblical days. The Pronunciation Unit does not like to move hastily: once a recommendation has been made those broadcasters who are on the BBC's staff are required to follow it. Great efforts are made to ensure accuracy. The prime minister of Grenada, Mr Nicholas Brathwaite, pronounces his name in various ways. After 14 lengthy calls to former ministers and leading Caribbean journalists, the Unit settled on the home-grown version, 'Brathert'.

In Britain, the Unit rings up every candidate in every parliamentary election to get the correct version of his or her name. BBC local radio stations compile lists of the worthies in their area, and these go back to the Unit as well. In the matter of place names, the Unit always checks two reliable contacts: the postmistress, say, or the local schoolmaster. It has learned to be wary of clergymen, because they usually come from outside. The Unit wants the local pronunciation of villages and some towns, though with others, and with cities, a standard version exists and 'Newcassel' or 'Hool' might sound mocking.

Yet even place names change. Outsiders move into a town or village and start pronouncing the name as it is spelt, rather than as the natives say it: 'Skelmersdale' instead of 'Skemmersdale', for instance. I asked about the choice of 'Daintree' or 'Daventry'; the index-card, furry with age, said 'Recommended pronunciation: davventri; daintree accepted as used.' Then it went on, 'From a contact at the home of the late Viscountess Daventry in Kensington, 15/5/57. Our contact was horrified at the idea of the pronunciation deintri, which she maintained was "modern", dating back only to the 1500s, whereas davventri went back to the Domesday Book.'

What enrages viewers and listeners most is the way they hear everyday English spoken. Regional accents have annoyed them since Wilfred Pickles was recruited to newsreading. When John Cole became Political Editor in 1981, his Northern Ireland accent aroused a frenzy of Home Counties criticism: now he is one of the best-regarded broadcasters in the country, a national figure who is genuinely liked and admired. Studies have shown that certain accents – West Country, Scots, Southern Irish – find general favour among viewers and listeners, while those of Birmingham, London, Liverpool and Belfast do not.

Some of the usages people criticise most fiercely derive from these unfavoured areas: 'DISpute' instead of 'disPUTE', for instance. Others come from the general haste which is an inevitable part of broadcasting: I often hear myself saying 'seketry' for 'secretary'. It is ugly, but producing the necessary dexterity of tongue and jaw to give the first 'r' and the third syllable their proper force isn't always easy. Within the BBC a guerrilla ('guerrEEya') war is being fought out between those who think it sounds sharper and better to omit the definite article before people's titles – 'Israeli prime minister Yitzhak Shamir said today . . .' – and those who feel that the time saved by such shorthand doesn't make up for the unreflective feeling it conveys. The habit comes from Fleet Street via commercial radio and is still spreading: though with luck it will never wholly conquer the BBC.

'FOR HEAVEN'S SAKE,' says a letter in the files, written in capitals to show extra anguish, 'INSTRUCT YOUR NEWSCASTERS, WHO INFLUENCE SO MANY, TO USE CORRECT ENGLISH.' But correct English is like the BEF on the retreat towards the Channel: it never gets the chance to regroup and make a stand. Since 1914 the pace of change in British English has been extraordinary, and it is unrealistic to expect that the BBC in general, or the three linguists plus their clerk in the Pronunciation Unit, could possibly halt it, even if English were in the habit of accepting codification, which it isn't.

In the 1930s, John Reith set up the Broadcasting Advisory Committee, precisely because listeners were continually complaining about the BBC's use of English. The Committee, like the Pronunciation Unit today, accepted that the language couldn't stand still, but its handbook, *Broadcast English*, recommended all sorts of usages which nowadays sound ludicrous: 'balCOny' not 'BALcony', 'cal-EYE-bre' not 'CALibre', 'HOSt'le' not 'hostile'. And yet in some sectors the front line remains surprisingly static; the Pronunciation Unit's files contain furious letters from the 1940s complaining about 'conTROVersy' and our old friend 'harASSment' as used in the case of Judge Clarence Thomas. The letters of complaint in 1981 were about precisely the same subjects as those in 1991: not a single new issue seemed to have emerged during the decade.

The greatest change, and the fastest, has come in terms of accent. I spoke recently to a university audience, and realised how different my accent and slang, the result of a 1950s childhood, seemed from theirs: all my 'jolly goods' and 'absolutelys', and all those vowels which are on their way to becoming museum pieces. Nor is this a new process: recordings of Gladstone or Neville Chamberlain seem monstrosities of affectation now, and the Queen herself had to tone down her English in the 1960s to something closer to that of her subjects.

Where, then, are we heading? My daughters, cultivated young women reading, respectively, Russian at Bristol and Classics at Oxford, display an encroaching Americanism which is no doubt the sound of the future. In casual conversation they leave out some of the basic building-blocks of language: 'I said' becomes, 'I'm, like' – as in 'I'm, like, "What am I supposed to do now?"' On their lips, of course, I find it enchanting, but I shall not be so happy when it becomes general. If, in five years' time, viewers and listeners write in to blame the BBC for it, they will be wrong: my daughters' generation hasn't picked it up from the BBC's own broadcasters, but from the great wave of American cultural and linguistic domination which started with talking pictures. Graham Pointon will have the difficult task of explaining this in his replies. And he will, perhaps, point out that he is merely the BBC's adviser on such matters, and not its dictator.

16 November 1991

HOIST BY HIS OWN CANARD

Stephen Spender

Salman Rushdie was sentenced to death a thousand days ago, by order of the Ayatollah Khomeni, a judgment which has been endorsed by his successors. Rushdie's offence was, allegedly, blasphemy against Islam, the prophet and the Koran in his novel, *The Satanic Verses*.

It was surely unthinkable, until quite recently, that a religious or political leader in a foreign country should openly and publicly pronounce sentence of death on a writer living in this country. It was also unthinkable that there should be co-religionists of the Ayatollah living in Great Britain who would publicly express their approval of the sentence so passed, and that they should make it so clear that some among them were willing to carry out the sentence, that the British authorities have been obliged to take Mr Rushdie into what is, in effect, protective custody.

These previously unthinkable things have become realities because, following on events such as the disintegration after 1945 of the British and other European Empires, we are living in one of the great periods of migration, when immigrants from over-populated and impoverished parts of the world – and from countries where there is political persecution – flow over their boundaries into the less populated, more prosperous and more democratic areas.

Some English (and French and Germans and, indeed, now Italians) deplore immigration and try to stop it. I must admit to having a certain sympathy for the way they feel, though not with their actions. It is sad for members of a nation to lose a sense of their own identity with all its traditions, culture, art, ideas and way of life inherited from the past and identified with landscape and towns. Nevertheless, I think that immigration, like the shrinkage of the world through modern communications, is inevitable.

In an interesting essay entitled 'In Good Faith' (published in the *Independent on Sunday*, 4 February 1990) Mr Rushdie defends *The Satanic Verses* on the grounds that:

> it is written from the very experience of uprooting, disjuncture and metamorphosis . . . that is the migrant condition, and from which, I think, can be derived a metaphor for all humanity.

He sees his task as a novelist as that which Shelley, in the modern world of scientific invention, saw as his task as a poet, 'to imagine that which we know'.

And what he knows in *The Satanic Verses* is his celebration of:

> hybridity, impurity, intermingling, the transformation that comes of new and unexpected combinations of human beings, cultures, ideas, politics, movies, songs . . . Mélange, hotch-potch, a bit of this and a bit of that is how newness enters the world . . . It is the great possibility that mass migration gives the world, and I have tried to embrace it.

What Mr Rushdie seems here to overlook is that it is mass immigration which has got him into the trouble in which he now finds himself: unpleasant as it is to have to admit this, it is the presence of large numbers of Muslim immigrants in English cities with, among them, a small minority of fanatics, which makes it necessary for the native British police to protect him from their attentions.

One cannot take it for granted that a global population hotch-potch of the kind which Mr Rushdie envisages would be a world safe, not just for him, but for democracy. Democracy is threatened in several countries now by immigration, partly because immigration provokes the most reactionary forces in the countries now receiving immigrants (Le Pen in France, neo-Nazis in Germany, neo-fascists in Italy), partly because the immigrants themselves are by no means always upholders of democracy.

There seems to be a rather widely shared assumption today that the breakdown of communism implies the triumph of capitalism and the market economy which go hand in hand with the triumph of democracy. Myself, I think that while Big Business may benefit from the forces released in a period of intense competition and rivalry, democracy may not necessarily, and inevitably, prove the alternative to the tyrannies which have collapsed or been overthrown. Events in Yugoslavia show how provinces may break off from their centres

without their necessarily becoming democracies in doing so, and how in some countries communists may remain in power, perhaps under another name.

As a result of internecine struggles in Russia, Yugoslavia and elsewhere there are likely soon to be millions of refugees; and wherever these are received as immigrants there will be reactionary forces opposed to receiving them, and there will be no guarantee that the immigrants themselves are democratic.

Salman Rushdie's vision in *The Satanic Verses* of a world consisting almost entirely of immigrants intermingling to the benefit of all, is inspiring and generous. But for migration to take place on such a scale without its resulting in a breakdown of democracy, is difficult to imagine. And if there was a breakdown of democracy, the immigrants in every country would be threatened with the kind of liquidation with which we were made all too familiar in central Europe in the years between 1933 and 1945.

Maintaining democracy is the essential pre-condition of immigration and, doing so, means putting it before immigration.

One lesson I draw from the Salman Rushdie affair is that immigrants should be required to obey the laws of the country or countries to which they migrate, especially where these are concerned with freedom. I wonder how far democracy is taught in English schools where there are large numbers of immigrants. I find myself thinking almost nostalgically of American schools, where children are made every morning to salute the American Flag, and wishing that there was a flag of democracy, symbolising freedom of speech, which children going into English schools – wherever these children come from – were made to salute.

Meanwhile, of course, I support the freedom of Salman Rushdie to express his visions, even when I do not agree with these. His case has come to symbolise the freedom of the writer, and to show how endangered this may be, and indeed especially, in the world of total migration which he appears to support.

16 November 1991

DIARY

Nigel Nicolson

In a few weeks I will be 75. I hope that my friends will be as astonished by that fact as I am, but I doubt it. For the first time the other day I read of myself as an old man: 'The old man shuffled downstairs, and the first I saw of him was a pair of scuffed boots.' 'Shuffled', 'scuffed', both untrue, but I suppose that they are legitimate attributes of old age if you wish to suggest it. I discussed with another visitor whether it has any advantages. Yes, four. You can plead irresponsibility, as once you did in extreme youth: people will excuse you for deafness or missing trains. Envy of other people's characters and attainments is replaced by admiration, for there is no longer time to catch up. Thirdly, forgetfulness: if this seems a strange sort of bonus, it has the advantage that you can read a great novel for the fourth time without remembering how it ends. Finally, and best of all, grandchildren, for whom you have no responsibility but abundant reciprocated affection. It is most unfair that penury should coincide with youth and relative affluence with senility, but it is up to the old man to make adjustments in favour of the young, and it gives him pleasure, which makes a fifth consolation for being 75.

But how little one knows about oneself. I read that Lord Longford, who will soon be 86, did not know the colour of his eyes. Meeting him the other day, I gazed into them. They are bluey-grey. He asked me if I knew the colour of mine. I didn't. Later, I looked in the mirror. Washy-brown. I suppose that one only notices eyes that are startlingly one-coloured, like brilliant blue. But no. When I was in the army (wartime only) I had as my adjutant a famous captain who had one eye blue, the other green. It was a formidable combination. He terrified us. I once danced with his wife. She was beautiful and scented. 'My word,' I remarked halfway round the floor, 'you do smell.' She made no reply, and we continued to foxtrot. I thought some qualification was necessary. 'Good, I mean,' I added three minutes later. She remained silent. My father once advised me that it is the things one hasn't done in life that one regrets, not the things one has done. But he was wrong. It is the failures, and the gaffes, that linger in the mind.

On Armistice Sunday I wept. I wasn't at the Cenotaph, nor even at my local church or war memorial. It was 10 p.m. and I was watching the re-run on television. Now, why did I weep? I wept because I suddenly thought of Corporal Drake. He was not a very good corporal, not even a good soldier. He was a Norfolk farm-boy who enlisted in the Grenadier Guards, was promoted (I can't think why) corporal, and was killed by a German shell on a Tunisian hill-side, not when we were advancing, but resting in reserve. I think of him every Armistice Day. Corporal Drake. Now, why was he killed? The formula is that he died fighting for king and country. But he wasn't fighting: he was sitting down. The King had nothing to do with it. 'Fighting' is a euphemism. Few soldiers actually fight. They wait; they stumble forward; they are hit by bits of steel, but seldom see their enemy except as prisoners; they are mutilated, or die. Death in battle is as accidental as death on the roads, and almost as pointless. So when I think of Corporal Drake (is he still remembered on the Norfolk farm?), I wonder what contribution he made to our Tunisian victory, and I have to admit that it was negligible. He killed no German. He gained no ground. But if he, and a hundred thousand other Corporal Drakes, had not been there, we would be celebrating a very different sort of Armistice. I wept for him because he is a symbol, not a cause, of our victory.

23 November 1991

WHY WE OVER-50S ARE QUITE HAPPY WITH EUROPE

Auberon Waugh

I was puzzled to find myself appearing on this page last week, my week off, when the space is filled by *The Spectator*'s Voice of Youf, young Charles Moore. He invoked my name as being among those who are 'old and grey and full of sleep' and so likely to be opposed to the exciting Euroscepticism of himself and what he refers to as his generation:

The great supporters of the European Idea are men

like Peter Riddell, Hugo Young, Auberon Waugh, Peter
Jenkins, Joe Rogaly. Their average is the wrong side
of 50.

The wrong side of 50? Do I read him aright? I do not know who Joe
Rogaly is and cannot find him in *Who's Who*, but I celebrated my 52nd
birthday last week, and surely all the others are well into their second
half-century?

He was making the point, for what it is worth, that 'the young' –
those of his own 35-year-old generation, including a further three
Spectator political correspondents and such political thinkers of the
Left as Julie Burchill and A.N. Wilson (*aet:su:*41) belong to this exciting
new club of Eurosceptics, so it must be the fun place to be, I mean,
y'know, where it's all at.

I confess I am a bit alarmed to find myself bedded down with
Riddell, Young and Jenkins, let alone the unknown Rogaly. Perhaps
their motives for welcoming closer commercial and political ties with
the rest of Europe are as described by Charles Moore:

> For those who became voters in the 1950s or early
> 1960s, the future role of Britain must have seemed
> a great question because Britain was a great power.
> How was a suitably grand role to be found if there
> was no longer an empire? The solution seemed to be
> that Britain must . . . become the leader of Europe.

I can only assure this young gentleman that, in my own case, he
has got it absolutely wrong. Having purged myself of all my leadership
urges defending (however ineffectively) a late outpost of the British
Empire in the eastern Mediterranean, I was under no illusions about
Britain still being a great power in 1959, and never sought a 'grand role'
for our politicians on the world's stage. One of the most attractive
aspects of the federal idea is precisely the limitations it sets on the
influence of British politicians and the British electorate. When Charles
writes of the younger Tories at the Conference being most vociferous in
their opposition to federalism (I can't go on writing Charles Moore; Mr
Moore would be absurdly pompous and Moore might provoke tears in
one so young), and lists some younger Tory candidates as being similarly
'decided in their belief that Britain should continue to govern itself',
he is not really talking about British youf. He is talking about young
Conservative activists, all of whom confidently expect to have a finger
in the pie of government.

My own observations of a slightly broader spectrum of British youf – my children, nephews, nieces and their friends – is that they are not tremendously interested in the Common Market; to the extent that they are interested, they welcome its political implications partly as offering an escape from Mrs Thatcher, partly as a means of frustrating their more politically active contemporaries – precisely the people Charles observed at Blackpool.

But it is no guarantee of the virtue of a cause that it is supported by the young. Rather the reverse, in fact. One complains about the ignorance and historical inanity of young Britons today – Charles proudly boasts that he had never heard of the British Empire until he was eight – but it is the British electorate, *tout court*, which really strikes terror. Gallup revealed last week that 77 per cent think 'everyone should have all the health care they need, no matter how much it costs,' although only 56 per cent were prepared to pay more in taxes to achieve that end. The idea of Britain governing itself under these circumstances becomes absurd whether you mean government by democratic choice or government by eager Young Conservatives.

Even if it were not an observable fact that the other governments of the old Six regulate their affairs better than we do – they have better pensions, better health arrangements, better legal systems – the case for an economic merger would be overwhelming vis-à-vis the threat of economic and political domination from across the Atlantic. If our electorate is alarming in its ignorance and stupidity, the American electorate is completely terrifying. Half of it is unaware of Europe's existence. The United States, like its citizens, is rapidly disintegrating into terminal self-absorption. Never mind the health risks, never mind the racial tensions, never mind the drugs, the violence or even the lawyers, although all these are either symptoms or contributory factors. The fact is that the United States is rapidly deteriorating into a market with which no outside country will be able to do business on anything like equal terms. If we allow ourselves to be dominated by the United States, we are substituting a market over which we have some participating control for one over which we have no control whatever, in whose councils we have no voice. We would be unequal partners in an arrangement entirely designed to disadvantage us.

It is the commercial and cultural domination of the United States – our reduction to a trans-Atlantic Puerto Rico – which we should chiefly seek to avoid within a semi-federal Europe. But the greatest advantage of the single currency is seldom mentioned. It has nothing to do with ease of travel or savings on exchange. Within a single currency area, no single national government will be able to inflate by printing money or overspending at will. At a stroke, it takes away the greatest power for mischief which our politicians possess. No longer will they be able to manipulate the economy with false booms or 'go' messages in order to secure their own re-election. No longer will our moronic electorate be able to decide that everyone should have all the health care he needs regardless of cost. Everything will have to be paid for on the nail whether by taxation or loan, and not by the attrition of savings through inflation.

I hope I have answered Charles's question: 'By what logic do familiarity with and affection for the continent of Europe lead to approval of economic and monetary union, or a common foreign policy . . .?' National sovereignty, in the context of what we are losing, means no more and no less than the power fantasies of a handful of young political aspirants. They are not too high a price for the rest of us to pay.

23 November 1991

ANOTHER VOICE

WHY IS MR WAUGH ON THE CONTINENTAL SHELF?

Charles Moore

We young people are notoriously hesitant to question the wisdom of our elders, but as *The Spectator*'s spokesman for my generation, I feel I must answer Mr Auberon Waugh's answer to me.

In this space last week, Mr Waugh (as one always, with instinctive deference, thinks of him) explained 'Why the over-50s are quite happy with Europe'. By 'Europe', he meant the EEC, rather than the great Continent that stretches from the Atlantic to the Urals. He advanced several reasons. One was that 'the United States . . . is rapidly disintegrating into terminal self-absorption' and into 'a market with which no outside country will be able to do business on anything like equal terms', so we must not allow ourselves to be dominated by America. Therefore we need to protect ourselves by an 'economic merger' with the EEC. There are a good many answers to this, but I shall content myself with one. Britain has a trade surplus with North

America of £2.5 billion; it has a trade deficit with the rest of the EEC of £9.9 billion, so where does the threat of domination come from?

Another of Mr Waugh's reasons was the 'observable fact' that the governments of the 'old Six' regulate their affairs better than we do. I am not at all sure that this *is* an observable fact, rather than an impression collected by the observation of a tourist naturally disposed to like places which are hotter and where the food is nicer and where he is out to enjoy himself, but let that pass. Let us accept that Belgium has good government and Italy has no bureaucracy and France protects civil liberties and Dutch euthanasia is a wonderful thing. If the 'old Six' do regulate their affairs better than we do, what has that got to do with a federal Europe? Until recently, the only important way in which the EEC governed its members was in the Common Agricultural Policy, and no one thinks that that is well regulated. Even now, most of the power of Brussels and Strasbourg has yet to be applied (hence the push for new treaties at Maastricht). So to observe smiling plenty and the rule of right reason in Paris or Bonn and to conclude that this shows how good a United States of Europe would be is a non-sequitur.

Mr Waugh's chief point concerns power. 'One of the most attractive aspects of the federal idea', he writes, 'is precisely the limitations it sets on the influence of British politicians and the British electorate.' And the best thing about the single currency, in his view, is that 'no single national government will be able to inflate by printing money or overspending at will . . . No longer will our moronic electorate be able to decide that everyone should have all the health care he needs regardless of cost.'

But if Mr Waugh is right, which he probably is, that most politicians are chiefly concerned with power, doesn't it give him pause for thought that most of our politicians *favour* greater EEC integration? They must have considered whether they will win or lose out of the deal, and concluded that they will win. That is what the endlessly repeated phrases about how we must not miss the bus and we must have a seat at the top table mean – they mean that a fittingly grand and powerful future for politicians is assured by a semi-federal EEC and the chance must not be missed.

Anyway, why single out the dangers of too much power for politicians in *Britain*? I do not wish to romanticise the British people or their elected representatives, but if you are seeking examples of the evils of popular will and the effects of power mania in this century, you will find rather more dramatic ones on the Continent than here. In fact, Britain is the only important country in the EEC where parliamentary democracy has been vindicated. Elsewhere, it has either permitted the rise of dictators, as in Germany, or proved at crucial moments too weak, as in France. This, not ours, is the historical experience on which the scheme for a federal Europe is based.

It is a scheme for avoiding fascist or communist dictatorship and popular power, for the two are seen as almost inextricably linked. M. Delors wants to run Europe as Colbert ran France, as the great bureaucrat who does not enact laws made by a parliament, but devises and imposes them himself. If he succeeds in increasing the power of the Commission as he intends, he will have created the greatest mandarinate in modern history, made all the more powerful by the fact that the mandarins, like M. Delors himself, will be politicians, not career civil servants freed from the dreary business of having to get votes to retain their jobs.

Now one can see some good effects of this. It probably will be harder for the single currency to be debauched by politicians than it is for them to destroy their national currencies. But it will also be easier for

the men who control that currency to impoverish a country, and to do so without fear of electoral wrath. Poorer nations will be bound to a currency which sets them impossibly high standards (as has happened with East Germany since unification) and so puts their people out of work. They will then live only on subsidies, and therefore at the whim of others. One or two incidents in history suggest that this can lead to disagreeable expressions of the popular will. I would rather have a pre-election boom than a fascist coup.

Some might wonder at the prejudices underlying Mr Waugh's arguments. Does he despise everyone who speaks English as a first language? Is there something about a Roman Catholic upbringing which makes one mistrust British institutions? I do not know, and it would be impertinent of me to speculate about such a venerable figure. But it is odd in this whole business that people keep on saying how awful the British political system is. It isn't. It has clearer lines of responsibility, a greater closeness to voters, a more important and franker forum for debate, a better ability to implement decisions, a wider public acceptance of its legitimacy than do its Continental counterparts. For two days last week the House of Commons discussed Europe, and did so with a thoroughness and sharpness and drama which has no foreign equal. I do not think our politicians are any more megalomaniac or our electors any more moronic than anyone else's, and I do think our constitution is better than that being concocted in the test tube of Maastricht.

30 November 1991

THE WRONGS OF WOMEN

Neil Lyndon

Does feminism count for anything today? Does anybody take it seriously?

Some of those who do seem to take feminism seriously are not to be taken seriously themselves; some figures who must be taken seriously, such as the Prime Minister and the Law Lords, might be surprised to think that their thoughts and judgments are influenced by feminism. As always, throughout its 25-year history, modern feminism doesn't know exactly what to think or to make of itself. According to some outward signs, it might seem that the most influential social movement of the postwar years is expiring in the last decadent gasps of redundancy.

Two weeks ago, a group of feminist-minded women writers and editors held a gathering to consider nominations for the Hooker Prize, spoofing the Booker Prize. Prominent in this band of sisters were the *Sunday Times* 'style' journalist and novelist Kate Saunders, the screenwriter Lynda La Plante, the columnist Jaci Stephen and Liz Calder, Publishing Director of the Bloomsbury publishing house. Riled by the absence of women writers from the Booker shortlist, they struck back by shortlisting Martin Amis, Clive James and Melvyn Bragg for the Hooker Prize which they awarded for 'male chauvinist writing'. First prize – 'the world's smallest condom' – went to Martin Amis for a passage about women's underwear in his novel *London Fields*.

The occasion had many marks of the dorm feast at St Trinian's – especially the trilling and giggling over naughty bits in modern fiction, read aloud with chortling wonder ('And then, you'll never guess what he does next: he gets out his THING; we all *screamed* with laughter').

The gathering was, however, decked out with the trimmings essential to the status of members of a dandified literary and journalistic set, declaring that these girls had graduated from the classroom of IVa to the ranks of the have-it-alls. The ceremony was held at the Groucho Club, where the *beau monde* goes to study its reflection and touch its own flesh. The girls awarded a special prize to Angela Carter as compensation for missing out on the Booker. It was, of course, a bottle of bubbly. Original.

The twittishness and chittishness of that sisterly gathering provide one style of answer to the questions about feminism: many of its adherents cannot be taken seriously. Kate Saunders covered herself with a toss of curls to describe the occasion. 'The award itself is a bit of a joke,' she said, but then, to get full advantage of both sides of the jape, she went on, 'but we all felt there were lots of women's novels that were as good as, if not better than, the ones which were selected [for the Booker Prize].' The joke, in other words, is impregnable to scepticism or scrutiny, both because it is a frippery and because it rests upon a serious proposition. The sisterhood has always been adept at having it both ways; and, even in jest, they have never taken themselves less than seriously.

Trivial vanity though it was, the Hooker Prize cannot be dismissed entirely as an irrelevance to our times. It is not important but it is slightly significant. It suggests that people who have some power may be governed in their thoughts by the muddled axioms of modern feminism, just as it was disturbing, earlier this year, to hear the QC Helena Kennedy declare, after a television film on the subject of rape, that the act of rape expresses the power which all men feel entitled to exercise over all women. Helena Kennedy may be a High Court judge one day. If, on that day, she still adheres to the feminist line of cant which holds all men to be rapists, our society (and the defendants who appear before her) will be in a spot of trouble.

By the same measure, Liz Calder, Publishing Director of Bloomsbury, is in a position which nobody would describe as being without influence. Book-publishing may be a financial minnow in the seas of a national economy (Marks & Spencer probably turns over more money in a single day on sales of socks than Bloomsbury's entire list generates in a year); but the business's power to influence opinion is not expressed in its balance-sheets. If the Publishing Director of an important house will give her name to the Hooker Prize, we may assume that she agrees with the first principles of the assembled group and we may assume, further, that they will have some bearing upon her work and her judgments.

Kate Saunders was a judge for last year's Booker Prize. For all the idiocy and flummery and the hoop-la surrounding the event, the judging of the Booker Prize is self-evidently an important role in our national culture, affecting the book-buying of a wide group of readers and immensely influencing the balance-sheets of publishers. Why should we imagine that the attitude Kate Saunders brought to her deliberations as a Booker Prize judge should be markedly different from that which made 'the world's smallest condom' the Hooker Prize – an unquestioning faith in the rectitude of modern feminism?

That view provided the Hooker Prize with its muddled point: the authors who were reviled (Dickens was also nominated) and pissed upon by the Trinians in the Groucho dorm had committed the offence of writing about sex. This is not allowed. A man may not write about the feelings of men towards women (or their underclothes) or of women towards men, even in fictional varieties and inventions of character, without opening himself, as an individual and as a writer, to the charge of 'male chauvinism'. Any male writer, dead or alive, Western or Eastern, Christian, Sikh or Buddhist, may be subjected to this charge. Regardless of the divisions between their times and their cultures and ours, Shakespeare and Hemingway, St Paul and Charles Dickens have had this accusation boxed around their ears – a philistine barbarity no less ridiculous and indefensible than the chanting of the Red Guards that Confucius was a 'cultural revisionist'. Some of the very same people who protest most vocally about the Rushdie *fatwa*, declaring that a writer may say what he likes even if he offends against the cardinal tenets of a religious faith, also take it as axiomatic that a man may not write or talk about women or sex in any terms other than those they approve: if a man breaches this informal prohibition, he is likely to be told that he has 'offended feminism' (another body of abstract faith) or that he is 'misogynous' or 'male chauvinist'.

Sex, sexual interests and desires, sexual relations and the politics which might attach to them have all been treated for 25 years as being the exclusive preserve, not just of women, but of the feminist sisterhood – their territory to define, to preserve and conserve. Any man who ventured a line of print upon this patch might find his reputation and his willy held up to scorn, presented with 'the world's tiniest condom' or with the chest-wig which was given to Clive James as second prize. (Odd how people who are so dedicated to the extirpation of 'sexist' observations about women's bodies are so pleased with themselves when cackling about men's bodies: imagine what their reaction might be if a group of men chose to award one of them the world's biggest Dutch cap or smallest bra.)

The sisterhood, better known as the hoods, has always been in a strangulating twist of moral division and descriptive confusion over the difference between the sexist and the sexual. Since the difference is impossible to locate, define and codify, the hoods have been driven back to the base line of all censorious intolerance which joins the High Court judge with Mary Whitehouse and Clare Short with William Rees-Mogg in saying that 'everybody knows pornography when they see it'. On the question of sexism, they are reduced to saying 'Everybody knows the difference between the sexual and the sexist.'

The truth is the opposite. Nobody knows that difference; and they never could. Twenty years ago, when I was an editor of *Time Out*, a group of young women who had founded the feminist magazine *Spare Rib* came to an editorial conference to tick us off for printing an observation, written by one of our number, that external female genitals looked to him like raw steak. This, they said, was plainly and incontestably sexist. They would not hear argument to the contrary. They would not admit the proposition that a writer may feel free to make any observation he chooses, nor that artists customarily see one thing as being like another. They could not be alerted to a paradox of those days which has survived into the present: the licence of expression which is denied to men is taken, with malice and derision aforethought, to be an incontestable right of feminist writers. The boy who wrote in *Time Out* was not allowed to give his view of a vulva but hoods such as Germaine Greer were quite free to give vent to any degree of physical loathing of male parts. A year before the *Spare Rib* hoods descended on *Time Out*, Greer had published *The Politics of Female Sexuality*, in which she wrote about 'the male genital, the visible doodle, the tag of flesh that could become as hard as a fist ... the tremulous dangling thing ... his tassel ... the pork sword'. Nobody saw these expressions as being sexist.

Twenty years later, some of those same sisters are running publishing houses, media companies, sections of major newspapers and magazines. They are sitting in judgment on the panels of the Booker and of the Hooker Prizes. They have acquired some influence both in law and in social custom and manners. They may have been and may remain exceptionally foolish, intolerant, morally perverted people who ought not to be taken seriously; but they have and have had some measure of their own way.

The Law Lords tipped their wigs in the direction of the hoods when they reinterpreted the law on rape to include acts between a married couple. Their Lordships were probably not aware of the particular feminist claim to which they were responding in their deliberations.

'It's a stretch limo . . . Stretch yourself out.'

The hoods have always claimed that heterosexual intercourse is, itself, a style of rape and that all women who consent to penetration are submitting to their oppressor. In *Sexual Violence: The Reality for Women*, composed by the London Rape Crisis Centre and published by The Women's Press in 1984, the authors declared:

> Once we see that rape is not an abnormal act, but part of the way men – not just strangers or maniacs but fathers, uncles, husbands, boyfriends, friends and professionals – treat us as women, we realise that we cannot make a distinction between 'normal' men and rapists. The silence around rape and the myths that obscure the reality have prevented women from realising that rapists are not recognisable as such. While men may choose not to commit rape, they are all capable of it and know this. When women know this too, we can stop relying on men for protection, start being angry and begin to find our own strength. In short, without this network of myths, society as we know it could not function as it does.

When their Lordships shifted the law on rape in marriage, they acceded to and gave established respectability to the idea that normal men are rapists. We may wish that they endure many hours of brow-beating perplexity in conducting this principle through the courts.

Another wisp of feminist orthodoxy got under the coat-tails of the Prime Minister two weeks ago and gusted him in the direction of Opportunity 2000 – his initiative which will require ministers of state and major corporations to take positive action, ensuring that women's names should appear on all lists of candidates for executive and managerial jobs.

Observing the conventions of cant and nodding amiably in the direction of political correctness, Mr Major said that men in authority, controlling appointments, might not like the emergence of women into positions of commercial power but they were going to have to get used to it. Everybody in his audience enjoyed a quick smirk of superiority. On this point, it is well-nigh impossible to find *anybody* who doesn't feel superior. Even the roly-poly Rotarians, trenchering and troughing at their monthly luncheons in the market town near my village, congratulate themselves and each other that, in their bank, in their building firm, in their small factory, in their legal firm, any woman can take any job for which she is fitted by ability and application. If there genuinely exists a seriously profit-minded group of male employers and executives whose members are averse to the hiring and promotion of women, I should genuinely like to meet them: they are such rare and antique specimens that they ought to be preserved as a national treasure.

The Clarence Thomas hearings in America revealed another measure of the extent to which the intolerant attitudes of the sisterhood have penetrated the life of the West, not so much in the evidence which was given as in the commentaries upon the case, in America and here.

Editors and columnists everywhere thundered the news that men must adjust their moral bearing to the new realities of professional and commercial life, in which women as equal colleagues had a right to pursue their work without unseemly leerings from the water-cooler and indecent boasting about the pleasures they were missing. These admonitions seem to be inherently decent and incontestable; but they do not take account of the deeply altered state of affairs at work for men and women: they do not allow for the truth that all places of work which include men and women in roughly equal numbers are hectic cockpits of sexual interest, flirtation, intrigue and scheming, in which women are just as likely as men to make advances and, if they are spurned, to be spiteful in revenge.

With the emergence of women in great numbers into work, all the rules of sexual manners in offices which guided our parents went out along with the carbon paper and the Gestetner. Like men, women do very often see their place of work as a theatre of sexual engagement. Many more men than women are still in senior positions, but women are being found increasingly in positions of power within companies and some of them don't hesitate to bend their powers to their sexual ends. Men who are fancied may get better work, more indulgent treatment of their expenses claims and enough free lunches on the company to choke a horse. Men who don't respond as desired may find themselves off the circulation lists for memos, lodged in the meanest hotel rooms for conferences and subjected to withering examination over their expenses.

Some ninny might call this sexual harassment; that, too, would be cant. As adults, both men and women must deal with the complications and frustrations of sexual engagement at work as best they may, with as much tolerance, forbearance and goodwill as they can muster. The vigilantes of sexual harassment and the corporate harassment counsellors who are appearing in American commerce will be made redundant when it is universally recognised that women may fancy men as much as men fancy women; and that desire, realised or thwarted, causes people to commit acts which may be unseemly, unjust or an abuse of office on both sides of the gender division.

The feminist orthodoxy insists that male sexuality is actively antagonistic to women, being barbaric, uncontainable and aggressive. They see and they describe the essence of male sexuality in acts of rape, the sexual abuse of children and the battering of women at home. In a book which I have just finished, I try to show at length that the incidence and extent of these acts have been wilfully and intentionally magnified by the hoods to make the case that all men menace all women; and I try to show that men, in their very being, have been represented as a sub-standard genetic form, a mutation of life, which must be contained and ordered if it is not to threaten all life on earth.

Does anybody take those propositions seriously? They do. All the rape crisis centres, the family rescue havens (previously known as battered women's refuges), the NSPCC, ChildLine and other charitable ventures depend upon the idea that male sexuality is, essentially, ungovernable and aggressive. Under the direction of Mr John Patten, Minister of State at the Home Office, police forces and courts have been instructed to 'crack down' on violent men in the home, assuming that there are such men in great numbers, which I have reason to doubt. Agony aunts like Claire Rayner repeatedly assure us that the sexual abuse of children is the untold secret of our social organisation and family life. This claim looks weedy when it is placed against the extreme infrequency with which social workers and police officers successfully bring cases to court on those charges; and it looks wild and self-serving when it is placed in the light of Lord Justice Butler-Sloss's urgings that the evidence for widespread incidence of sexual abuse of children should be treated with the utmost caution.

The hoods and their accomplices in government and media will not admit that women, too, may be violent, both towards their men and their children; that women may be suspected of sexually abusing children; and that women may act reprehensibly, deviously and deceitfully at work in pursuing their sexual desires. Their absolute and totalitarian insistence is that all evil proceeds from the male and that the male is all evil.

At the bottom of these movements and policies is a terror of Eros. The hoods succumbed to the terror when they were very young women, stunned by the fissiparous shock which had arrived in all our lives through the invention of infallible contraception. The intolerance they released upon the West was intended to exclude and to silence men. The admonitory and censorious movement continues, most recently given shape in the little condom awarded to Martin Amis. Men must keep their place, according to the tastes and definitions of the hoods; or they risk public disgrace, humiliation and mockery.

Whether or not you take it seriously depends upon your calculation of the effects and consequences of that movement and the view of masculinity upon which it depends. I can see few things more serious in our society than the presence among us of a totalitarian group, legitimated by fashion, office and place, whose wicked and vain orthodoxies are influencing the operations of courts and of commerce and are inhibiting expression in all our most compelling forms of art.

23 November 1991

UNLETTERED

Mrs Andrew Boyle sent us this explanatory note together with a letter (below) she received from the Kensington branch of Barclays Bank.

> The executor of the will of my late husband, Andrew Boyle, recently wrote from his office in Grays Inn asking Barclays Bank, Notting Hill Gate, to close his account. Enclosed is Barclays' reply, addressed, as you will see, to A. P. M. Boyle, Esq., at his former home address. I dare say it might well have met with his requirements, had he been here to have any.

> A. P. M. Boyle Esq.

> Dear Mr Boyle
> Further to your recent letter, as requested, we have today closed your Deceased Account Number 60192686 and enclosed is a cheque for the outstanding balance of £2158.78.
>   We hope this meets with your requirements.

> Yours sincerely
> Miss A Ilyas
> Accounts Department.

23 November 1991

FOOD

IMPERATIVE COOKING: THE CAN'T BRIGADE

Digby Anderson

Who can be blamed for the appalling food served in Britain at Christmas? One small word is the clue.

As the season of dinner parties, buffets and large family meals looms, you will start to overhear the word 'safe'. Beef is safe. Chicken is very safe. And there is nothing safer than turkey. Goose is not so safe. Liver is decidedly unsafe – any liver, even duck liver – and so are tripe and lampreys. Pheasants and partridges approaching any degree of reasonable highness, say ten days or so, are not safe.

This has nothing to do with salmonella. The ladies talking about such weighty decisions immediately go on to explain what the 'safe' business is all about: 'We're having beef again. Beef is so safe. You can't go wrong with beef. Everyone likes beef.' It is safe to serve beef because everyone likes it. What emerges is that there is a whole catalogue of food which is unsafe because someone or other won't like it, not in the sense that they would prefer something else (we all have our preferences) but in the sense that they 'can't' eat this or that. 'I'm sorry, but I can't eat liver.'

I have had guests who 'can't' eat eggs, can't eat oysters, crabs, can't eat whelks, can't eat hares, cockerels or anything cooked in blood, can't eat Gorgonzola, can't eat good blue beef or pink lamb, can't drink espresso coffee, can't eat fat, can't eat kidneys, can't eat tomatoes, can't eat aspic.

I'm not talking about those unfortunate persons – who are in fact very few in number – who have genuine food allergies; or those absurd and ungrateful wretches, the vegetarians – who are far too numerous. The ones I mean have no obvious reason, good or bad, why they 'can't'. Pushed, and it's worth pushing them, 'What do you mean, you can't eat kidneys?', they mumble, 'I'm sorry, I just couldn't,' hoping you'll let the matter drop. Don't. 'What do you mean, you couldn't? What would happen if you did?'

At this point, some just repeat the refrain, 'I can't', others make allusions to various vague physical consequences: dark hints that their sluggish bowels might be livened up a spot or that they may not fall instantly to sleep. Yet others try a half-hearted counter-attack, 'Everyone has something they can't eat.' 'Nonsense.'

For it is nonsense and peculiarly British, perhaps Anglo-Saxon, nonsense. In general Frogs and Eyeties will eat most things if they are cooked correctly. The French jib a bit at mint sauce, but they'll eat it. They regard the British as barmy to eat Jerusalem artichokes, but they ate them when they had to in the war. Of course they prefer some foods to others, but they do not exclude whole categories of raw materials or dishes because 'Je ne peux pas'.

If you have one of the whining 'can't' brigade at your table, persist, push the enquiry: 'Come, Stephen, you're a grown chap, time you got over this nonsense and started to enjoy food which a consensus of tradition has established as wonderful. These goose livers. Now what exactly is the problem?'

Sometimes the trouble is that Stephen was given rotten liver at school. But then most of us were fed rotten religion and rotten versions of Jane Austen at school, but we don't keep up the self-denying vendetta for ever. Or perhaps there is a silly disgust at things which are 'slimy' or which creep and crawl. Again, time to grow up. Or Stephen may be afraid of the unfamiliar lamprey or afraid of enjoying the 'rich' blood sauce. Whatever it is, it's a moral defect. If he is afraid, what he needs is courage.

So on no account must his whining be indulged. It is not a kindness to permit these morally flaccid persons to continue in their craven condition. All the force of ridicule, social stigma, emotional blackmail and even physical force must be used to crush them.

Why? You ask why! Because of the cumulative damage the blighters do. Add together all these meats and vegetables, fishes and dishes that someone 'can't' eat, and you're left with a narrow range of dull, lowest-common-denominator food: 'safe' food, which ruins Christmas for those of us who like good food. For if there is one group of people who are to blame for the tedious, predictable pap served in and around the British Christmas, it is the 'can't' brigade and the capitulation of better eaters to their miserable demands.

Christmas is followed by New Year. Don't just wait to come across a 'can't' coward, seek one out and make it your duty in the season of goodwill to be as beastly to him or her as possible. Who knows? A good resolution to face up to the joys of eels may follow.

23 November 1991

CAMBRIDGE'S PRIGGISH TENDENCY

John Casey

A friend of mine recently overheard a don whispering urgently to another don in the Senior Combination Room of King's College, Cambridge: 'Frank [Kermode] has been praising Roger Scruton. *Whose side is he on?*' The traditional centre of Political Correctness in Cambridge has long been King's – of which I was once an undergraduate. In King's, as elsewhere, the thin trickle of PC merges into the great ocean of English censorious priggishness.

The other day, in the Combination Room of another Cambridge college, a very distinguished elderly don was playing chess with a younger colleague. The older man was smoking a cigar. A classicist fellow of the college – a well-known member of the sanctimonious tendency – flounced up and shrieked: 'You are smoking! How disgusting! Don't you know that smoking is vulgar?' The scene ended with the older don having to leave the room (where smoking is not, in fact, prohibited), taking his chess-game with him.

Political Correctness is not confined to King's. It is the air which, in Cambridge, we breathe. My own lack of PC over the years has ensured that in Cambridge I have been turned into an ogre.

This has been a curious experience – and the myth is taking ever more curious forms. The undergraduate newspaper, *Varsity*, this term reported an undergraduate's criticism of me: 'In lectures he's very highbrow and wears a gown.' Whatever next?

But this is not the real reason for my unacceptability. That goes back a bit. In 1982, I gave a talk on immigration to the Conservative Philosophy Group, which I allowed (with some misgivings) to be published in the very first issue of the *Salisbury Review*. This meant that it was read by a few hundred people. The talk attempted to construct a Burkeian account of civil society, and to discuss the question of immigration in – as I thought – ironically pessimistic terms.

It was noticed in the press, and was taken to be a suggestion that some immigrants might be repatriated. The *Telegraph* and the *Guardian* published letters from me in 1982 in which I insisted I meant no such thing.

I soon came to think that much of the article was crazy and

inhumane, and I never allowed it to be reprinted. None of it was 'racist', but in the aftermath of the riots of 1981 it had an apocalyptic quality which I have long thought historically misjudged and wrong-headed. In the articles I have since written in newspapers and magazines, I have not returned to the subject. Or, if I have touched on it at all, what I have written implicitly repudiates what I said in 1982.

But Cambridge is a sort of Black Hole, sealed off from the outside world. One has very little sense that either dons or students actually read the newspapers. The result, in my case, has been a sort of oral tradition, mixing weird apocryphal stories with garbled accounts of my opinions *circa* 1982.

Someone seems recently to have read a copy of the *Salisbury Review* article in the University Library, and decided that it was Politically Incorrect. The result has been a campaign mounted for the last 12 months to dissuade people from coming to my lectures. Posters have been put up, and pamphlets handed out. So far, I have noticed no effect on attendance at my lectures.

The climax of the campaign came this term, when an unofficial 'alternative course' of lectures was set up in opposition to me. The campaigners had to choose which course to oppose, since I was giving four: on Aristotle, Aquinas and Augustine; on Joyce; on T. S. Eliot; and on Aesthetics and Criticism. They chose the last.

My aesthetics course is clearly political dynamite. Topics covered include: 'expression'; 'imagination'; 'on drawing an object'; 'thought and emotional quality'. I was so struck that this course should have been singled out that I offered a bottle of champagne to anyone who could find anything political in it; and two bottles to anyone who could find anything Politically Correct.

Varsity publicised this offer, but – possibly because some sub-editor could not believe that such weighty matters could be humorously dealt with – garbled it. I was made out to be offering two bottles of champagne to anyone who found anything 'politically corrupt'. Obviously the only thing to do was to make a further offer: anyone who found anything 'politically corrupt' could claim a case of Sparkling Cape Burgundy, and a year's subscription to *Sunday Sport*.

Meanwhile, the 'alternative lectures' were going ahead in King's. They were to be on such exciting, up-to-the-minute topics as feminism and 'specific concepts of writing'. The guest lecturers were to include members of the Radical Philosophy Collective, and the Oxford Marxist, Terry Eagleton.

A friend of mine dined and had drinks with me, and then sheepishly admitted that he had been persuaded into giving one of the alternative

lectures – on that redoubtable Nazi, Heidegger. (However, it turned out that he had been double-booked, and was unable to perform.)

Finally *Varsity* agreed to publish an article by me. I explained the evolution of my opinions; made some jokes at the expense of the prigs; and took the opportunity to remind students that the notion that people should not pursue their thoughts freely and sincerely, even if they might come to mistaken conclusions, was entirely at odds with the idea of a university.

The response of the campaigners was wonderful to behold. Having got wind that my article was to appear, they produced a poster, with which they festooned all the colleges and arts faculties. It was full of ludicrous mendacities – for instance, that *Varsity* had published my article only because I was 'a family friend' of the members of the editorial board (which I was not), and that I had threatened the paper with legal action if it did not publish my piece (which I had not). They simply could not bear the fact that an opinion contrary to theirs was allowed to appear in a student newspaper.

This finally aroused the writers of *Varsity* to a response. They published letters and editorials thunderously in favour of freedom of speech. One undergraduate even suggested that the Politically Correctives ought logically to burn the works of Voltaire and J. S. Mill.

The reaction was extraordinary. Large numbers of undergraduates made plain to me how much they despised the campaign. And the organisers themselves altered their tack. Far from discouraging people to come to my lectures (they explained), their new policy was to say that students should come both to mine and to the alternative course. (This was a bit difficult, since they had been scheduled at the same time.) Perhaps their next move will be to make attendance at my lectures obligatory.

One of the people at the centre of the campaign remained unbowed. He wrote a letter to *Varsity* in which he said that I had written an article in the *Evening Standard* last year 'pointing to the impossibility of a multi-racial society'. He added that, no doubt, I relied on undergraduates being unaware of what I write. I had in fact written in the *Evening Standard* to quite the *opposite* effect, e.g., 'Patriotism does not depend upon race and can survive in a multi-racial society.'

We have long known that the Left in the universities hates freedom of speech. What is more striking is that these campaigners needed an ogre, and were furious that he melted into air as they grasped at him. Like all the members of the Politically Correct tendency, they assume that opinions are not the result of arguments, which one might follow to surprising conclusions, but simply reveal good or bad ('unacceptable', to use the current cant word) states of soul. (This is a vulgarisation of the Marxist idea that there are no objective opinions, only 'ideologies'.) So they genuinely cannot understand that someone might change his mind, whilst not repudiating the way of arguing that led him to his original conclusion.

The Heavenly Host of the Politically Correctives do not rejoice in the spectacle of even one thinker that recanteth. Instead they give a very passable imitation of vampires presented with a bunch of garlic.

30 November 1991

LOW LIFE

HOME, SWEET HOME

Jeffrey Bernard

From where I am sitting, facing south and from right to left, I can see the Regent Palace Hotel, the Swiss Centre, the Odeon Leicester Square and the clock on the tower of St Anne's Church, Soho. From the bedroom window I can see Centrepoint. Am I already dead and in heaven? I have seen the Rockies, steamed up the Mississippi, down the Nile, entered the temples of Thailand, the Hermitage in St Petersburg, walked on the gallops by Lambourn at dawn, seen storms at sea, sunsets in the West Indies, women who could break your heart from a hundred miles, but never ever have I seen anything quite so stunningly beautiful as the rotting fruit and vegetables in Berwick Street Market just outside the front door of this block of flats. Home, sweet home. At last.

Not even Ulysses had to live out of carrier bags for five years. Neither did he have to put up with the landlords, landladies, neighbours and household pets that I have had to endure. There was a dog in Kentish Town that used to evacuate its bowels every morning on the lupins in the garden. That was as painful as seeing a work of art destroyed. There was the woman in the basement in West Hampstead whose screams of ecstasy made my bedroom windows rattle. In Covent Garden I was cheated out of £1,000. Then there was the Peeping Tom of Maida Vale and the landlady who disappeared with my £650 deposit. After that there was the tower block in Westminster whose windows persistently beckoned me to jump.

As I have said before, it has only been the joint efforts of Keith Waterhouse and Peter O'Toole that have prevented me from going quite bananas. And what strange spin-offs there have been from the play. Yesterday, a company that makes films for television telephoned to ask me if I would be willing to recite, so to speak, my obituary to camera. Since they pay properly I said I would be willing but I am horribly superstitious about it. One more trip down a staircase or off a pavement could do it for real.

I shall sit here and stare at the backside of the Regent Palace. My brother Oliver sent me a card yesterday saying, 'There's no place like home so don't go out for a few weeks'. He is very likely right but it is tempting and like a breath of fresh air to me to step outside into the squalor of Soho. No more taxis, thank God, and no more thanking me for not smoking.

The only cloud I can see on the horizon is the prospect of another six sittings for the portrait. I don't suppose it ever occurred to anybody that having your portrait painted entails wearing the same clothes for every wretched sitting. And now the man who commissioned the picture wants my daughter to sit for the artist, Michael Corkrey. I am sure she will but the trick is to find her. I am damned if I can and I need her help to unpack some things that have been in store for an age and to open the champagne I have on ice. I shall never be able to open a bottle of fizz again thanks to the bust arm and elbow and I won't miss it much, but a flat in Soho needs a christening. So Isabel, if you are reading me loud and clear, for God's sake telephone me. Where? In the bloody Coach and Horses.

7 December 1991

AN ARMY IN SEARCH OF A STATE

Anne McElvoy

Zagreb

The grandmothers of eastern Croatia are an incongruous sight, trapped in the fake luxury of the Intercontinental Hotel. Black scarves tightly knotted, skirts billowing behind them, they hug their bulky cardigans tight around them as if to ward off the memory of what has been and what is yet to come. One has hung her handbag over the lumpen abstract sculpture in the lobby and perched herself at its foot. Here she takes out her knitting and clicks away furiously, pausing only to wipe away a stray tear. On the notice board, which in other days channelled foreign businessmen to their respective conference halls, the 'Guests from Vukovar' are bidden to breakfast in a back room, away from the rest of us. A pointless segregation: the Intercontinental's clients now consist solely of refugees and journalists: no surer indication that a country is at war.

If we needed any further reminder, a note from the management in every room begins, 'Unfortunately, our country is being severely attacked by the "Federal Army" by all weapons from land and air . . .' and proceeds with instructions on keeping to the blackout rules at night: 'Otherwise we shall feel obliged to disconnect your electricity.'

The first refugees arrived a few days after the fall of Vukovar in mid-November, transported from cellars, where they had spent weeks cowering from the army's attentions, through the ruins of their town and into this strange haven of chrome chandeliers and haughty receptionists, whose pursed lips make clear that they never thought they would have to dispense rooms with a view to peasant families from remote areas near the Serbian border. Since then, they have been joined by others from Zadar on the Adriatic coast, and Slunj, a medium-sized town south of Zagreb, from where the entire population fled and which is now being repopulated by Serbs.

These are the fortunate ones: their accommodation is warm and food is provided. Those arriving later are sent to coastal hotels, many without heating and scarcely any cooking facilities. Even here, the children are pale, their mothers fraught with anxiety and their fathers morose. They have lost everything. Vukovar is in ruins. It is Croatia's Carthage, a triumph of destruction.

Alen Voric, aged eight, sits close beside his mother and recalls his last day in Vukovar: 'We came out of the cellar and went in a bus and it went to our house but it had fallen down,' he explains. Asked who is to blame, he replies, 'The men with beards,' and adds that when he grows up, he will fight Serbs.

The grandmothers, at first sight pitiable, are in fact the most resilient. Amalia Josipovic is 78 and fled the village of Svinjarevci near Vukovar, together with three elderly friends, when the army rolled in. 'We heard the tanks coming and ran for the fields,' she says. 'They shot at the people trying to leave by car so we went five kilometres through the cornfields on foot.' She has no relatives to look after her in Zagreb and has been told that she will be resettled on the coast, at which thought she displays the first sign of fear. She has lived in the village all her life and has never seen the sea.

Svinjarevci has had a mixed Serb-Croatian population since the Germans were driven out after the war. 'If the politicians tell you that we could not live together, they are lying,' she said. 'We shared our plots of land, looked after the fowl together. Now they have fled to Serbia where they have nothing and we have fled to Zagreb where we have nothing. So no one is at home and no one is happy. What is the point?'

It is a question asked with increasing frequency on both sides in the conflict. Croatia's hapless president, Franjo Tudjman, who has long lost touch with the feelings of his people (if he was ever in touch to start with), has prosecuted a strategy of incompetence threaded with steely cynicism. President Tudjman is an old man in a hurry, and he tried to gain in a few weeks for Croatia the independence it had sought for eight centuries. He led the country into a war for which it was materially and mentally unprepared, against an enemy whose aggressive capability and will were already well documented. Against the warnings of his strategic advisers, he tried to fight a defensive war, from the start banking on early intervention by Europe which did not come.

Croatia's president has thrown the lives of many of his country's young men away for a rash dream of independence without concern for the price involved. His popularity has ebbed drastically in the last weeks – in the front-line areas, they snarl at the very mention of his name. His television addresses are fiascos, paranoid ramblings about Serb infiltration accompanied by rhetoric about the blood of the dead nourishing a new Croatia. He is kept afloat by the war, but his rule is already considered by most of his population to have been a failure. Ten thousand dead, half a million refugees and a third of the republic's territory controlled by the enemy – an appalling balance with which to end the year. The manner in which Croatia has fought for its independence will probably have lost it territory for ever. As one wit here remarked, a future film of President Tudjman's life could well be entitled, 'Honey, I Shrunk the Country'.

While covering the war over the last six months, one of the most depressing spectacles has been Zagreb's slide from a proud and smart Habsburg city, its fashions, attitudes and attentions turned towards the West, into a militarised Balkan *strudel* of endless conspiracy theories and gun-culture, while at the same time averting its gaze from the true plight of Dalmatia, Slavonia and even the nearby central front.

At the Saloon Bar disco, favoured by the nearest thing here to the *jeunesse dorée*, in their Italian jackets and mock-gold earrings, national guardsmen are politely requested to leave their rifles in the cloakroom. There, each rifle has a raffle ticket stuck to it to avoid confusion. The fighters from the ultra-right Croatian Defence Force whose hand-grenades dangle from their belts, clanking like Christmas tree baubles, swagger into the cosy bars of the old town demanding attention. Zagreb has not been mobilised, so this is more style than substance. The wearers are in their late teens, boy-men in black bandannas, outsize crucifixes and layers of co-ordinated combat gear. Here Narcissus goes to war only sometimes and preferably not

will arrive from Belgrade. 'What would Marshal Tito have thought of the current state of Yugoslavia?' I asked him. His eyes filled with tears. There was no answer.

And I reflected that if the army's actions are too much for General Cad to stomach after 40 years of service in the JNA's ranks, we in Europe should blush with shame at our studied impartiality.

Yugoslavia is no longer a state which needs an army, but an army in search of a state. Contrary to popular depiction, the interests of the JNA and Serbia are not identical; it just happens that they have coincided in the present exigency. There are few certainties at the end of 1991 in Yugoslavia except that Yugoslavia itself is dead.

Even if one proceeds from the unpalatable assumption that the JNA secures a military victory in Croatia, it has an inglorious future as Greater Serbia's private army, defending territories in which guerrilla warfare will thrive. It is an overblown force, employing some half a million people and unwilling to abandon the fat and comfortable living to which it grew accustomed under Tito. Meanwhile, the war is already making hefty inroads into the Serbian economy and barely a week goes by without the parliament in Belgrade approving some 'loan' or other from the country's households to finance the war. Even discounting the inner political turmoil which comes of being headed by a retrogressive dictator like Milosevic, the country's economic future is grim. Already, we hear whispers of the next Balkan battle: the civil war inside Serbia.

21/28 December 1991

VANITY, FEAR, AMBITION, IDLENESS

Rodney Leach

Twenty-two years ago, when I was engaged in public combat with Robert Maxwell, something happened which I had not previously encountered in my career and was never to encounter again. There came to my office a stream of letters, voices and visitors telling nightmarish tales of betrayal, fraud and violence. The accents were often Central European, the authors anonymous, the visitors fearful and insistent on secrecy. I had no way to check their stories. So far as I knew, fantasy or revenge could have prompted them. But I retained an indelible impression of a murky sub-world in which nothing was as it seemed and in which people saw themselves as Maxwell's victims. Among the visitors was a nameless man with illustrious connections who asked me if Pergamon's structure lent itself to the laundering of KGB funds. I felt he knew the answer to his own question.

At the time I was a director of N. M. Rothschild; our client was Leasco, Saul Steinberg's company, and we were charged with completing Leasco's agreed acquisition of Pergamon, a public company run and substantially owned by Maxwell. The acquisition never went through. We pulled out when we found the true state of the Maxwell companies' accounts.

The credit for stopping the bid must be shared. Jacob Rothschild had the surest insight into Maxwell's character; my colleague Ivor Kennington the most tenacious grasp of his irregularities. Leasco's accountants uncovered the detailed evidence of Maxwell's methods. Together we assembled the jigsaw. I shall never forget the moment that it dawned on us exactly how he was cooking the books – by creating bogus sales to his own private companies.

Now the great and the good descended on us to offer themselves as brokers of compromise. For them, political mediators by instinct, the affair was negotiable. They came, they failed, they went, baffled by our intransigence – Lord Goodman, Lord Aldington and others.

These famous men were to me an unwelcome surprise. Others did not disappoint. As the drama unfolded we had become adept at reading Maxwell's mind.

The unfailing guide to his actions was to assume that every step would be precisely calculated for his own self-preservation, to the exclusion of all other considerations, but would be accompanied by threats and false promises designed to confuse the issue. One day, armed with these assumptions, which served us like radar in fog, we concluded that Maxwell would adjourn the special Pergamon shareholders' meeting called for his dismissal. We sought an *ex parte* injunction to prevent him. A peppery judge in chambers, irked at our late arrival, told us we had ten minutes to convince him and that he was not minded to be sympathetic to our cause. Abandoning our prepared explanations, we plunged straight in – 'The man's not straight.' We gave some chapter and verse. '*That* sort of fellow, is he?' exclaimed the judge. 'Injunction granted.'

The Board of Trade Inspectors, Sir Ronald Leach and Owen Stable

QC, despite a massive campaign of obstruction and vilification against them, pronounced that Maxwell was unfit for the stewardship of a public company. They painted a compelling word-picture of his impermeability to advice, his disregard for the truth and his blustering, domineering methods.

Yet still no prosecution came. Leasco won a victory in the civil courts in America, but the Director of Public Prosecutions in London, who again and again seemed on the brink of preferring charges, stayed immobile. Was there political influence to protect Maxwell? It is a question for an investigative journalist. What is certain is that if Maxwell had been jailed then, his subsequent depredations would have been on a relatively minor scale.

Nevertheless, after all that was revealed in the 1970s, it remains astonishing that within 20 years Maxwell was able to take the banks for over £1 billion, ruin the investors in two public companies and rob his own employees' pension funds of many hundreds of millions. I take it to be unlikely that these crimes are all of recent origin, the 'desperate acts of a desperate man' who had overpaid for Macmillan. On the contrary, they are of a piece with his whole former business life; and his payment, shortly before his death, of £100 million to the pension scheme of a company which he had previously sold, suggests that his discovery of the attractions of such funds goes back a while.

Personal venality is a poor explanation of the City's and Wall Street's gullibility. Of course, Maxwell easily seduced left-leaning journalists and directors, but they did little more than form a shield of useful idiots. No, the real reasons why Maxwell got away with it on such a colossal scale were the age-old human frailties – vanity, fear, ambition, idleness.

The vanity that led bankers to abandon their traditional maxim that character is all-important, in favour of charisma and participation on the fringe of great events; or that led an industrialist like Lord Kearton to say that Maxwell could be controlled by a strong chairman. The fear that silenced those who knew a fragment of the fraud and kept them from piecing it together with others. The corporate ambition that, in stretching for profits, overlooked the risks of paper collateral. The idleness that set superficial impressions and casual enquiry over hard questions and diligent research.

It follows that as the writs swell and the regulators ponder which stable doors to shut, nothing much will be achieved beyond society's desire for revenge. As usual, there will be cruel misfortune and surprising fortune, in who escapes and who is punished. Some, close to the epicentre, who closed their eyes or acquiesced in terror, will never be able to explain, save to a few of generous wisdom and compassion, how they came to sign this or that document. Others, who had nothing to fear but who lent their names to Maxwell will have to choose between looking like fools or knaves. They will choose foolishness. On both sides of the Atlantic, men who are paid a king's ransom for their business acumen will plead ignorance and portray themselves as dupes.

Meanwhile over the last two weeks I have started to accumulate a growing file of bankers, investors, businessmen and writers who have written or called to thank me for some warning given long ago, as a result of which they decided never, so long as they lived, to have anything whatsoever to do with Robert Maxwell. It is a pity there are not more of them.

21/28 December 1991

FORBIDDEN PLEASURES

Michael Bloch

I am not a regular smoker; that is to say, I may smoke an occasional cigarette just as I occasionally eat asparagus or visit the aquarium at London Zoo. The first cigarettes I bought, at the age of 19 some 20 years ago, were from Bacon's in the Cambridge Market Square, a splendid old establishment with much oak panelling and a retired squadron-leader sporting magnificent moustaches. No doubt I drifted in there seeking an occupation of some kind. As in all good tobacconists, a medley of sweet odours assailed one as one walked through the door, conjuring images of the spice trail, the opium wars, rahat lookoom and the harbour at Funchal. This came from the house-blended pipe tobaccos; but the cigarette I was recommended by the genial, whiskered proprietor amply lived up to his shop's perfumed promise.

Sullivan Powell Special Turkish Number One was its name. It was oval in shape and clung to one's lips; there was a hint of incense about it, and a strong thick sweetness like liquorice; it pricked the nostrils in a sensual way, and if one blew one's nose afterwards, tar emerged. It became one of the secret joys of my university years; I suppose at the height of my habit I was smoking about 15 a week. It was not a habit to be indulged in publicly, but at solitary moments when one was listening to Chopin, dreaming of romantic adventures, or reading *Les fleurs du mal*.

After this first experience of smoking, all Virginia cigarettes and all filtered brands have seemed tasteless, insipid and frankly horrible. Sullivan Powell eventually became part of the Gallagher empire, but they had a shop in the Burlington Arcade up to a few months ago, where they sold a filtered cigarette which they continued to call Special Turkish Number One. But the assistant seemed to know nothing about tobacco when I last went in there and these filtered items bore no relation to the Sullivans I smoked 20 years ago. I tried breaking them up, discarding the filter, and rolling them up again in cigarette paper; but there was nothing to remind one of the sweet tarry delights of yore.

Bacon's also sold a Turkish cigarette of real Turkish manufacture. It was called Yenijé; it was even stronger and sweeter than Sullivan but quite tiny, being almost half the size. I enjoyed smoking these occasionally, though they left me feeling sad as they lasted such a short time. When I visited Istanbul in the autumn of 1989, I was looking forward to sampling them again. It was with tremendous shock that I discovered that Turkish cigarettes are obtainable nowhere in that city, whose inhabitants now smoke only Marlboro and other American brands. I did, however, meet an old tobacconist who believed Yenijé might still be made in Izmir and sold in Ankara, though he did not seem very sure.

In the mid-Seventies, feeling the need for a change, I gave up Turkish and started smoking Scott's Burma cheroots. No one who knew these delicious things, which came in gorgeous brown-and-yellow packets, will ever forget them: they tasted of cinnamon, and were so tightly-packed and slow-burning that one could keep them going for up to five hours. Then, in 1977 I think, the entire Burma tobacco crop was wiped out by some weevil, and they never reappeared. The other day I discovered a packet in a drawer; it must have been at least 13 years old, but the cheroots still smoked perfectly and tasted wonderful.

When I came to live in London, I went quite often to Fribourg & Treyer's lovely bow-fronted shop in the Haymarket, where they sold their own Turkish cigarettes in every strength, shape and size. None of them matched up to the original Sullivans (which had now disappeared), but they were very good nevertheless, and the men who sold them wonderfully knowledgeable. When it closed down about ten years ago, it seemed as if what remained of civilisation was coming to an end. It has been replaced by a store dealing in fancy stationery. In Cambridge too, Bacon's, having tried to survive by extending its merchandise to include hip flasks and walking sticks, has folded, giving way to an emporium selling frocks to tourists – though a brass plaque bearing the lines of Calverley's *Ode to Tobacco*, dedicated to the original Mr Bacon, still graces the wall outside.

With the demise of Fribourg's, the English market in eastern cigarettes was cornered by Benson & Hedges, which continued throughout the Eighties to offer four varieties – Turkish, Egyptian, Balkan Sobranie and Orientals. They all came in beautiful boxes but, with declining sales and absence of competition, the quality did not improve. The Orientals, great fat things which took about a quarter of an hour to smoke, started out with a wonderful heavy sweetness like the old Sullivans, but eventually began to taste like a coarse North African cigarette such as Gitane or Gauloise. The Turkish and Egyptian ovals were quite pleasant in their way but became almost indistinguishable.

Still, one was grateful for them all; and it was with anguish that one learned that, under some European Community directive, they were all to cease manufacture before 1 January 1992. I knew a splendid Colonel Whitehead at the Savile Club, a former military adviser to the Iraqi monarchy, who had for years relied on the Turkish Bensons in their bright blue boxes and did not know how he would manage without them; he had the luck to die in February 1991, the very month they disappeared from the shelves.

Some good Oriental cigarettes, such as Andron and Rameses II, continue to be produced by Greek firms in America; and no doubt aficionados will go there to savour these forbidden delights just as those who wish legally to enjoy hashish visit Amsterdam or Barcelona. As for myself, I stocked up with several thousand of Benson's Turkish and Egyptians during their last days of sale. They are a pale shadow of what I smoked 20 years ago, but enough to revive memory; if I smoke two or three a week, they should last me the rest of my life.

21/28 December 1991

ANYTHING TO DECLARE?

Vicki Woods

I find it an endearing national characteristic of the British that in the small things the rule of law lies lightly upon us. We are not a pettifogging people. Don't you quote by-laws at me. We won't keep off the grass, and we will open on Sundays. We bend the rules. You have to draw a line, of course, and clearly the late Robert Maxwell was a good few yards the wrong side of it, but in the main, we don't like rules and regulations and despise those who lay them down: Eurocrats, town clerks, traffic wardens, tax-collectors, park-keepers, prefects, men from the ministry and VAT inspectors. There's a level of ordinary, commonplace, everyday sort of downright law-breaking that most Britons cheerfully put up with in themselves and in other Britons: 'Bloody little tin Hitler. I was only doing 85. Should be out there catching car thieves, not sauntering up and down the M4 laying speedtraps!'

So, as we stood at Heathrow and watched the luggage coming up from the Casablanca flight and falling heavily on to the carousel, I was very interested to see what everybody else had done to avoid paying duty on their Berber carpets. Some smartyboots had clearly taken large empty suitcases out to Morocco to bring their carpets back in. We had failed to have this foresight. Some people had bought cheap camel-leather grips in the souk, and had stuffed their carpets inside. We had failed to do this, too. One traveller had stuck 'fragile' labels on his camel bag, in order to help this pretence along. You could see the camel bags a mile off, loudly proclaiming 'Inside – undeclared Moroccan carpet'. Our carpets had been wrapped up by the Berber traders in black glasscloth and tied up with string. They weren't in disguise at all.

We pushed two luggage trolleys through the green channel, both piled high. The luggage was all mixed up and belonged, variously, to me, to my husband, to my son and daughter and to my daughter's honorary godmother. She and I were doing the trolley-pushing. My husband was in a foul mood, and not just because of the carpets.

Two customs officers looked at each other as we swung round the corner and moved to stand in front of us: a young blonde girl and a rather formidable-looking woman around my age. 'Have you anything to declare?' they asked. 'Spirits? Tobacco?' 'No, no,' said I, with confident voice and a brash smile. 'Where have you come from?' they asked. 'Oh, ah, from Marrakesh. From Morocco. Via Casablanca.' More brash smiles, from me and the daughter's honorary godmother. 'Mmm, on holiday were you? How long for?' 'Oh, ah, two weeks, yes? Two weeks.' 'Did you buy anything while you were out there?' Did we buy anything? I find the lie direct about the hardest thing I ever do in English, but one ploughs on. We both began to speak together, turning from one customs officer to the other: 'Well, a few bits and pieces, didn't we? We bought, erm . . . souvenirs. Wooden ah, boxes. A few souvenirs. And bits and pieces, yes.' 'Mmm, would you mind if we had a look through your luggage? Can you bring it over here to this table, please?' We pushed the trolleys over, but the customs officers barely looked at them and looked at us instead. 'Did you bring a tortoise with you?'

Well, it was like being hit over the head with a shoe. I was completely thrown. It was flummoxing. Did we bring a tortoise with us? Why us, for heaven's sake? Do we look like the sort of people who'd bring a tortoise with them? Why a tortoise particularly? What's going on? Do they ask everybody who lands from Casablanca if they brought a tortoise with them?

The tortoise, a sleepy little thing smaller than the palm of my hand, was lying in my wicker basket, lightly covered by a pink fringed scarf. Its name, apparently, was Arthur. My daughter had bought it in the souk in Marrakesh that morning for 100 dirhams: it was the only one in the ludicrously overcrowded cardboard box which still had all its claws on its tiny feet. It was going to have a long and happy life. In England. She refused to change its name to Abdul or Hassan or something more evocatively Moroccan than Arthur. She had bought lettuce to feed it with. She had carried both tortoise and lettuce in a stout box which she had safely stowed underneath the seat in front of her on the aeroplane and we had transferred the animal into my wicker basket in the ladies' lavatory just the other side of customs.

My daughter's colour began to rise. Twelve-year-olds, once they start blushing, blush hard. The young woman customs officer, not long out of girlhood herself, cleverly fixed the blusher with a knowing eye, and lowered her voice to a caressingly gentle level. 'Have you brought a tortoise with you?' she said. Silence. 'We know you had a tortoise. Where is it?' she asked. Silence. 'Little girl, have *you* got the tortoise?' she said, and my daughter, now brilliantly encrimsoned, said 'No!' At which point, I realised I couldn't have this. 'I can't have this,' I said. 'No, no, this must stop; talk to me, not to her, she's not actually lying or anything; she's quite right: entirely accurate; *she* hasn't got the tortoise; *I've* got the tortoise, it's here. Look. There you are. One tortoise.'

Arthur crawled slowly across the table towards the customs officers, looking very small. The customs officers said, 'Oh, how cruel!' and I blustered furiously. 'Cruel? Nonsense, not at all, plenty of air and light, only in the basket five minutes, better placed now than it was in Morocco! Crawling all over each other, losing their claws, look, it would have died in that damn box in the souk!' The senior customs officer said, 'If tourists like you didn't buy them they wouldn't keep them in a box in the souk.' Having heard the same arguments rehearsed by my husband all the way out to Marrakesh airport, I opened my mouth but then shut it again.

'Right, what else have you got in here?' asked the senior customs officer, waving a hand at the mass of luggage, and we realised we were going to be in for a long day. We were on a flight from Casablanca. People smuggle all sorts and conditions of stuff from Casablanca. Visions of small back rooms and rubber gloves rose in the mind. My husband, black with rage, began unlocking suitcases, undoing straps, untying bits of string and unrolling carpets. He then lit a Hamlet. He completely ignored the tortoise. He also ignored me, and the sudden, rather puzzling sight of our neighbour, the law lecturer, who happened to stroll through the green channel on her way home from holiday and give us a wave. We were clearly going to be the talk of the pub before we got back to the village.

It takes me forever to pack, and I hate it, but packing is a doddle compared with watching the dainty fingers of lady customs officers gamely unrolling a ball of teenage boy's dirty sock and prodding it for spare tortoises or worse. Every lumpy bundle began to look like two pounds of marijuana, and turned out to be a charming little wooden box, or tray, or picture-frame, and both I and the daughter's honorary godmother joined in the knicker-ravelling, in an attempt to be as helpfully law-abiding as possible. There did seem to be an awful lot of souvenirs.

'May I look in your handbag?' said the young customs officer. Oh,

God, the handbag. I'd forgotten all about the handbag. I started to gabble about the handbag in a fury of embarrassment and impatience, but I shut up. She delved in, and came out with the most unbelievable object, the size of a rugby ball, carelessly wrapped in brown paper. Not a handbag sort of a thing at all. She laid it on the table and gave me a speaking look. It was a squishy, very Moroccan-looking parcel. I said, 'You're just not going to believe this.' She said, 'I think you'd better tell me.' I said, 'I promise you, you won't believe me.' She started unwrapping the brown paper. I said, 'It's a lettuce.' The tatty green leaves of a Moroccan Webb's Wonder began to fall off on to the table and she stared at me as though I was mad. I said, 'It's for the tortoise to eat.' She wrapped it up in eloquent silence and put it back in my handbag.

Then the vet came. She was terrifically cheerful, and wore green wellies and a Barbour. She said to my miserable daughter, 'You've probably saved its life, actually. It's a Kleinman's tortoise, only about two weeks old. It's not an endangered species, but it's vulnerable. It would certainly have died in that box in the souk. It'll go to the Animal Quarantine Station for 14 days and they'll keep it under a sunlamp. You might be allowed to keep it after that. You'll have to apply for a Cites permit from the Department of the Environment. It might take some time, but the tortoise will be fine. It'll go and live with a tortoise expert, near Bristol.' My daughter, who is at school in Bristol, lost her fierce cranberry colour and began to wonder about access and visitation rights. She began to think about Bristol, a relatively calm and ordered English sort of a place where you did your prep and didn't wander through mediaeval souks and smell extraordinary smells and see chameleons and flies and poor baby tortoises and donkeys with horribly bleeding flanks, and have men in long frocks popping out of every doorway and shouting 'Thirty thousand camels!' at you.

They gave me forms to fill in. Hours later, having repacked, and gone through certain other embarrassments about carpets and handicrafts and what a green channel is actually for, I finally asked the senior customs officer how on earth she'd known we had a tortoise. She said, 'It was a fellow-passenger who informed on you. He saw your daughter with the tortoise at Marrakesh and at Casablanca, and came to tell us when he got off the plane.' I thought about this for a minute and became filled with murderous rage. I said, 'Was he *English*?' and she said, 'Oh yes. He's a tortoise-lover. He's got two tortoises of his own.'

I returned to work on the Monday and rang the customs about an import licence for the tortoise. 'The vet misinformed you,' said the customs officer. 'I thought she was wrong at the time, and she was. She told you we'd detained the tortoise, and that you could apply for it on an import licence, but you can't, because you took it through the green channel. So the tortoise will go to a Kleinman's tortoise expert, and he'll look after it and try to breed from it. You won't see it again, but you can tell your daughter that she certainly saved its life. I'll have to report this upwards. The vet was mistaken to say that we'd detained the tortoise.' I said, 'But you did. You did detain it.' 'Oh, no, we didn't,' said the customs officer. 'We didn't detain the tortoise. We *seized* the tortoise.'

We then had a brief conversation about the law of the land with particular reference to customs seizures and confiscations, and then she added, in a kindly tone, 'You were well over your allowance on the carpets and handicrafts, you know.' She brought up the question of the school sneak again, anxious for me not to think badly of him. He was a tortoise-lover, she said, who had clearly been acting magnanimously, with only the best interests of the tortoise in mind. 'In your different ways,' she added, 'you could say you were both doing your best for the tortoise, weren't you? If that's any comfort.'

21/28 December 1991

BASTARD

Alan Brownjohn

Into a suddenly sunny spring dawn
A bastard creeps out through a crack in some
Until-then, immaculate-looking woodwork.

He inhales the air and smiles, and everything
Looks good to him. And so he takes a few
Experimental paces, trying out

His legs and wondering what clothes to wear:
A city suit? Some jeans and a baseball cap?
Or an 'I ♥ my building society' t-shirt?

– Because he plans to walk into an Organisation,
To stir things up inside an Organisation.
He is going to Go For It and get others Going,

And he's past Reception already, and up
In an express lift to a penthouse suite already,
And they have an office waiting for him already,

And his first dictated letters on a screen.
In the other offices, behind their hands,
They are talking about him, quite a lot,

They are saying, 'How did that bastard get that job?
I'd like to know where the hell he came from!
I'd like to see his qualifications for doing

What he does.' – All talk, and he knows it, it's safer
To talk than to act, the smaller bastards
Know the truth of that from long experience,

They've learnt to carry on and keep their heads down
To protect their own bit of woodwork.
                                        So all goes well,
With the faxes slithering out from other bastards

In other penthouse suites all round the world,
And the graph turning upwards on the wall-chart in
The Bastard's Conference Room, the spread-sheets glowing

With the marvellous figures the Bastard envisages;
And his desk is clear and shiny, and people's smiles
Are amiable and innocent, or seem so.

Or seem so . . . In his deep suspicious brain
The Bastard worries occasionally that their lips
May be smiling, smiling for him, but not their eyes.

Still, for now, things go splendidly, the Bastard is seen
On 'State of the Art' and 'Man of the Week', and has
A 'Room of my Own' and a 'Holiday of my Choice'.

– And then one day a casual conversation
Stops short when he enters a room without warning,
And another day the people do not stop

When he comes round the door, but self-consciously keep talking
With knowing looks, and ever widening smiles.
The Bastard pretends he hasn't noticed, but

He goes back to his office and he thinks
'Those bastards could be ganging up on me . . .
I must watch that little bastard with the earring.'

The Bastard is full of fear and fantasy,
And the fantasy that made his world for him
Becomes a fantastic fear of losing it:

His mirror tells him always to guard his flanks,
And never leave his knife-drawer open when
He turns his back on even his secretary

– But he does have courage. It tells him to have it out
Face-to-face with his team of Assistant Bastards
And find out what the hell is going on.

Oh no, they'll never tell him half the story,
Oh yes, they'll sit and talk behind their hands,
But he can still fire the lot; or he thinks he can.

Today they are gathered round a table, with vellum pads
Which some of them are writing or doodling on,
And some are self-confidently leaving quite untouched.

It's the ones who pick up no pencils and take
No notes who are the most dangerous. They know
The result they want without fidgeting about it;

Especially the little bastard with the earring.
He speaks in code, but it's clear what he's implying:
The Bastard is letting the Organisation down,

It ought to do better; and all the smallest bastards,
The shareholders' democracy, have been stirred
To demand a different bastard at the top.

This year they're eager for a different scene,
This year they're after a man with a different style,
This year they'd like a bastard who wears an earring.

The Bastard's hand is turning clammy on
His thoroughly doodled vellum pad,
The sky is blue for other bastards now.

He sees what is coming next, and he'll speak out first.
He rises from the table, he looks at them
With steady eyes, and steady eyes look back,

Though the lips are smiling. 'I've seen your game!', he shouts,
'I've sussed it out – you're just a lot of *bastards*,
A lot of dirty, crooked scheming *bastards*!'

When the door slams hard behind him they look at each other
And shake their heads with humane and pitying smiles.
'Poor bastard,' one compassionately murmurs.

The earring says, 'It wasn't easy, but
It had to be.' And a third: 'I'm so relieved
It's over and we can breathe.' And a grinning fourth

In a flak jacket moves into the Bastard's chair
As the sun sets golden, and the immaculate walls
Begin to look like very porous woodwork.

21/28 December 1991

YOUR PROBLEMS SOLVED

DEAR MARY . . .

Mary Killen

Q. I am giving a number of dinner parties over Christmas and would like to ask your advice on a point of control. What can one do when people just carry on laughing, talking and drinking when you have told them that supper is ready and have asked them to come through to the dining room? It is particularly annoying if you are having soup or a soufflé, which I am planning to. Can you advise a foolproof way of getting my guests to come through when they are asked to?

M.P.C.M., Wilts

A. That first flush of intoxication which characterises the moods of many guests at the beginning of a dinner party tends to render them unco-operative about 'coming through'. Often they are mid-anecdote with a new person and the alcohol has diminished their sense of responsibility when the call to table is given. You should have no trouble in getting them to come through, however, if you switch off the lights in your drawing room shortly after your announcement is made. The pitch darkness will bring your guests to their senses and you will find that they blunder swiftly out towards the light and the dining room.

Q. Your kind advice please! It used to be a simple matter to give our dustmen a Christmas box. The refuse lorry always arrived round about the same time every Monday, a four-man team collecting and loading mostly in sight of each other. On hearing the lorry, which amusingly used to make much more noise just before Christmas, I would go out and give the money to the driver, asking him to divide it equally among the team. Thus most or all of them would witness this. At the beginning of this year, however, our local authority placed this service in the hands of a private firm, and the programme is different. One man now arrives in advance and places the black refuse bags from our dustbins in our drive. The refuse lorry then collects them at widely unpredictable times – sometimes when we are not in. How can I ensure that my Christmas box to these dustmen will reach its rightful recipients this year?

E.W.H., Holly Bank, Ormskirk, Lancs

A. A number of readers have written with similar queries, many of them concerned that the one dustman who calls in advance, and whom one might see close to

the house, should not siphon off the entire Christmas box for himself. My advice is that one of your refuse sacks should have Sellotaped to it a large sheet of white paper on which is printed in bold letters: 'REFUSE VAN DRIVER – PLEASE CALL AT THE HOUSE TO RECEIVE CHRISTMAS BOX.' If you are likely to be out when the driver might call, leave a similar notice on your front door which reads: 'REFUSE VAN DRIVER – PLEASE CALL AT IVY BANK [or another adjacent property belonging to a co-operative neighbour] TO COLLECT CHRISTMAS BOX.' Readers should note that the dustmen's anticipation of Christmas boxes means that this is the best week of the year for getting rid of old fridges, garden refuse and other bulky items which dustmen normally refuse to take.

Q. What is the best Christmas present to give to someone who you do not like?

D.L., WC1

A. A xylophone would be an ideal present for people who have children. The instrument would give equal offence and annoyance to an unmarried adult.

21/28 December 1991

IF SYMPTOMS PERSIST . . .

Theodore Dalrymple

At the end of the consultation my patient took a small manila envelope from her handbag and slid it diffidently across my desk.

'I'm so grateful for what you've done, doctor,' she said, 'I'd like to buy you something for the hospital.'

Gratitude! It's the last thing I expected: you could have knocked me down with – well, with a small manila envelope.

I tore it open as soon as she left. It contained £5. Her donation reminded me of one of the handsomest gifts I ever received. I had treated an old African villager for malaria, and he returned soon afterwards with a small plastic bowl filled with sawdust in which nestled five eggs, very precious in those times of near-famine. His humility shamed me.

I should have bought something for my ward with the £5, of course, but the devil entered me and I decided to go through the proper channels. I called the administrator: his secretary answered.

'He's at a meeting,' she said. 'Can I be of help?'

I explained the situation and asked what I should do with the money.

'Well, we'll have to send an acknowledgment, of course,' she said. 'That's routine. But I'm not sure what we do with the money in a case like this. I'll have to ask the administrator when he returns from the meeting. Can I have the name, address and date of birth of the donor?'

It took me a few minutes to dictate them. The cost of the acknowledgment was rising.

Three hours later, the administrator's secretary called me.

'The administrator's spoken to the accountant,' she said. 'And he says the money'll have to go through the books.'

'Why?' I asked.

'Well, you see, if we write an acknowledgment – which we must – someone going through the files might ask where the £5 got to. Besides, the patient really gave the money to the whole hospital, not just your ward.'

'So we have to divide it up?'

'Yes, we do.'

There are 24 wards in the hospital: they will each receive 21 pence – less administrative expenses, of course.

'Could you pop the money in an envelope with a covering letter and send it here in the internal post?' asked the secretary.

It once took 14 days for a referral letter to reach Ward 8 from Ward 11 through the internal post.

'Certainly,' I said. 'A pleasure.'

I dictated the covering letter: it took only ten minutes of my secretary's time. I'm sure it didn't take long to file, or alternatively to lose.

As for the £5, it will in due course be paid into the bank. The covering letter won't take long to write.

So far, then, my patient's little gift has cost the hospital quite a lot of money. If you add my time, the administrator's and the accountant's

'I'm afraid you've got diabetes.'

time, my secretary's time and the administrator's secretary's time, the postage and stationery, I estimate that my patient owes the hospital about £175, or £7.56 per ward.

It's lucky for her that it's the thought that counts.

4 January 1992

TO SIR OR NOT TO SIR

Simon Courtauld

Brian Redhead was interviewing Lord Carrington on the future of Yugoslavia. It might have been interesting to hear what the present chairman of Christie's (and former foreign secretary) had to say to the listeners to the *Today* programme about the prospects for peace between Serbia and Croatia; but my attention was distracted when I distinctly heard Mr Redhead call him 'sir'.

I wondered for a moment whether Mr Redhead, who is sometimes accused of allowing a left-wing bias to creep into his interviews, was being the tiniest bit satirical. But the tone of the questioning did not suggest this. Or was he perhaps deferring instinctively to a peer of the realm? It seemed more likely that he was merely according a mark of old-fashioned respect to one of his elders and betters.

This was remarkable not because anyone would expect Mr Redhead to be discourteous but because not many people are addressed as 'sir' these days – least of all, one might think, by someone of the politically correct tendency.

Time was when the 'S' word came naturally to the lower classes when addressing their social superiors, and to a young man (though not so usually a woman) when talking to his seniors. Having had a public-school education, he would be expected to say 'sir' to anyone of his father's age whom he might meet at home or in the course of business. Now some schoolmasters invite their pupils to call them by their first names, and a father who asks that his friends be addressed as 'sir' by his son will probably be thought to be making a pointless joke.

It does not necessarily follow that there is less respect around today but – whether because this is supposedly the age of equality or because people are now more apt to acquire an, often misplaced, sense of their superiority when young – 'sirring' has largely gone out of fashion.

Now that I am, as Auberon Waugh describes it, on the right side of 50, it does not trouble me that no one calls me sir – except, very occasionally, one of my children's male friends. But having been brought up to use the 'S' word selectively, I shall certainly continue with it on occasion, though not any longer to senior officers in the armed forces, many of whom are my contemporaries.

Not long ago I greeted a slight acquaintance (then a major-general) at dinner with a jocular 'Good evening, sir' – mainly because I had momentarily forgotten his name – to be met with the response, 'You don't have to call me sir: I'm only a few years older than you.'

In New Zealand, I am told, married men of my generation never get on to first-name terms with their fathers-in-law; 'sir' or 'mister' continues as the accepted form of address for as long as the marriage, or the father-in-law, lasts. I have never come across this elsewhere, not even among Americans, though they are often noticeably respectful towards their elders: these days, however, only the private school or business school graduate is likely to go on saying 'sir' for a few years.

If, in the past, too many 'sirs' were sprinkled around when introductions were made, or in the course of conversation, it may be right today to reserve the appellation for men who by their age and distinction command real respect. Excepting male members of the royal family (whom one is obliged to call sir), I can think of dukes such as Buccleuch and Devonshire, politicians such as Lord Home and Julian Amery, the explorer Wilfred Thesiger, whom I have met in the past five years and addressed quite naturally as 'sir'. Who else, one wonders, still receives this mark of Brian Redhead's respect? And who else deserves it?

4 January 1992

IF SYMPTOMS PERSIST . . .

Theodore Dalrymple

It was a naïve domestic little murder, but I think you'll be amused by its presumption.

A man should not strangle his wife, of course, nor a wife her husband, even when provoked: the law and morality are agreed. Nevertheless, a certain erosion of this unexceptionable principle seems to have occurred of late, to the detriment of domestic security. For if excuses are to be accepted in such matters, who among us will sleep easily in his or her bed?

I was called last week to the local police station by the custody sergeant who was worried that his prisoner – a wife-strangler who had just been arrested – was medically unfit to be detained. The prisoner was curled up in a ball, the sergeant said, not responding to anything that was said to him. From time to time, he would hurl himself at the cell wall and bang his head against it.

'Sounds quite normal to me,' I said. 'For a murderer, that is.'

'Give me some credit, doctor,' said the sergeant. 'I've been in this game 12 years, and I know when something's wrong. His eyes have gone.'

So I set out to examine the murderer whose eyes had gone.

I found him curled up in his cell, just as the sergeant had described, underneath the notice which informed him that writing on the wall was an offence and would result in an additional sentence.

I asked him what had happened, and he spoke with perfect clarity.

'I strangled my wife,' he said. 'I shouldn't've done it, doctor. I've messed everything up.'

At that moment I felt proud to be British: even our criminals use understatement.

'I never thought I'd do it. I just lost my temper, like. She was seeing another man, and I warned her, but she wouldn't listen. I couldn't take no more, doctor.'

Unbeknown to me, the sergeant had his ear to the judas-hole. Suddenly the murderer began to moan; he clutched his head, jumped up and started to scream. He ran to the wall and banged his head on it.

'Give me some pain-killers, you bastards, give me some fucking pain-killers before my fucking head fucking bursts!'

I told him in no uncertain terms to stop, and he did.

'Sorry, doctor,' he said, 'but I've got a terrible headache.'

I turned to go, and just caught sight of the sergeant scurrying down the corridor between the cells. Back in his office, I told him there was nothing wrong with the murderer beyond a certain understandable anxiety.

'But there must be, doctor,' he said. 'I mean, look what he's done.'

'He's harassing someone else!'

It emerged then that the murderer was not previously unknown to the police: the week before he had been arrested for causing what is known in the trade as a *domestic*. This involved smashing up the house and threatening to kill his wife with a knife, a threat he repeated in front of the policemen who went to intervene.

'Didn't you charge him?' I asked.

'No,' replied the sergeant.

'Why not?'

'His wife wouldn't press charges.'

Whatever are we to make of the police? It seems they are willing to prosecute only when they have made up the evidence themselves.

11 January 1992

NOVEL AND UNWELCOME COINCIDENCES

Susan Hill

I am not yet so paranoid as to believe that the fates are conspiring against me – that way madness lies – but the theory of the collective unconscious is beginning to seem attractive. And now that it – whatever it may be – has happened again, and this time worse than all the rest, I realise that it does go back some considerable way.

When I was a child, I frequently visited my maternal grandmother who lived with her sister, my great-aunt. They were the last survivors of a family of seven sisters and one brother. His photograph, in army uniform, stood on the piano. He, the pride and joy, the youngest and best beloved, had been killed at the Battle of the Somme on his 19th birthday. His name was Owen. To them his memory was green, and they spoke of him constantly, and of that war – *the* war, though they had lately lived through a second (this was the late 1940s).

Graham Greene said that everything of importance to a writer's career has happened to him by the time he is 12 years old. I have found it to be so. My obsession with the First World War and everything to do with it began in those years of early childhood, seeing my great-uncle Owen's photograph, listening to the old women's talk, and as I grew older, I read as much as I could, fact, fiction and poetry, to do with it. My imagination was fired again on hearing the first performance of Benjamin Britten's *War Requiem* in 1962, and eight years later I plucked up courage enough to write a novel about the love of two young soldiers, in the trenches of Flanders. *Strange Meeting* was published in 1971. It was not, of course, the first novel about the Great War, and the whole period has been the domain of many artists. But, in that ultra-sensitive state immediately following on the completion and publication of a novel, I was plunged into depression when another, about the love of two young soldiers in the trenches of Flanders, Jennifer Johnston's *How Many Miles to Babylon?*, came out shortly after mine.

Still, these things happen; at least mine had come first, and in the two decades since, it has not suffered, never been out of print, and seems to have a particular place in the affections of many. I have been rather clinging to that fact, of late.

In 1981 I had an idea for a story, which came to me all at once and so whole and complete that it did not alter in essentials from the first notes I made as an *aide memoire*. The whole outline was there from the beginning, theme, period, setting, characters, even some of the names. For various reasons, I did not continue work on it at the time, though I was aware that eventually I would.

A couple of years later, David Puttnam was looking for a love story to film, and when he approached me for any ideas I might have, I remembered the outline, which had always seemed a very visual and filmable one to me. He agreed, and liked it enough to commission a screenplay, which I struggled to write for some months, before facing the fact that I am not, and never could be, a film scriptwriter, and allowing the outline – by now considerably fleshed out, but still essentially the same – to sink to the bottom of a drawer.

So that it had already been part of my working life, as it were, for some time, when I came upon it again in 1989, realised that I had not done with it, and almost at once began to write it as the novel it was always destined to be.

Air and Angels was completed and sent to my publisher, Christopher Sinclair-Stevenson, thereupon in May 1990. It is set in Cambridge, *circa* 1912, and the principal male character is a don and cleric who falls unexpectedly and passionately in love with a 16-year-old girl. As well as being a theology tutor, he has a strong leaning towards the biological sciences, and is a serious ornithologist and naturalist.

By August of that year, I was awaiting the first proofs of the novel. One fine Sunday morning – I remember everything about it with astonishing clarity – we were having coffee at a café table overlooking the Royal Shakespeare Theatre and the River Avon at Stratford, each reading a newspaper, when my husband looked up from his *Observer* and said quietly, 'There is an interview with Penelope Fitzgerald here that you had better read.' Alerted, though somewhat puzzled by the seriousness of his tone, I set aside my own paper and did so. I discovered that Mrs Fitzgerald was about to publish a new novel called *The Gate of Angels*. Its hero was a clergyman with a scientific bent, who falls passionately in love with a very young girl. Its setting, Cambridge, *circa* 1912.

I recall that everything around me seemed oddly unreal, as though the scene were painted, like a stage set, and that a lump, like cold lead, had formed itself in the pit of my stomach.

It was, of course, complete and absolute coincidence of the most bizarre kind. I admire and enjoy Penelope Fitzgerald's novels, and I once met her, but it was many years ago and I would not claim to know her. We have never corresponded or spoken about our work in any way whatsoever. We have different publishers, and neither of us had spoken publicly about our work in progress. Few writers do. It is said that there are only a handful of plots in the world's fiction, and the theme of an older man falling in love with a young woman is probably one of them. It is not the central theme, but what a writer does with it and how which makes his or her work distinctive. It was the coincidences of detail, date, setting and so forth which made the similarity between Penelope Fitzgerald's novel and my own so remarkable, let alone the appearance of the key word 'Angels' in both our titles.

I did not read her book. I could not, which is a pity, for it is the only one of hers I have missed. Otherwise, I think no harm has come of the business. We did not appear to get in each other's way at all; both novels had their own, quite independent success.

I would have shrugged my shoulders. One novel with striking similarities to my own about the First World War had appeared, but afterwards. I had produced a book with the same theme, setting and period as another, and though mine had appeared later on this occasion, it had at least been finished and out of my hands by the time I learned of the existence of the other. One might simply have given a wry smile, had a third, and far more grievous blow not fallen.

When I was nine, I won a school prize and chose for my book – I am unsure exactly why – a children's account of the explorations of Shackleton and Scott in the Antarctic. On the day I began it, I became irrevocably and totally hooked on the subject. Since then I have read, and if possible bought, everything I have come across about it and by now have a small library devoted to Antarctica and its exploration. I have read Shackleton's *South* and Apsley Cherry-Garrard's *The Worst Journey in the World* a dozen times each.

As with the First World War, it took a long time for me to get up courage to tackle my obsession in fiction, but I had a trial run 20 years ago, in a play for Radio 3 called *The Cold Country*, about three men stranded in a tent in the Antarctic during a blizzard. Then, two years ago, I began to make notes for a novel loosely based around Scott and his companions on their last, fatal voyage. I have never written this kind of fiction-with-real-life characters, but I was encouraged to do so by James Hamilton-Paterson's fine first novel about Edward Elgar, *Gerontius*.

The notes were taking shape and I planned to begin the novel this time next year. All seemed well.

Just before Christmas, on the 8.50 from Oxford to Paddington, I opened my copy of *The Bookseller* and saw an advertisement for a new novel by Beryl Bainbridge. It is called *The Birthday Boys* and is based on the last voyage of Scott and his companions to the Antarctic.

The moral? Well, there isn't one I suppose. Two years' work has gone down the tube – for however different my approach might have been I could never write my novel now. I can scarcely bear to walk by the Antarctica collection on my bookshelves.

I have never met or corresponded with Beryl Bainbridge, and so far as I know neither of us made public details of our work in progress. I haven't read her book – I couldn't, which is a pity because, as with Penelope Fitzgerald, I enjoy and admire her work greatly. I've read the reviews of *The Birthday Boys*. They have been excellent, and I am delighted and wish the novel tremendously well, for of course it is close to my heart, whoever its author.

Fate. Chance. Coincidence. The collective unconscious. Who knows? The only thing to do is get on with something else and not whinge. Above all, I am grateful I had not almost completed my own Antarctica novel.

It's a rum world though. A few years ago, a man accosted me in the foyer of Broadcasting House. 'Ah-ha!' he said, stabbing an accusing finger, 'I know who you are! I recognise you. You're Beryl Bainbridge.'

At the time, I denied it.

18 January 1992

SPECTATOR SPORT

THE GENEROUS GENIUS

Frank Keating

I hope the packed throng will sing one of his own hymns at John Arlott's memorial service at Alresford on Monday. Perhaps the one he used to call, with a chuckle, 'my harvest festival hit single' – 'God whose Farm is all Creation':

> All our labour, all our watching,
> All our calendar of care,
> In these crops of your creation,
> Take, O God: they are our prayer.

According to David Rayvern Allen, the BBC producer and devoted collector of Arlottiana, John was asked by the BBC in 1969 to put new words to three traditional English melodies for their new *Hymnal*. 'Sure,' said Arlott, 'I'll let you have the words tomorrow.' 'Don't be silly,' said the rather staid lady commissioning the work, 'you'll need more time than that.' Said John, 'It don't take long to write a lyric,' and the three hymns were duly delivered next day. John once said of the harvest festival 12-liner, 'It has been about a hundred times more remunerative than anything else I've written in my entire life. It's in virtually every modern hymn book in the English language. Quite amazing.'

Although he will be fondly remembered for as long as tape recording exists, mostly for his beguiling cricket broadcasts and his writings for years as the *Guardian* cricket correspondent, he wrote regularly for *The Spectator* in the 1950s – on anything and everything; even, in January 1955, on a boxing match:

> Four times Johnson's upswinging fist made a strange angular line in the space where Marcos had been a moment before. Tobacco smoke had turned the steam-heat into a swamp mist. Punches landed with the sound of a boot clapped into a puddle . . . Marcos

ran at Johnson and hit him and hit him again with a
feminine intensity.

Or how about his 'perfect meal', chronicled for *The Spec* in 1954 –
in a little trattoria at Monrupino, where Italy topples on the edge of
Yugoslavia, with the house wine

> so dark that it clouds the teeth grey-black. It is lusty
> and round in the mouth, warm in the stomach. We
> drank it contentedly with *prosciutto crudo*, the salted,
> uncooked ham, sliced casually and eaten on crusts of
> bread from a bare wooden table, with another glass of
> the wine in place of a savoury, and another instead
> of coffee.

The marvellous and generous man was still at it almost to the very
end. In the four or five years before he retired from cricket, in 1980,
it was my unparalleled luck (and joy) to travel with him often: to the
Test matches to knock off for the *Guardian* a little sidebar piece of
waffle alongside his report; but best when we zig-zagged round the
shires, him in his element planning the alfresco lunch we would have
– and with whom – me carrying his battered old typewriter case, and
keeping the scorecard up to date when not being gently ordered to
nip out of the ground and across to the county stores for another
couple of slices of rough terrine or an extra hunk of Cheshire. He
would always keep the safe hold on his briefcase, which held four
bottles nicely, and be in charge of the corkscrewing. Also, he would
be *maître* of the onion-slicing, paring with the meticulous relish of
a needy peasant the pungent, tear-jerking bulb – just so – with his
penknife.

Once I got out of bed on the wrong side and wrote a crosspatch piece
in these pages about the ultimate pointlessness of writing on sport.
By return of post, kindly admonishment from John, handwritten in his
famous purply-black Quink:

> It is clear that sports writing is not – or should not be
> – important in the pattern of literary life; just as sport
> is not – or should not be – important in the shape of
> world history. The fact remains that many unimportant
> – and important – people retain a deeply romantic and
> nostalgic feeling for sports, for the great sportsmen of

their childhood, and abiding interests and loyalties in
the sporting events of today.

I suppose John Arlott will be the only genius I shall ever meet.

18 January 1992

DOORS

Hilary Corke

At last we found a house that had a room
And squeezed the car beside a cow-shed stall.
The sun a green half-bitten apple sank
Precisely then between black writhen whips,
Sooty declension. Sandwiches and ale.
Along the narrow dogleg corridor
Planks creaked on different notes, and numbers hung
Handpainted on small hooks along the wall.

Later I sailed that passage in some gap
Between two greying hours with slow footfall
Feeling in quarter-light (and could not find
The switch) for where the bathroom's welcome lay.
The floorboards sighed; then at a doubtful tack
Behind some number still illegible
Seeped through the very whitewash that I touched
A kind of trickling sobbing like a tap.

I stopped, my heart stopped with me; all the dawn
Seemed nothing but instinct with hopeless tears
That would not staunch. There were no comfort words.
Flowed on and on. And at my coming back
Flowed on and on. I almost thought to try
That gate of sorrows, swing it in the dusk
And put my hand upon a blinded head
And put my arm round shoulders in a bed.

But this was now and England. English Breakfast
Served in the Dining Room, and check the tables:
Two girls with hiking-legs; the little couple
Who pass each other jam; the curly boy
With V-neck sunburn; the brash family
Who leap from joke to silly joke like goats;
The man who reads and cuts his toast in fours:
And all the faces just as closed as doors.

18 January 1992

'UNTING IS ALL THAT'S WORTH LIVING FOR

Raymond Carr

The contempt in which the literary establishment holds the works of Robert Smith Surtees is only equalled by the contempt in which his readers, like myself, hold the literary establishment. Since a colleague could accuse a fox-hunting head of an Oxford college of 'discrediting the University by his degrading antics', it is to be expected that some dons sustain the prejudices of 19th-century radicals and low churchmen, scorning a writer whose novels, admired by Thackeray and Kipling, are concerned with fox hunting and the state of English agriculture. Surtees is not regarded as a suitable subject for English Literature or much consulted by historians as an incomparable source for the study of mid-Victorian rural society. It is astonishing that none of Surtees' works was in print in 1979. It is the achievement of the Surtees Society, founded by Sir Charles Pickthorn in that year, to have brought out his most important novels with those original illustrations that have etched his characters on the mind's eye for many of us since childhood. The Society now publishes Frederick Watson's study of Surtees. It is a useful but not a great book, illustrating Surtees' character with lengthy quotations from his works. It was written in 1933 before farming became a mechanised agro business and the traditional rural community was still a social unit, as A. J. P. Taylor put it, 'complete with squires, fox hunting and gnarled yokels'. Watson writes of 'yellow stooks upon the stubble under a still autumn light'. Not many stooks about the place now.

Surtees himself was no rural romantic. A satirist, he recognised the limitations of satire: as Watson remarks, 'he could only write with genius about ignoble people'. But what magnificent characters they are, their utterances now part of the folk memory of the sporting world. Jorrocks, the cockney grocer MFH, not above touting his tea at meets; Facey Romford, a mercenary itinerant Master of questionable morals living off his subscribers; a whole gallery of professional huntsmen from the flashy Bragg on the look-out for a rich and inexperienced Master to exploit, to Jorrocks' huntsman, the immortal James Pigg. All are redeemed by their enthusiasm or skill as fox hunters. Jorrocks is a pusillanimous rider. 'Come hup, I say, you ugly beast', he roars, pretending to put his horse at a stiff fence, 'but in reality holding him hard by the head'. But he lives for hunting. Pigg is a foul-mouthed tippler, but for him 'there's nout like huntin''. Facey Romford is a rogue, but he kills his foxes; when his hounds check, the intuition of genius tells him where his fox has run. Surtees' greatest literary creation is Soapy Sponge, the anti-hero of his best novel. Sponge, Surtees himself wrote, is 'a characterless character', whose only reading is Mogg's *Cab Fares of London* and whose only occupation is fox hunting. Yet he is as memorable as Mr Micawber. It is not only the capacity to create unforgettable characters that invites comparison with Dickens: at its best, Surtees' comic dialogue is as good as anything in Dickens; at its worst, it must be confessed, it is terrible.

Watson sets Surtees in his context. Born in 1805, he died in 1865. He therefore witnessed the great sea-change in fox hunting. From the occupation of provincial notables, farmers and tradesmen it became a national sport centred on the crack Midland packs. The chronicler of this fashionable world was Nimrod – the pen name of the inventor of hunting journalism, Charles James Apperley. Apperley was a snob, impressed by the long corridors and liveried servants in the mansions of the great hunting magnates and much given to Latin quotations. (It is a sign of the cultural decadence of our times that there is not much Latin in sporting journalism today.) Surtees disliked Nimrod – there is a cruel parody of his inflated style in *Handley Cross* – and everything he stood for. Surtees disliked fashionable hunting and the hard riding for riding's sake and the loose living that went with it. His heart was in the provinces whence he came. He never hunted, Watson observes, with crack hunts and his own experiences as a master in his native Durham were unrewarding once his hounds took to worrying sheep. The great aristocrats kept magnificent hunting establishments: but

Lord Ladythorne is more interested in flirting with attractive girls than in killing foxes. The Duke of Tergiversation adjusts his hospitality on 'the debtor and creditor principle' to his political and social ambitions. Lord Scamperdale lives on bacon in one room but flatters farmers' wives as all good masters should. No one saw more clearly than Surtees that should farmers, exasperated by inconsiderate fox hunters, turn against hunting, the sport was doomed: from being a bond of union it would foster a rural class war.

But there is no streak of sentimentality in Surtees' scenes from provincial life, little compassion. Hence the failure of his novels to appeal to the Victorian public. As Watson points out, there is no mention of the sufferings of the agricultural labourers who appear as clots who misdirect hunts. He was an enthusiast for improved farming; his obsession with proper drainage appears time and time again in his novels and in a curious passage Jorrocks dreams of a steam-driven combine harvester. Surtees was, as Watson rightly argues, a progressive and a prophet. The small farmers who lack capital for improvements, like weasels, must go to the wall. Men must adjust to the times. At first he believed railways would drag squires to London and a race of

absentee landlords would unleash a French Revolution; but he came to see railways as a civilising influence. Rather than destroying a harmonious rural society, railways might save it by 'bringing wealth and salubrity' to an isolated countryside. His *Hints to Railway Travellers and County Visitors to London* (1852) told the squires how to buy tickets and find the cheapest floors in hotels. Detail always delighted him and he bores his readers with paragraph-long descriptions of clothing, down to the last button. He is a provincial puritan: he detests gambling, 'low' sports like cock-fighting and bear-baiting, scratch hunts organised by publicans. He disapproved of coursing as artificial and deplored the fact that shooting, once the healthy exercise of a man and his dog to replenish the pot, was on the way to becoming an organised massacre, exterminating 'in one day what should serve you a year'. Jorrocks is all very well in his way in fiction, but in real life 'the fact is that a man won't do for a Master of Hounds unless he is a gentleman'.

He embodied in his writings all the prejudices of his caste. He hated social climbers in the hunting field and outsiders from 'trade' who bought estates to acquire gentility. Sir Moses Mainchance was one; Mr Jawleyford another. 'Paper-booted, pen-and-ink landowners', they screw their tenants, fail in their obligations to the countryside and come a cropper financially. His deplorable anti-Semitism stemmed from his belief that Jews were behind the racecourse gambling world he so hated. In *Ask Mama*, the Miss Jewsons turn up their 'oily hook noses at everything'; 'cigar-smoking Israelites' loll about in their carriages at races 'like half-drunk sailors on a spree'.

Why did this north country landowner take to writing at all? He may, in his youth, have needed the money, but not after he inherited Hamsteley; his early journalism may have relieved the tedium of studying for the bar in London. He certainly rejected fame as a spur since he wrote anonymously. He knew he was no good at plots and his novels are a succession of episodes. I think writing was, for him, a means of pitching into those aspects of landed society and the world of fox hunting of which he deeply disapproved: the rise of the *nouveaux riches*, the use of the hunting field as a marriage market where ambitious mothers and their daughters pursue a promising husband as the field pursue a fox. Jorrocks was meant to shock the fashionable world of Leicestershire, so buttered up by Nimrod, who must have found it inconceivable that a retail grocer should become an MFH.

In much of his writing Surtees is tilting at windmills that have long been dismantled, castigating pretensions that now assume other forms in a world where social advancement is achieved by dining pop

stars rather than MFHs. Surtees has been neglected because his major
novels centre on fox hunting; he may survive outside that world, now
threatened with legislative destruction at the hands of townee MPs,
through the sheer vitality that this reserved country landowner injected
into his best work – and some of his work is quite terribly dull. For the
opportunity to taste it at its best we have to thank Sir Charles Pickthorn
and the Surtees Society. With luck, the collected works of Surtees may
one day shine from the shelves of English Literature libraries. Frederick
Watson's quotations demonstrate that at least they are more amusing
than much of the stuff that nestles there.

25 January 1992

AT THE EDGE

P. J. Kavanagh

Was it the blouse-and-skirt combination, the cut
Of the fair hair of the near-silhouette
Against yellow sea, that made me peer and stare?
I walked by white cliffs with my son who was not
Your son, when he came you were gone.
I screwed up my eyes, unfocused, to see less clear
And keep you a moment longer, hold you there.
It has happened before, of course, as though round a corner
Impossible things may appear. A middle-aged woman
I saw when I secretly led us to where
I could see with my back to the sea, who had nothing in common
With you save stature and stoop and short-cut yellow hair.
We continued. Not self nor pain nor fate is here or there,
But relentlessly turns us to souls that peer and stare.

25 January 1992

ALL THE QUEEN'S MEN

Hugh Massingberd

Next week – on 'Ruby Thursday', as I heard one of the Queen's queens refer to it – will see what Her Majesty herself calls 'the 40th anniversary of my father's death and of my accession'. Note the sense of priority: King George VI has cast a long shadow over his elder daughter's reign.

In her Accession Declaration, she vowed that 'I shall always work as my father did', a promise echoed in her latest Christmas broadcast: 'Over the years I have tried to follow my father's example.' Certainly the Queen tends to like things to go along much as they did in her father's day – notwithstanding the energetic efforts of her husband, Prince Philip, to rid the Court of what he has called 'fundungus'.

'To survive,' Prince Philip has said, 'the monarchy has to change.' No one more took to heart Lord Altrincham's rather prissy strictures of the 1950s about the Queen's 'tweedy' entourage and 'a tight little enclave of British "ladies and gentlemen"'. But as one contemplates the Court today, it is striking how little has really changed.

The trouble is that there is nothing so inflexible as instant tradition born of insecurity. And naturally the House of Windsor, whose very name was born during the Great War in reaction to its German origins, felt particularly insecure after the Abdication. Many of today's hallowed 'precedents' for monarchical conduct and Court procedure turn out, on examination, to be barely half a century old. Even the tradition that the sovereign does not pay tax effectively only dates from King George VI's accession.

The whole question of royal finance continues to cloud the monarch's horizons and it is not one which is going to go away – for all the sycophantic guff we are hearing at the moment to the effect that the Queen is a ruby beyond price, God bless her. The problems caused by the 'accountability' of the Queen and her increasingly unsatisfactory relatives cannot any longer be brushed aside by well-bred bromides.

The public relations of the royal family has been a disaster area in recent years and, while it may be tempting to blame it all on those horrid tabloids and us nasty scribblers, I am inclined to point the finger at the Queen's advisers. They are supposed to keep the monarch abreast of public opinion, to tell her candidly where she and her family are going wrong, and to come up with practical new solutions (such as, say, the Queen giving up the Civil List and emulating the Prince of Wales by living off estate revenue and voluntarily paying a proportion to the Treasury). But one gains the impression that they would never dream of daring to do so.

Whether the Queen's men like it or not, her reign has seen the powerful emergence of the public relations industry, which has transformed the nature of politics. Somehow, however, it has passed the Palace by. When, the other day, I referred to the fragrant Belinda Harley as the Prince of Wales's 'new PR adviser', an anguished royal flunkey ticked me off for perpetrating such a grievous misstatement. Miss Harley is indeed a public relations executive by background, but in Court circles 'public relations' remains a dirty phrase, though it is at the heart of the monarchy's problems.

Who is responsible? Well, the buck stops with the Private Secretary, one of the most unsung and yet most vital posts within the British Constitution. Historically the job has called for men of quite exceptional statesmanlike qualities; with the best will in the world, for he is undoubtedly a decent and honourable chap, that is hardly a description of the present incumbent, Sir Robert Fellowes, whose father was agent at Sandringham to both King George VI and the present Queen.

Fellowes, a former discount broker and a brother-in-law of the Princess of Wales, succeeded Sir 'Bill' Heseltine, an Australian acclaimed as the first 'Commonwealth courtier' and credited, during his stint as Press Secretary, with initiating the 'walkabout', setting up the revealing royal family television documentary and generally polishing up the media image. Heseltine, in turn, had taken over from the rather grey figure of Sir Philip Moore (now Lord Moore of Wolvercote), a career civil servant who seemed set on making the Palace tick over on the lines of a government department.

Of all the Queen's men, Sir Martin Charteris (now Lord Charteris of Amisfield) proved the most human and engaging Private Secretary. Her Majesty's speeches suddenly took on a more relaxed, even humorous vein. It was fun to watch Charteris slapping his knee with merriment at his own jokes as delivered by the Queen. 'I think everybody will concede that on this of all days I should begin my speech with the words "My husband and I"', she quipped at the silver wedding celebrations the year Charteris took office. It was impossible not to warm to him when he remarked on *Desert Island Discs* that he loved the Queen 'very much'.

The Private Secretary's duties were set out in the lapidary memorandum to the Select Committee on the Civil List in 1971 by

Charteris's predecessor, Lord Adeane, who followed his grandfather, Lord Stamfordham, into the post, though his son, Edward Adeane, ended the dynasty's connection with the Court when he parted company with that difficult master, the present Prince of Wales. The outline of the job is arranging royal tours, drafting the Queen's speeches, administering the royal archives, the Palace secretariat and the beleaguered press office. But this list gives no idea of his constitutional significance.

As the Queen's first Private Secretary, Sir Alan ('Tommy') Lascelles, very much one of the old guard, put it, the job is not 'by any means beer and skittles'. Of all people, that doctrinaire Socialist bore Harold Laski best explained how 'the royal secretary walks a tightrope below which he is never unaware that an abyss is yawning'. Laski pointed out that 'a bad Private Secretary, one who was rash, or indiscreet, or untrustworthy, might easily make the system of constitutional monarchy unworkable unless the monarch himself was a person of extraordinary wisdom'.

A key part of the job – not least with the prospect of a 'hung' parliament – is, in Laski's words, to be 'the confidant of all ministers, but he must never leave the impression that he is anybody's man'. From Churchill, who was more than 50 years her senior, the Queen has progressed through nine Prime Ministers – including Margaret Thatcher, six months older, and John Major, nearly 17 years younger. All have been impressed by the Queen's remarkable command of detail contained in her 'Red Boxes' – Her Majesty is celebrated for her love of facts – but few appear to have established a particularly warm rapport. 'What one gets,' observed Jim Callaghan, who hit it off with the Queen better than most, 'is friendliness but not friendship.'

Amid the embarrassingly excessive euphoria of the so-called 'New Elizabethan Age' of the early 1950s, it was easy to cast the young Queen as 'Gloriana' while the veteran war leader Churchill was portrayed – historical metaphors becoming somewhat confused – in a role analogous to that of Lord Melbourne guiding the young Queen Victoria. But much as the Queen enjoyed certain aspects of her audiences with the old boy – particularly their chats about her greatest passion, the Turf – the relationship was by no means in the 'dear Lord M' mould. That self-appointed royal adviser Lord Mountbatten – admittedly an unreliable source – once told me that there had even been some sort of constitutional showdown between the Queen and her first Prime Minister over the question of the royal surname. Churchill, stoutly backed by Queen Mary, would not countenance the House of Mountbatten and so the House of Windsor it remained.

The wisecracking Harold Wilson claimed to have enjoyed particularly cordial dealings with his sovereign, whereas Eden and Heath are supposed to have vied for the Tuesday evening wooden spoon. As for Thatcher, the two women (neither a feminist, nor noted for their 'gender solidarity') probably got on better than is generally thought – despite fierce differences of opinion over the Queen's romantically idealised 'great Imperial Commonwealth'. In any event, the Queen – generally rather cheeseparing about dishing out gongs – was notably quick off the mark with Lady Thatcher's Order of Merit; and Her Majesty was said to be distinctly unamused by the way in which her Prime Minister of 12 years was bundled out of office by the machinations of the Tory party *apparatchiks*.

Many people wrongly assume that because the Queen is obviously conservative (with a small 'c') she must be a dyed-in-the-wool Tory. Hard as it may be to grasp, she is genuinely apolitical. Her father and that most underrated of all the Queen's men, the historian Sir Henry Marten, Provost of Eton (who gave her a thorough grounding in constitutional history and law), brought her up not to favour any political party. 'The Queen doesn't make fine distinctions between politicians of different parties,' said Sir Godfrey Agnew, a former Clerk of the Privy Council, in a nicely double-edged observation. 'They all

'He's a bit sensitive about mother-in-law jokes.'

roughly belong to the same category in her view.'

The Privy Council – memorably described by Richard Crossman as 'the best example of pure mumbo-jumbo you can find' – in theory provides the Queen with a wealth of constitutional wisdom on which to draw. Yet, though in her younger days the Queen may have sought out such elder statesmen as the late Marquess of Salisbury (the diehard High Tory and High Churchman 'Bobbety', who succeeded in putting the kibosh on poor Princess Margaret's chances of marrying Group-Captain Peter Townsend), the idea that she calls on a magic ring of constitutional advisers is largely a myth. To suggest that there is a cosy knitting circle made up of such figures as Lord Blake, Lord St John of Fawsley (God bless the Master of 'Emma's' collection of royal knickers) and the voluble Commonwealth 'expert' Sir 'Sonny' Ramphal would be to enter the realms of fantasy – though there is the odd licensed jester like the egregious architect Sir Hugh Casson.

No, on the whole, the Queen relies on the resources of her Court – and a pretty uninspiring and unimaginative crew they are. As the best of royal biographers, James Pope Hennessy, observed, royalty is fine taken neat; it is only when diluted by courtiers that it can be difficult to swallow.

The calibre of the Queen's men, it must be said, has declined more than a little since the days of Sir Henry Ponsonby, the great Victorian *éminence grise*, and his son 'Fritz'. In his introduction to the latter's *Recollection of Three Reigns*, Antony Lambton observes:

> It was conceived a good idea after the war to democratise the monarchy by making ex-servicemen courtiers, to bring a sense of realism to the throne. In practice this meant the new equerries, unused to the world of the Court, insecure in their social position, never dreamt of talking to the late King George VI or Prince Philip and the Queen as Ponsonby would have done.

In Lambton's view, this is a loss which will not be righted until the payment of equerries is commensurate with their importance as advisers to the Queen. 'Apparently,' he says, 'some merchant banker gave idiotic, parsimonious advice on this issue: a change would appear to be a priority which would establish better relations between the royal family and the public.'

The current crop of courtiers are indeed drawn from those whose reflexes are conditioned to obey orders rather than to frame them. The much-vaunted 'meritocratisation' of the royal household has, in short, failed to produce people with an instinctive grasp of statecraft and the long view born of an independent perspective.

Part of the problem is that the Queen, cursed with her grandmother Queen Mary's crippling shyness, is not a sociable monarch, unlike, say, Charles II, George III or Edward VII. She has never shown any inclination to go on royal progresses, on which she might stay with a broad spread of the landed aristocracy. In this she takes after her father who prided himself on not being 'smart' or fashionable.

In this vacuum she and her family have shown an uncanny knack of befriending the least attractive elements of the upper classes – whether pompous dullards of the old school or such bounders from the polo field and the racecourse as Major Ronald Ferguson (father of the irrepressible 'Fergie', Duchess of York) and the late 'Porchey', Earl of Carnarvon, an appalling old ham and reprobate. His son, the present Lord Carnarvon, a chip off the old block, is one of the Queen's closest friends and occupies the position of her racing manager. As such, in the notorious West Ilsley scandal (wherein the Queen's paralysed but still highly competent trainer, Major Dick Hern, appeared to be the victim of an old-fashioned eviction from the royal stables), Carnarvon achieved the remarkable feat of making his royal mistress so unpopular on the Turf that there was even speculation that Her Majesty might be booed down the course at Ascot during the Royal Meeting.

In the run-in to the Queen's Golden Jubilee it looks as if it might take a new set of all the Queen's horses (a long-hoped-for Derby winner among them, perhaps?) and all the Queen's men to put the royal soap opera together again. Instead of the existing farrago of toadies, stuffed shirts and 'jobsworth' bureaucrats, those concerned for the long-term interests of the monarchy should look for an intelligent combination of statesmen and PR professionals whose own excesses could be tempered by the wise counsel of what Lambton unblushingly calls 'the best families'.

Above all, we look to the Queen herself to come into her own at last as a great matriarchal figure and fill her mother's shoes as she has her father's. So far her devoted subjects have yet to see the real 'Lilibet' behind the intently dutiful, occasionally acid-drop exterior. 'All her experiences are received,' Callaghan once tellingly remarked. 'She has very little direct experience except in one field – horse-racing and breeding. She will tell you very frequently what someone else has said about something; that is her means of judgment. She can't form her own judgment direct.'

An analyst scrutinising the 'Royal Firm' (as King George VI liked to call it) might well conclude that, with its boss lacking the confidence to impose her personality and her understrappers lacking the initiative, and the bottom, to give her objective advice, it might be time to sell one's shares in the House of Windsor (OK, 'Mountbatten-Windsor', Dickie, you old fraud). But I hope that the best of Elizabeth II is yet to come. Churchill may not have been the Queen's Melbourne, but she does need a new Disraeli – with an eye to Europe rather than the Commonwealth – to encourage her on a fresh and triumphant course.

1 February 1992

LETTER

DEFENCE OF THE REALM

Sir: I am writing to comment on the mischievous and provocative article by H. Massingberd ('All the Queen's Men', 1 February). He is entitled to his opinions and so am I, having served the monarchy for 50 years and having met most of the names he mentions.

I cannot comment about the Queen's private secretaries as I have no knowledge of their work but I have met most of those mentioned. They are men of the highest calibre and I am certain they give loyal and devoted service and very sound advice. To quote from the article: 'The Royal Secretary walks a tightrope' and none of them has fallen 'into the abyss below'. So much for the writer's unsubstantiated comments.

Massingberd says the Queen's Household consists of uninspiring and unimaginative men. How does he know? Has he served the Queen in any capacity to make such judgments? Does he really think equerries should go round giving orders to the Queen? Does he really believe Lambton's laughable remarks about the Royal Family being socially insecure? Does he know any equerries? I suspect he has never met one otherwise he wouldn't make such ill-informed comments. Statecraft is the business of the Private Secretary, equerries have different duties. He should know this.

In the third paragraph from the end of the article he talks about the Royal Soap Opera. The one thing you don't want is to turn the Royal Family into a soap opera. Goodness knows the media do their worst to achieve this. Massingberd goes on: 'Instead of the existing farrago of toadies, stuffed shirts, bureaucrats' etc. Let's tidy up these innuendos. Looking at the Household List, I see it contains the names of a number of as distinguished men and women as you will find in any organisation anywhere. In his blinkered view anyone working for the monarchy automatically becomes a brainless flunkey or a stuffed shirt. (The press loves to use the word 'flunkey' or 'brass hat'. Take either, you must by implication be stupid or worse.) He suggests the employment of a statesman but he doesn't say

where you find such a person. As the Queen sees the
Prime Minister every week she probably can get all the
advice necessary. I thought the press office was staffed
by professionals already.

The writer does not appear to know anyone in the
Household because if he did he wouldn't write such
rubbish about it. Perhaps he hasn't been asked to a
Garden Party! I am told he writes well about houses.
He should stick to that.

In conclusion I say this. I am surprised that a
right-wing magazine such as *The Spectator*, to which
I subscribe, should print such an ill-informed article
at this time, when a general election is in the offing
and we need all our stable institutions.

A.G. Way
Kincairney, Dunkeld,
Perthshire

22 February 1992

DIARY

Ludovic Kennedy

Why is the word atheist still so pejorative when that's what at least
half the population now are? People of all sorts think that admitting
to it, as I often do, is slightly bad form. This is because in the popular
mind and despite falling membership, the Church still occupies the
moral high ground, and believers and even 'don't knows' see atheism
as a departure from the norm. Many also interpret atheism as being
positively anti-'God' whereas in fact thoughts about him rarely enter
my head. I mention this because a week or two ago I appeared in a
radio show called *Sunday* to discuss 'God' with a Methodist minister
and a rabbi. They said what you would expect them to say. I said
that all religions were man-made and that every society had always
created in its own image the god best suited to it; also, that all gods,

including that of the Christians, were ideas in the mind and so to say that Jesus was the son of 'God' was a nonsense. Creation, I concluded, was a marvellous mystery we could never solve and let's keep it that way. After the programme I received 40 letters: 25 writers said how refreshing to hear views which coincided with their own, 15 that Jesus and God were waiting for me, and if only I could give myself to them, how happy I (and they) would be. If I was rich, nothing would give me greater satisfaction than to endow an annual lecture to explore the huge gulf between believers and non-believers, explain how it is that men and women of equal intelligence can differ to the extent that the first lot think the second lot are missing the truths of a great spiritual experience, while the second lot think that the beliefs of the first lot are fantasies based on fear, wishful thinking and self-delusion.

Does that mean that as an atheist I look forward to a day when all churches have become museums or bingo halls and bishops and archbishops, wise or foolish, are no more? Not at all. The churches, however ailing, add a dimension to life which it would be tragic to lose and because, as Cardinal Hume has put it, they are a sign that goodness is achievable. I'll be even more contradictory and say that when I die, I would like a priest, if willing, to conduct my obsequies, not because he (or maybe she) is a priest but because one of the grave ceremonies of life ought to be carried out professionally. Who else but a priest can do this? When my friend Derek Hart, the broadcaster, was cremated, there was no priest to conduct the proceedings, and it was one of the emptiest and most dismal ceremonies I can remember.

8 February 1992

'LET'TH JUTHT THIDDOWN . . .'

Vicki Woods

As I plough through the accounts of the Mike Tyson rape trial, I have some sympathy with the plight of young Desirée Washington. Not because of feminist fellow-feeling, but because I too entered Mike Tyson's bedroom one night, freely and of my own volition. I was interviewing him for *American Vogue*, to go with a handsome set of pictures they'd taken of him and his (then) inamorata Naomi Campbell, the south London super-model. I flew to Las Vegas and waited for Don King's office to make the call. Don King is Tyson's manager and has himself served time for homicide.

I sat around in the Las Vegas Hilton for a day and a half watching Americans put money in machines, until a laconic man called Aaron Snowell came to pick me up. The interview was to take place in a house Don King was renting. We drove there in complete silence. Snowell pushed open the door and left me in the hall. It was the noisiest house I have ever been inside. The walls heaved. Some of the walls were made of television screens six foot high by five wide, all switched on and belting out an incredible level of boom-boom racket. The rooms all ran into each other, and the place was packed with heavyweight boxers and a couple of dozen assorted men built like heavyweight boxers: trainers, managers, minions, hangers-on, cooks, waiters, minders and limo-drivers. Don King, Tyson's manager, was standing at a desk in front of a bank of six telephones, yelling into two of them while the others rang continually. It was dark. I felt like a helpless mamma coming home to find a teenage party in full swing, heaving with gate-crashers. In my hand I held a notebook and a tiny tape-recorder. I began to see this wouldn't be the easiest interview I'd ever done.

Across the room, I picked out what I thought were two Olympic gymnasts clinging to Mike Tyson's legs. Then I realised they *were* his legs, naked thighs in little baggy shorts. He caught my eye and smirked at me, waving me over, so I scuttled across and began to shout questions at him above the din from the televisions. Sitting down, he's as big as four people my size. It's disconcerting. He's shy, gauche and awkward, which is disconcerting, too. And he talks in a tiny, tiny voice, which you have to bend close to hear, and he has a lisp like Violet Elizabeth Bott. Me, fortissimo: 'I hear you're keen on Damon Runyon, Mike.' Mike, in a baby voice: 'No, I'm not; it'th rathitht crap.' Mmm. 'What are you reading at the moment, Mike?' '*A Hundred Yearth of Lynching*.' 'Gosh. What's that about, exactly?' 'Lynching niggerth in America.' Tyson didn't want to be interviewed. Don King wanted him to be, but he didn't; it was pretty clear. I ploughed on, trying to get on to boxing, but he wouldn't. 'I don't want to talk about any of that thtuff.' I tried lighter topics. 'Whose clothes do you like, Mike?' 'Gianni Verthace'th.' For two hours, against the nightmarish din, I tried every question I could think of, both germane and pointless, trying to break him down. He began to come across a very little bit when he'd established my Englishness:

he likes England. 'My biggest fanth. England and the Brathilianth.' He then established my married state, the ages of my children and where I was staying. He was getting less mulish and unco-operative, but there was altogether too much social intercourse and not enough interview. 'You theem like a very charming lady to me,' he said. I shouted, 'Oh, thanks.' He said, 'You thouldn't cut your hair tho thort.' I yelled, 'Oh, really?' He was clearly beginning to melt and brushed the hair off my forehead with a giant hand. That was *seriously* disconcerting, but what the hell. And then he suddenly yawned and began to look much more relaxed and cheerful, and I began to feel as though I might actually get an interview out of him when he leaned across me and said, 'How much . . . do you weigh?' I felt like a chicken leg.

Unfortunately, Don King went into hyperspace at this point. He seemed to have a German banker on three of his six telephones, and Don was demanding of Tyson that he come over and concentrate on a deal he was doing that was going to be worth 90 million, or 90 billion. The size of the deal raised the roof, and Tyson had had enough. Nobody could watch a six-foot-by-five television with this sort of racket going on, so he swung off the sofa and walked towards the stairs, shouting for me to come up to his bedroom. Well, I grabbed the opportunity as fast as any 18-year-old American fame groupie, picked up my tape-recorder and hopped up the stairs after him.

Freely and of my own volition, I made for the bedroom. Nobody caught my eye, but I saw tongues popping into cheeks all over the room. Up I went, along the corridor and into a very tidy bedroom with children's drawings stuck on the walls, and a big double bed, and a day bed. Inside there was absolute silence. Tyson shut the door behind me. My God, at last. Peace and quiet and no televisions and a slightly more co-operative interviewee. Well, now. Here we are in Mike Tyson's bedroom, ladies and gentlemen of the jury. In the blue corner, on the day bed, is a man with gold teeth, a tiny pair of shorts, the brain of a 12-year-old, the body of a tank, an entourage of faithful hangers-on and an earnings potential of 90 million, or 90 billion. He is patting the seat beside him and saying, 'Let'th jutht thiddown and relaxth and hang out a little!' In the red corner, wearing a suit, is a 40-year-old woman journalist with an empty tape-recorder, a headache, a deadline to meet, a ticket back to London, and a slight unfamiliarity with the American vernacular.

Hang out a little, eh? Well, how do you hang out, exactly? Let's maybe not hang out a little, perhaps. I hopped around the room pointing animatedly at the pictures. 'Gosh! Lovely picture! Who drew that?' and so forth. He patted the day bed. 'Gosh! What a lot of clothes you have!' He didn't respond. 'Erm, can I look in your closet?' I asked. It's American for wardrobe. At which point, and who can blame him, he leapt off the day bed, opened the wardrobe, pointed silently at about 200 suits and said he had to go into town and thee thome people. A limo drove me back to my hotel.

After the piece appeared in the magazine, *American Vogue* had a letter from a reader complaining about my piece. It was a well-written letter. She said that it was full of slights and cheap jokes about Mike Tyson and Don King and everyone else I had met. She said that it was racist. She said I had clearly been unnerved by finding myself in a roomful of black Americans. She complained that I had told the readers nothing about Mike Tyson the man or Mike Tyson the boxer, and she was very scathing about my having ducked the bedroom scene.

'Just what did your writer imagine would happen to her in Mike's room?' she asked, and concluded with a very telling thrust: 'She should have used her opportunity to get a better interview.' Well, it's a point of view. And I did feel bad about ducking out of the bedroom, all the way back to London. Maybe if he hadn't been wearing shorts, who knows?

8 February 1992

BOOKS

HOW TO BE VERY, VERY POPULAR

Anita Brookner

A DUBIOUS LEGACY
by Mary Wesley
Bantam, £14.99, pp. 272

It is not necessarily very intelligent to look askance at the success of Mary Wesley, whose popularity and whose sales have eclipsed those of younger and more earnest novelists. Her latest book, her eighth, is darker in colour than the previous ones, but will no doubt enjoy just as great a success. A critic, perhaps a little morose at being excluded from what seems to be universal enjoyment and appreciation, may be allowed to wonder at this. For the novel is slight, slight to the point of transparency, yet there is no doubt that Mary Wesley has joined the pantheon of established female entertainers, and has, moreover, become enthroned as a kind of icon, as Angela Thirkell once was – although Angela Thirkell was the superior writer.

The plot of *A Dubious Legacy* is minuscule but convoluted. To a country house, Cotteshaw, owned by Henry Tillotson, come two young couples, Barbara and James, and Antonia and Matthew. Henry's poisonous wife Margaret lies enthroned in bed: she is perfectly well but makes only brief incursions into real life, as she does for instance at an ill-judged dinner party, when she dances on the table and tears the head off a pet cockatoo. Barbara and James marry: so do Antonia and Matthew. Both the girls, however, are in love with Henry, who becomes the father of their daughters. All is known, half-known, or not known by the various other characters, the maid Pilar, two homosexual tenants called Jonathan and Jonathan, and the handyman, Trask. The working out of this plot, which moves along rather shakily, takes several years, beginning in 1944 and ending in 1990. A certain doggedness is needed to keep one's eye on the page, and yet the author's confidence is unmistakable.

Much is made of the idea of inheritance: Henry inherited the house and farm from his father, much as he inherited his wife, who was bestowed on him by an act of paternal philanthropy. Henry does not chafe under this burden. Indeed, he finds that it gives him a certain freedom. Henry, it is agreed, is 'flawed'. He seemed to me the one convincing character in an unconvincing assembly. But the countryside, and the weather, are fine. Maybe this is the secret. However unconvincing the cast, one is in appealing territory.

There is a certain type of doughty English female writer – Agatha Christie, Catherine Cookson – who wins respect for sheer longevity and volume of output. Mary Wesley is not quite of this number, although her productions are every bit as stereotyped. Photographs show her looking sardonic, in the shadow of a dashing hat. And she is undoubtedly sophisticated, even cynical, in the brittle throwaway style of the Thirties. But this cynicism hides a deep sentimentality, a nostalgia for summer weather, for houses of 'honey-coloured stone', for young love, and for happier times. Much has been made by her publicists of her rakishness, of the spectacle of a woman in her eighth decade writing about sex. In fact she does not write about sex, which she seems to view as enjoyable but insignificant. Her novels simply reveal her as a woman of some experience. This is thought to be highly unusual, although it is not. Women on the verge of 80 do not talk about their amorous pasts because they were brought up in a tradition of reticence, and also, it must be said, because no one is particularly interested.

There remains the question of her overwhelming popularity. She has proved as reassuring to men as she has to women; those readers who appreciate her are addicted to her. Perhaps her novels contain a lesson on how matters should be handled: romantically, lightly, dashingly, tastefully, and with no dialogue more complicated than the he-said she-said variety. There is also a sense of her ancient eye casting a speculative glance on one's own less well-bred arrangements, deficient as they are in advantageous accessories. She has acceded to a state beyond criticism, and she has done this through her own courage (the sheer grit of composing a novel a year) and a style and substance which are perceived as being filtered through a residue of happiness, the sort of pre-war happiness that was a golden age for the fortunate, of whom she is surely one.

Her basilisk profile (the photograph again) defies one to put her down, to feel for her anything but admiration. I thought *A Dubious Legacy* very slight, very unreal, very tedious. The lady herself is clearly more than the sum of her books. One can only feel pleasure that her efforts have brought her success, while at the same time wondering why her readers gain so much nourishment from what are after all little more than astutely controlled fantasies.

Women writers on the whole are well served in England. The process by which some of them become 'well-loved' is mysterious. Perhaps it has as much to do with personality as with literary worth. Mary Wesley has, in the space of a few years, become 'well-loved'. And only a critic would cavil at this accolade.

8 February 1992

DIARY

Dominic Lawson

Who said, on television last week, 'All of the democracies are bankrupt now, because of the way the services have been planned for people to grab'? Milton Friedman? Margaret Thatcher? It sounds too extreme to have been uttered by John Major. In fact, it was said by Her Majesty the Queen to a frantically nodding Ronald Reagan on board the good yacht *Britannia*. It was the most fascinating moment of a fascinating BBC film, commemorating the 40th anniversary of Her Majesty's accession. Strangely, this unique example of the Queen publicly giving vent to her political opinions was not picked up by the legion of 'royal' columnists, who were all far too busy chortling over the Queen's admittedly memorable put-down of Mr Edward Heath. I was even more surprised that such republican newspapers as the *Independent* and the *Sunday Times* did not link the Queen's remark to their running campaign against the Government's handing over of £50 million or so a year to our non-taxpaying monarch. Of course it is not entirely clear what the Queen was trying to tell Mr Reagan, in between her attempts to find the former President some decaffeinated coffee. Did she mean all public services, or just what we have come to call the social services? Either way, it suggests that the Queen must view with some dismay her Government's decision this week to give public sector employees all the wage increases their review bodies demanded, no questions asked. We are even more bankrupt now. Those who reviewed the film pointed out that the Duke of Edinburgh was notable by his absence except, we are told, from the cutting-room floor. But I sensed the Duke's strong influence on the Queen's remarks about bankrupt democracies and people who grab, just as one could sometimes sense Denis Thatcher's influence when his wife switched from the democratic to the demotic.

Elizabeth R was simultaneously broadcast in France. A relative – of mine that is, not of the Queen – who saw the French version tells me that there were no subtitles. All the voices were dubbed, including the monarch's. Apparently the voice of the French 'Queen' was not at all smart, but I suppose the French could claim that the Queen's eldest uncle favoured a kind of royal cockney. I wonder if the French even changed the bit where Her Majesty says, 'Ah, Monsieur Mitterrand, vous connaissez Monsieur Heath?' Perhaps they did, since the French monarchs never used anything but 'tu', reckoning that they need not accord anyone the respect of the second person plural.

15 February 1992

A CRICKETER UNDER THE JAPS

E.W. Swanton

This weekend sees a sombre jubilee. I suppose that the picture of the last days of the Battle of Singapore will stand out equally clearly in the recollection of most of my fellow survivors. We had ample time to relive the chaotic scene in the three and a half years from the Allied surrender on 15 February 1942 to that of the Japanese in Tokyo Bay on 15 August 1945.

On Thursday 29 January, 17 days before the largest capitulation in the history of British arms, we slid into Singapore harbour, the only significant reinforcements to have arrived there since the Japanese invasion of Malaya seven weeks before. As the American troop-ship SS *Wakefield*, carrying 54 Brigade of the 18th Division, was being berthed, the decks thick with men in full order, a flight of 27 Jap bombers flew straight at us. If ever there was a sitting duck we were it. Almost overhead they came, then veered off and dropped their bombs on the pre-selected prey, a gasworks perhaps. The leader ignored the target of his dreams, for in the Jap code obedience came before initiative. It was my first glimpse of his mentality.

The Australian truck drivers who took us to a staging camp in a rubber plantation told us we had arrived too late. By contrast, an official communication from Army HQ at Fort Canning suggested things were normal enough. A letter from the Deputy Provost Marshal requested a photograph in duplicate for the issue of an identity card – this when by the weekend or thereabouts the advancing Japs would have arrived at the Johore Strait dividing the island from the Malayan mainland. It was incidental in my case that the signatory of the letter, Lt Colonel Brian K. Castor, the pre-war secretary of Essex County Cricket Club, would have had no difficulty in recognising his cricket partner in a pre-war opening stand or two.

The shape of Singapore Island is much like a full-blown rose, twice as wide as it is deep, with the city on its southern coast. The naval base and the causeway connecting with the mainland lie centrally, with the military area of Changi to the north-east.

This was the area assigned to our 18th Division, which was composed of Territorials from the eastern counties. With what remained of the Indian 11th Division, we took up positions on the 31st, the battle-weary Australians and the other Indian and British troops who had been fighting a gallant, hopeless retreat on the mainland being deployed on the left flank. Churchill, in Book IV of *The Second World War*, notes that there were no permanent fortifications on the landward side and, what was 'even more astounding', no field defences had been attempted after the war in the East had begun. This is the exact truth. Not a coil of wire did we find, and when we sent to the RAOC depot on the afternoon of Saturday the 31st to get some, we found they had closed down for the weekend.

We made what defensive provisions we could in that first week of February, and provided some custom to an Officers' Club bar with well-laundered staff down by the shore. I signed my last chits there (thinking a bottle or two of whisky would come in handy) on 8 February, the very night that the Japs (after a strong bombardment, in small craft and with blood-curdling cries) penetrated the north-west coast.

The 18th Division, wrote the Prime Minister to General Wavell, the Supreme Commander, on 10 February, 'has a chance to make its name in history'. Vain hope! After two years of hard home training, commanded by General 'Becky' Beckwith-Smith, in whom we had confidence and who held the affection of all, we were denied any such glory. Leaving us unscathed, apart from spasmodic bombardment from the air and artillery on the mainland, the Japs made such inroads in the north-west that by 11 February (my 35th birthday) all troops east of the causeway were withdrawn to a circular perimeter in defence of the city. Units were thrown in piecemeal to plug the gaps. Beckwith-Smith saw his beloved division dismembered bit by bit.

Once the Japs had gained a foothold on the island, surrender was inevitable. In 17 days I never recognised a single Allied aircraft, only Japs either bombing from high altitude or, in the final days, spotting disdainfully for their guns almost at tree-top height. They even had balloons doing the same job. Denied any vestige of air support, even the finest fighting troops would have been pressed to maintain morale.

On 12 and 13 February, the 25-pounder guns of 148 Field Regiment supported the centre-right of the perimeter defence of the city facing the MacRitchie, the southernmost of the three island reservoirs, with the Bukit Timah golf course just west of it. From a convenient observation post, I had the satisfaction of directing heavy concentrations of fire from the 12 guns of 419 Battery at and in the area of the clubhouse and down the Sime Road.

The left of the line came under the heaviest enemy pressure, and on 14 February we received orders to conform to a further withdrawal. It was in establishing a new OP that I came to grief. Wireless communication between OPs and guns was extremely unreliable, making archaic telephone lines essential. While my OP Ack was away directing the signallers laying the wire, I saw up an adjacent tree a pair of spectacles glinting in the sun. Using my Ack's rifle I aimed a few shots into the foliage, but was rewarded by no falling body. A while later, rather forgetting the fellow, I got up to investigate the wire-laying situation. In a burst from, I suppose, his sub-machine-gun I was hit by a single bullet at the right elbow. I was taken to an advanced dressing-station, being succeeded at the OP by my battery commander, Major Bill Merry. During the night of the 14/15th the situation on our front rapidly deteriorated and in the early morning of the day of surrender poor Merry, in the act of rallying some straggling infantry, was killed.

I, by contrast, had been wonderfully lucky. The bullet had passed through my arm an inch below the funny bone. Sent back to Singapore General Hospital, I passed through corridors lined with civilian stretcher cases, and was directed to the last but one vacant bed.

I found there a medley of emotions: frustration ('We were thrown away,' says a staunch bombardier, recalling the moment), indignation in some, indifference in a few, and in many – for those at the guns' end had had no direct contact with the enemy – sheer surprise. For our losses were negligible, four killed out of 202, one of them our battery commander.

In his summary of the immediate reasons behind the surrender, General Percival mentioned dwindled food reserves, shortages of ammunition, petrol and water. I can vouch for the water shortage, for in 24 hours at the General Hospital I received one cup, which was the ration. (It was ten days before the water supply was restored to this teeming hospital.) Once the Japs took the MacRitchie reservoir, the struggle was over. Could the General have exposed the civilian population of nearly a million to the threat of death by thirst? His only alternative to surrender on the morning of 15 February was a counter-attack to regain possession of the reservoirs and the food depots. His commanders ruled out this option as impracticable. They doubted – with ample reason – whether their forces could resist another determined attack – which would have meant Jap troops running loose in the city.

So the white flag was hoisted and, shortly after dusk in the Ford factory at Bukit Timah, General Percival acceded to the demand of unconditional surrender made by his opposite number, Lieutenant General Yamashita. The Jap army had shown all the military virtues, as well as a capacity to inflict acts of unbridled savagery that boded ill for their captives. After the action at Muar, non-walking wounded were massacred in cold blood. At the Alexandra Military Hospital at Singapore two days before the surrender, 150 patients and staff, having been confined all night to a space allowing standing-room only, were executed the next morning.

The feeling that we were implicated, however helplessly, in the humiliation of Singapore, coupled with the sudden change from normal food to a diet exclusively of rice and jungle vegetables, did nothing for morale in the early days of captivity. I recall a dark moment in March or April when a string of heavy Jap cruisers – we counted 11 in line ahead – steamed past Changi to the naval base. Our release at that moment seemed a very long way off. There was no means of knowing that the spring of 1942 marked the limit of Jap expansion, that in early June the Americans shifted the balance of naval strength by destroying four of their carrier fleet in 10 minutes in the Battle of Midway. This astonishing victory, John Keegan has written, 'turned the tide of the war at a stroke'.

For most of us, I think, depression lifted when there was work to be done. In River Valley Road camp in Singapore city, as the so-called camp Welfare Officer, I formed a library of several thousand books brought back by working parties employed by the Japs to clean up the European quarter. They were the sort to be expected on the shelves of expatriate Englishmen: Priestley, Waugh, Galsworthy, Bryant, H.V. Morton, Gunther. When we were sent away to make the Burma–Siam railway, two books a man were doled out. The result was that in the next three years modest libraries were set up all along the railway, once the line had been laid and work pressure eased. The tattered contents were kept in reasonable shape by book-binders using paste and remnants of gas-cape for covers. At one point my 1939 *Wisden* was in such demand that it could be lent out only for periods of six hours.

In September 1942, I found myself transported up through Malaya by rail. There were, luckily, only 22 to our officers' cattletruck and not the usual 40, so that, over the several days of a journey punctuated by station stops to consume pails of rice and water, we were just able to lie sardine-fashion head to tail. From the rail-head at Banpong, we marched 25 miles (with all the belongings we possessed or could carry on a tarmac road in much heat) past amiably curious Siamese to Kanchanaburi, and thence by jungle track to the headquarters camp at Tarsao. This was the route travelled by all the Allied POWs engaged on building the railway: there were 66,000 of us, of whom 16,000 failed to return. These were military casualties exclusive of Tamils, Malays, Chinese and other sources of impressed labour who died like flies.

Soon after we started up the track, a tropical storm descended on us. Heavily laden and soaked to the skin, we were slipping and slithering on when an extraordinary thing happened. The troops, who had cursed terribly in the heat, suddenly began to sing and went on doing so, louder and louder. I will never forget the look of utter incredulity on the face of

'Personally, I'm delighted they got taken over
by a Japanese firm.'

the Nip (in captivity, Japs were known invariably as Nips) plugging on beside me. I suppose the rain reminded us of home.

The most devilish time was the 'speedo' period from March to 17 October 1943, by which date the Emperor had decreed that the line must be completed. It was – at the cost of prisoners, weak as they were, ravaged by dysentery, malaria and beri-beri, working 12 hours a day on a diet of rice and vegetables, plus an occasional egg and still rarer vestiges of meat, driven on by the Nips and in many cases dying on the job. When the south-west monsoon broke in May, one was never dry.

I was first at Wampo, then Tonchan and Kinsayok, in camps bordering both the Kwai-Noi river and the railway track, as it was hewn yard by yard out of the jungle. My duties were mostly in camp, building huts and digging latrines, and, in a laughably so-called Welfare capacity, organising a talks programme, quiz sessions and singsongs in the evenings. I recall, however, some timber-carrying days when British and Dutch officers and other ranks, Tamils, Malays, Chinese, Jap engineers and several elephants were all engaged on building a bridge. Speedo was the word.

I owe it to the memory of Colonel Sir Philip Toosey and to my fellow Far Eastern POWs to object to the portrayal by Alec Guinness of the British colonel in the film *Bridge Over the River Kwai*, which, though purporting to be a version of the fictional book of that name by Pierre Boulle, was assumed by the public to be fact.

The building of the bridge at the junction between the Kwai Yai and Kwai Noi was the essential first step in the construction of the railway that was to follow the line of the Kwai Noi up to the Burmese border at the Three Pagodas pass. As the senior British officer in a group of prisoners that swelled ultimately to 2,600, including many Dutch, Toosey was ordered to command the camp at the site and provide all fit men for the work, which was supervised by the Jap railway regiment.

He protested without avail that under the Hague and Geneva Conventions prisoners must not be used for tasks helpful to the war effort as, of course, did other senior POW officers elsewhere, but equally to no avail. He therefore pursued a policy of limited co-operation, which he considered the best way of ensuring that as many of his men as possible should survive captivity. By insisting on strict discipline – no beards, by the way, for fear of lice – keeping constant pressure on the Nips to improve food and conditions, and protesting against every instance of brutality, he succeeded marvellously. In many ways the film gave a graphic, realistic picture of the scene apart from the character of the Jap-happy, half-crazed 'Colonel Nicholson'.

Sir Alec Guinness won an Oscar for a virtuoso performance that was nevertheless seen by Toosey's fellow-prisoners as a gross calumny against one of the heroes both of the war in Malaya and of the captivity.

If circumstances thrust Philip Toosey most prominently into the spotlight, other senior officers of the 18th Division shouldered with outstanding success throughout our captivity the utterly wearing, frustrating, dangerous duty of representing their fellow-POWs in negotiations with the Nips. They lived with the knowledge of secret wireless-sets, illicit traffic in money and medicines, and other matters which, if the Nips had known of them, would have resulted in torture, if not death. Two lieutenant-colonels, H. H. Lilly of the 1/5 Sherwood Foresters and A.E. Knights of the 4th Norfolk Regiment, known as 'Knocker', small men both but tough as old boots, were respected up and down the river.

I eventually got down to the 'hospital' camp beside the golden temple at Nakom Patom. The 'hospital', by the way, was so only in name. We still slept all together on bamboo platforms, though perhaps there was a little more head-room, say 30 inches each, rather than the uniform 18 inches.

The railway layers passed us at Kinsayok on 30 July 1943, after which the work pressure eased and the camp death-rate decreased, perhaps from five or six a day to one or two – or even none. In a clearing we made a sort of open-air chapel, with a wooden altar and cross in case a padre came our way. A Harvest Festival was planned, and one of the Korean guards, who was a Christian, contributed to our meagre display a hand of bananas. This was noticed. The guard was beaten up and I, the Welfare Officer, apparently a subversive influence, was slapped a time or two and sent down to headquarters at Tarsao.

The journey down river in a pom-pom would have been agreeable but for the prospect of being handed over to the tender care of the Kempe-Tai, the secret police. Luckily, the camp commandant dismissed the frivolous charge and I was passed on down to the new hospital at Nakom Patom. At Tonchan I recall the climax of a much more serious case. At a transit point on the march up through the jungle, Major I. J. Mackinlay of the Scotch whisky firm was so provoked by the Nip NCO in charge that, with a blow to the jaw, he knocked him senseless. The Nip was dragged off by other guards, feet first. Astonishingly, next morning Mackinlay and his party, under another Nip, were moved on with no word said or action taken. Now, weeks later, the boss of the Tonchan camp, Sergeant-Major Hiramatsu, known as the Tiger, called for Mackinlay Chosa and confronted him with the NCO he had KO'd. Mackinlay for a while protested he had never seen the fellow before, but finally gave in. Thereupon there was laughter and back-slapping and the three sat down to sake and food.

The normal penalty for striking a guard was death. There was a jovial side to the Tiger, but he did not come by his sinister nickname for nothing. At the War Crimes Trials at Singapore in 1946, he was sentenced to be hanged, as were others of our tormentors such as Noguchi, commander of the Kanchanaburi camp for officers, set up in January 1945 when the Nips, anticipating an Allied invasion, separated officers from other ranks. It was Noguchi who, for some imagined insult to Japan while Captain Bill Drower was doing his job as an interpreter, gave him a savage beating and kept him for 77 days in solitary confinement in an underground shelter, with no washing facilities or change of clothing, on a subsistence of one meal a day of rice and water. Only the surrender saved Drower's life.

The trials, which took place under the authority of the Judge Advocate-General, imposed the death sentence on many; others were committed to various terms of imprisonment; a few more acquitted. Notorious sadists like Donald Duck, the Frog and the Undertaker – the worst of them all had their labels – were strung up on evidence given by senior Allied officers.

These included some of those who administered 300 lashes and worse tortures to Leonard Wilson, Bishop of Singapore (accused of spying), as told so dreadfully by his chaplain, John Hayter, in his book *Priest in Prison*.

To the natural comment 'you must have had a terrible time', when the subject of our POW life has since come up, my answer is equivocal. On the face of it, conditions were appalling. Yet the body can be extraordinarily adjustable to conditions, however horrific, while the spirit takes courage from friendship, the feeling of burden shared, and the sense of humour it nourishes, macabre though it often was. The American wife of an RAMC officer incarcerated in Changi Prison put it this way: 'It wasn't unrelieved gloom. I wouldn't have missed it in terms of human experience. It made me grow up. I became a little less self-concerned.' I would go along with that.

Many have found it difficult to live with the stigma that attached to the Malayan campaign and capitulation. Yet the odds facing the Australian, Indian and British forces were enormous. The aerodromes, foolishly sited pre-war in northern Malaya and manned mostly by obsolete or obsolescent aircraft, were overrun within the first few days. The truth was that British Far Eastern strategy was based from pre-war days wholly on sea power: hence Singapore's big guns and static defences all faced seawards, on the assumption that it would be necessary only to protect the fortress from an attack by sea until the Allied navies arrived within a matter of days. From the moment that the *Prince of Wales* and *Repulse* failed to survive their first encounter, our fate was sealed.

When, in 1945, my father met me off the boat-train at Waterloo station, he walked straight past me on the platform. He hadn't expected such a slim-line version. My weight was ten and a half stone, five stone lighter than when we'd said goodbye four years earlier. I had lost something physically which was soon put right. But I had gained much that would always remain.

15 February 1992

FOUNDATION COURSE IN WOMEN

Kate Berridge

'An unnecessary part of human behaviour.' You would think that this view of sex came from a leather-elbowed academic in the good old days of single-sex public-school education. In fact it belonged to the housemaster in charge of the girls (of whom I was one) admitted for the first time at sixth-form level to a boys' public school. In the 19th century, when the school's success peaked, this was probably a very popular view. In the 20th century it is not.

Much has been written about the impact on boys of contact with girls and the worries such integration causes staff and parents. Less often considered is the impact on girls, when the cosy and remarkably limited landscape of the girls' school is exchanged for the tough and loveless jungle that characterises most boys' schools. Consider what it is like to move from offers of tea and seed cake with Miss Eadis, 'so that we can go over the areas you're finding difficult', to a hairy monster of a male teacher screaming, as if injured, 'The only thing you'll pass is water!' If admitting girls, particularly at sixth-form level, is seen as providing the boys with a sort of Foundation Course in Women and the opportunity for some hands-on experience, for many girls the whole business is less fortunate. For some it is a humiliating ordeal resulting in lasting cynicism.

Our arrival was like the installation of a new attraction at a theme park where everyone was bored with the existing rides. There was great interest but it was almost entirely in how we looked. Because there was no girls' uniform, we all looked remarkably different. Our entry into Chapel in the first few weeks was like a beauty contest in which the commentary might have gone something like this: 'Sarah (30, 22, 36) is reading French, German and History. She likes Laura Ashley clothes and riding. Here she is modelling the barefaced pastoral look in a fetching floral print. She has never had a boyfriend but is writing to a boy she met at a three-day event in the holidays.' At the other end of the scale, 'Lucy (38, 24, 34) just loves Latin which she is taking with History of Art and English. Her boyfriend works in the City, which is what she wants to do when she leaves. Lucy is wearing a figure-hugging dress by Piero de Monzi which her boyfriend bought her in Milan especially for her new school wardrobe.'

Inevitably, the Lucys fared better than the Sarahs. We were very harshly judged; we were also audibly judged – on our way to lessons we would have to endure shouts of marks out of ten from windows. We were seen as simply sets of breasts, legs and novel sexual bits. Crater Face, Thunder Thighs, Legs Astride and Mattress were just some of the names that quickly and widely circulated. These names were not in the spirit of friendly teasing: they were used long before anything resembling friendship had occurred. Schoolboys always call each other rude names, so perhaps we were being treated no differently from Bladder Jones and Wanker Wellings. The difficulty was that we were completely unused to this sort of treatment.

Boys will be boys. But the response of masters to girls is even more fraught and less talked about. They also got things wrong, but in many cases it was not their fault. There is a certain breed of schoolmaster, the withdrawn classicist, who, having performed brilliantly in his time at the school and getting the highest degree in his year at Oxford, invariably returns to the safe, womanless haven where he spent the happiest days of his life. We must have been very unsettling for these striplings in the classroom with their cherubic faces, copperplate handwriting and voices that through years of being silent in libraries could not be raised above a stage whisper. Their experience of women seemed confined to the classics; we became for them frail Dickens heroines permanently on the brink of tears or fainting fits. With them we got away with much.

Alternatively, there were those who were so keen to treat us just like boys that they were inclined to a level of toughness which was inappropriate. One childless housemaster, with his cheroot-smoking wife (we called them Mr and Mr), was in this category, devising endless punishments – 'sentences' – which he meted out according to his mood. These included gravel-shifting, log-chopping and cutting a hedge with scissors for offences which even now seem incomprehensible. On one occasion, a girl who was happily singing in the corridor was 'sentenced'; and I remember a girl who one evening missed the informal tea and reading which took place after prep and was 'sentenced' (she had just had a phone call telling her that her grandmother had been killed in a car accident). Worse, there was an element of sexual rivalry and possessiveness between us and some masters for the affections of certain boys, and competition between masters and the boys for us. All this, and we were expected to sail through the toughest exams of our school career and on to university.

Before our arrival, the only exposure the boys seemed to have had to women was confined to a handful of matrons, the wives and daughters of masters and dirty magazines where a 'two sets of bare breasts per study' pin-up rule was observed. When we arrived it was as if an essential nutrient that had been missing was suddenly available. Depositing a handful of young girls amidst boys whose sexual hormones are at their most active and who have been so isolated from girls is unfair on all parties unless you are prepared to accept the possible outcome of such a combustible mixture. A couple of weeks ago, for example, Rugby expelled a boy and a girl pupil after they had been discovered *in flagrante.*

More than 18,000 15-year-old girls took formal advice on contraception last year. Boards of governors, parents and staff must start to address the fact that their charges in the public-school sector are not so different from their contemporaries in state schools in what they want to get up to. They must also face up to the fact that for each canoodling couple caught there are many more who won't be. In my year at least two girls were on the pill when they arrived; the majority had fairly innocent relationships with boys but some had very intense sexual relationships. One liberal master lent a love-struck couple the art-room keys for assignations and, in another case, a serious flirtation between a girl and a master developed into an affair after she left. One boy and girl got married but divorced three years later.

We have a long way to go before we get the right formula for the treatment of girls at boys' schools, and perhaps we will never be as relaxed about it as the school in Los Angeles which announced this week that it was putting condom machines on the premises.

As things stand, boys' schools continue to experiment with girls. If their new girls fall in love they may do less well academically, as indeed will the boys who fall for them, and if they are caught making love they will be expelled. But if the girls last the course they will have gained academically and will have enjoyed better facilities than those at their old girls' school. They will also learn one very important fact of life: girls with big breasts have the best time.

15 February 1992

CONFESSIONS OF A SUPERGRASS

Wilfred De'Ath

On 14 December 1991 I was arrested in the Queen's Hotel, Southsea, and charged with obtaining services by deception, i.e. using someone else's credit card. I spent two reasonably comfortable days in police custody and was placed in front of Portsmouth magistrates on the Monday morning, after spending a few uncomfortable hours in a kind of cage – dog-kennel dimensions – under the courtroom. To my solicitor's relief, I was granted bail but the condition was made that I should reside at the Dickson House bail hostel in Fareham, Hants, pending further court appearances.

On the Monday afternoon, I was provided with a rail warrant by the Portsmouth probation service for the short train journey to Fareham, which I made in the company of a long-haired, effeminate young man named Simon, charged with burglary and a number of drugs-related offences. This was not my first sojourn at a bail hostel (I once spent seven months in Clark's House, Oxford, a relatively relaxed place), but it was to be by far the most harrowing.

Dickson House set out to rehabilitate its still technically innocent charges with a routine of structure and discipline. A plump Scotswoman named Lena with a very genteel accent was assigned to be my personal counsellor; she spent an hour or so telling me that I was on no account to bring drugs into the place (a most unlikely contingency, since I am profoundly opposed to drugs) and to report back to her anything I saw or heard. She then showed me into a room for three which I was to share for a week or so with a very fat, tattooed burglar named Ian and a very thin child-molester named Andy.

It didn't take me long – one sniff – to realise that pot had recently been smoked in the room; the next 24 hours were an orgy of pot-smoking, both in and outside the room, apparently involving nearly all of the bail hostel's 28 residents, who told me that the drug helped them to 'lighten up' a little in the stressful situation in which they found themselves. Bored with all this, I did what I had been asked to do and 'grassed' Ian to the hostel staff, for which he threatened to 'bury me six feet deep', which he again threatened to do when I remonstrated with him for playing his stereo, with unmelodic vocal accompaniment, until 3 a.m. I sensed that Ian was 'all mouth and no trousers', as they say, and unlikely to do me much harm.

Things took a more serious turn about two weeks later, after a fairly miserable Christmas and New Year, by which time I had been moved into a double room with a con man named Big Steve, a devout Roman Catholic, who was even more profoundly opposed to the drug culture than myself. We two soon became known – and feared – as the Dickson House twin 'supergrasses'. On the morning of 3 January, I inadvertently 'grassed' a rather charming young man named Little Steve – not for drugs but for constantly rapping on our door during the night. The staff had been waiting for an excuse to get rid of Little Steve and used my complaint to 'breach' him. He was sent to Winchester prison. This action brought down the wrath of almost the entire hostel upon me, not because they cared particularly about Little Steve or his fate but because he turned out to have been their main supplier of drugs. Deprived of their regular supply of 'lightening' narcotics, the residents rapidly reverted to their violent animal natures.

It all came to a head at supper the next evening when the dining-room was set out with two tables – one for the grasses and one for the non-grasses. The tension was palpable in the small, claustrophobic room. Big Steve and I were made to sit at the grasses' table. Of course, sauce bottles were thrown, and an ugly full-scale riot seemed about to develop. I retreated to my room to consider what to do; Big Steve, more courageously, went across to report to the hostel office where, as ill-luck would have it, a lone and rather inadequate female was on duty that night.

Big Steve returned to join me in our room and we waited. We did not have to wait for very long. A howling mob of our fellow residents, actually only five in number but sounding like many more, headed by the hostel's senior bully and narcotics 'fence', Tony, a former army training sergeant, had soon kicked down our door. Then Tony picked me up with his left hand and threw me into the room across the way where he and a young man with a long record of violent crime, Barry, proceeded to beat me up. I tried to smash the window with a view to jumping from the first floor, but it was double-glazed.

All the things you hear about such moments are true. My past life, all 54½ years of it, flashed in front of my eyes. I had not been so frightened since I had looked down the barrel of a gun belonging to an ETA terrorist in San Sebastian in 1973. The terrorist had been intent on killing me and I had no doubt that Barry and Tony, in their drug-deprived frenzy, intended to kill me too. But my room-mate, Big Steve, with great presence of mind set off the hostel's fire-alarm by holding a lighted match to the room's smoke warning device. At the sudden jangling of fire-bells, the two criminals who were pulverising me reacted and ran like the rats of psychologists' dreams.

Would it be an exaggeration to say that Big Steve had saved my life? We both returned to the safety of the staff-room for the rest of the night, in the course of which our room and possessions were smashed and scattered beyond recognition by our assailants. My little wooden locker was reduced, literally, to powder. The female staff member had had a direct panic button to Fareham police station but had apparently decided not to press it. The deputy warden of the hostel had been telephoned at his nearby home and told of a 'violent incident' but had chosen not to come in.

Next day, I was removed to a nearby cottage for my personal safety. Tony, who had somehow avoided capture, traced me there and attempted a forced entry. This time I really thought the end had come but, after hiding under a bed and in a cupboard, I decided to dial 999. It is the one and only time in my life that I have been pleased to see a policeman. Tony was arrested and now languishes along with the other assailants in Winchester prison.

Throughout all this, the bail hostel staff were pathetic. The best they could come up with for me was a transfer to another hostel (Winchester!), where, as they admitted, the chances of one of my attackers turning up after re-bailing were fairly high. I had had enough of them all by now, and, on the afternoon of Monday, 13 January, I quietly took the law into my own hands and 'breached' myself. As I did so, I felt strangely happy as well as free.

15 February 1992

A DARK BLUE DAY

Alan Brownjohn

I have to call it something like despair,
Forgetting the name of somebody who came
Across a room, and very suddenly
Set herself down in an opposite chair
And placed her two stockinged feet on the arm
Of my own chair at twenty-five past three

Thirty years ago! Because, I could tell she guessed
No one else would be watching, the window only showed
The rooftops and part of the sky, which we could see
Had turned a dark blue, darker than the rest,
And I missed the chance she offered . . . I recall it snowed,
With the flakes failing to settle, just timidly

Wafting over the brickwork of the grey
Terraced streets which rose up slowly from the river
Like an adjunct of its mist. – And I think I know
That the town could be found once more, that dark blue day
And those grey streets reappear, if I could ever
Call up her name; which would persuade the snow

To fall again, and the room to still be there
With its window onto rooftops, and cloudy light
Shining into a narrow space where two people meet
Thirty years ago, each stuck in a deep armchair
Pretending to guess if the snow might fall all night
– And the man would settle for stroking the woman's feet.

15 February 1992

DIARY

Keith Waterhouse

The race is on to make *Maxwell: the Movie*, with at least three contenders at the starting post. My money is on Mike Molloy, former editor-in-chief of the Mirror group, who has a wealth of first-hand Maxwelliana in his television film treatment – for example, the time Cap'n Bob was reduced to a cowering wreck by the arrival of Mother Teresa and a heavy mob of nuns, hell-bent (if heaven-sent) on relieving him of a million pounds before they left the office. (He didn't have his cheque-book.) Then there was the highly placed woman executive who accompanied the old rogue on a business trip to Tokyo, where he tried to send her out to buy him a pair of socks. The lady was most indignant. 'Bob, you are paying me many tens of thousands a year for my professional skills. They do not include sock-buying.' An apparently contrite Cap'n Bob dug into his pocket and produced a brick-thick wad of yen which he pressed upon his offended senior employee. 'My dear, I'm most truly sorry and you must forgive me. Now you've been working very hard and I want you to take the afternoon off and devote yourself to shopping. Buy yourself something very silly.' As the mollified executive made for the door he added, 'And bring me back a pair of socks.' If Molloy's version gets off the ground, I have offered to play a small cameo scene. When Robert Maxwell was trying to persuade me not to transfer my act from the *Daily Mirror* to the *Daily Mail*, he asked whether I belonged to the Mirror pension scheme. I told him that as a freelance I had my own arrangements. Sloshing more champagne into my glass, he invited me to outline my private pension plan, listening, as I did so, with the amused tolerance of a rich uncle hearing a favourite young nephew boast of having saved up four and sixpence. At the end of my account he patted me confidentially on the knee, and in a fog-siren purr promised, 'I could enhance that pension scheme, Keith.'

The writer Alan Williams thought he would take his two-and-a-half-year-old daughter to see Guy the Gorilla, so named because he arrived at London Zoo from the French Cameroons on 5 November 1947. He was the biggest attraction at the Zoo for 30 years, until he expired under anaesthetic while being treated for an impacted tooth. He was the only ape ever to make it to the obituary columns of *The Times*. After a visit to the taxidermist, Guy was transferred to the Natural History Museum where he continued to pull in the crowds, and there, last week, Alan Williams's small daughter expected to find him. No Guy. 'We don't display him any more,' explained a tight-lipped female. Why not? 'We consider it offensive to him.' Why? 'It is demeaning. We don't display personality animals now.' But what about the stuffed lions and tigers? Don't they have personalities? 'They're not personality animals in that demeaning sense.' So the Williams tot had to make do with an ice-cream. Political correctitude strikes again.

22 February 1992

UNLETTERED

A reader wrote the following letter as a covering note to her application for the job of personnel manager at Clarks Shoes.

> Dear Mr Baker
> Re: The Position of Personnel Manager
> Looking at my CV you probably think I have not read your advertisement properly. I do not have union negotiation experience; nor do I have a proven record of managing a team.
> But I think you should interview me. I will explain why when we meet.
> Yours sincerely
>
> Annette Pettman

This was the reply she received:

> Dear Ms Pettman
> I am afraid I am going to have to disappoint you. Your

somewhat peremptory letter arrived this morning when I have already had almost 160 candidates for this job.

This letter may appear to be somewhat reactionary to you but I felt I should explain to you why your style did not impress me or indicate that you were an appropriate person for this job.

I accept that the idea of a covering letter is to catch the attention and imagination of the person who reads it, but frankly yours turned me right off. You sounded arrogant, self-centred and presumptuous. You may not realise it but that is the effect that your letter has: arrogant because you seem to believe that your unique qualities are more important than the skills, knowledge and experience that we require; self-centred because you seem to think that you can go to the front of the queue; presumptuous because you seem to think that you are going to get an interview.

I do not wish to denigrate your achievements which are considerable, but I do not think that your style of approach would fit in here at all. It may surprise you to know that there are at least 40 candidates that we think are more suitable than you.

Yours sincerely

Jeremy Baker
Management Development Manager
Clarks Shoes Limited

22 February 1992

LOW LIFE

GROG BLOSSOM

Jeffrey Bernard

I dozed off after a lunch in the Groucho Club one day last week and when I awoke I found that Sue Townsend had left me a nicely inscribed copy of her book, *Adrian Mole: From Minor to Major*, by my side. I opened it at random and read one of young Master Mole's entries which was a one-liner saying, 'I am having a nervous breakdown. Nobody has noticed yet.' Oh, I know the feeling. Or at least I used to know it years ago.

The next morning we had a farewell drink together. Sue lives in Leicester, and we said we both felt that one's childhood was one long nervous breakdown. Mine lasted until I was able to escape school. It is odd that most parents assume that their children are more or less blissfully happy. There is such a lot they don't notice.

And talking of childhood we discovered that we had been and still are addicted to rivers and streams. Sadly for Sue, somebody has dumped a rusty old car in her stream, as people will. Mine probably dried up years ago. It ran by a ruined Norman castle near Peterchurch in Herefordshire. The edges of it were all watercress and buttercups and even on the hottest summer days it ran icy cold and clear and we cupped our hands and drank deep of it. Where could you or would you dare to drink from a stream today?

'For God's sake! Stop being so negative.'

And the great game was to build dams. I still think of drinking that water now when I wake up in the heat and anxiety of the night and light my umpteenth cigarette of the day. How odd it seemed to be sitting in a club bar and talking to Mrs Mole about playing and picnicking by streams.

Something Sue said reminded me of a childhood daymare almost as bad as a nightmare, which was to imagine I was doomed to spend my life serving behind the counter in an ironmonger's shop. You have to wear a brown coat for that and put up with the smells of creosote and turpentine. 'A pound of three-inch nails? Certainly, madam. And here is your galvanised bucket.' I wonder why ironmongers should have first struck terror and boredom into me.

But I waffle, and we did, and a nice change it made from the usual bar talk. The day hadn't started all that well. I received a letter from the Health Education Authority about an anti-alcohol campaign they are launching to persuade young people not to take to it like so many ducks to water. They want a slogan or two for their posters and a black and white photograph of me looking awful to hold up to the youth of England so as to warn them about what 'just the one' can do to a man's face.

I don't mind. My appearance has become a source of copy to journalists and just a few days ago Peter Tory, writing in the *Daily Express*, headed his piece 'Facing the Awful Truth'. An old library picture was captioned, 'Bernard as he was in the Sixties' and a recent picture was captioned, 'Now . . . Bernard's decline is a sad sight'. Well, it may be a sad sight in the shaving mirror but I don't see why it should be to anybody else.

But what is the point in warning young people about the evils of alcohol? They know them already and can see them every day in the streets or in the House of Commons when they are sitting. I have never taken a peek into the House of Lords but I should imagine there are a few grog blossoms in there too.

22 February 1992

YOUR PROBLEMS SOLVED

DEAR MARY . . .

Mary Killen

Q. As I am a comparatively well-off bachelor, I have been made godfather to a number of friends' children. I am perfectly happy to be generous and usually quite good at remembering their birthdays, but I do find it rather annoying when they don't write to thank or even acknowledge that they have had the cheque or present – or whatever I give them. How do other people ensure that their godchildren perform this simple act of politeness?

H. V., W8

A. One popular godfather who found himself in a similar position eventually tackled the problem by sending only a card on the birthdays of offending godchildren. The message inside would read: 'Happy Birthday. I enclose [for example] £10', yet he would not enclose any money at all. He found that the godchildren wrote back with alacrity to point out his oversight and, unable to merely make the bald request that he forward the promised cash, were forced to write a few lines of personal news. He continued to use it with satisfying results for many years. The understanding grew up, though neither godfather nor godchildren ever referred to it, that they must write their thank-you letters in advance.

Q. May I follow up on last week's 'Dear Mary' hygiene special with a problem of my own? Over the festive season, I noticed that women were being kissed, willy-nilly, by a number of elderly men, i.e. relations, old family friends, whom they would normally keep at arm's length, as it were. The problem is not sexual harassment but halitosis: these men are increasingly

proud of the fact that they have kept many of their own
teeth, whereas in former times the offending molars
would have been replaced by dentures. How can one
avoid this situation, bearing in mind that it usually
occurs the moment one has opened the front door?

F. M. B., Isleworth, Middlesex

A. The best way to avoid unwelcome oral assaults is
to be prepared. As soon as you see a likely offender
moving towards you, throw yourself clumsily against
him. This will enable you 'accidentally' to kiss a part
of his body – such as the side of his neck – which is
out of fumes' reach and should preclude the need for
any further intimacy.

Q. I do have a problem. I just cannot stand your
column. Do you have any suggestions?

R. E. L., Frinton-on-Sea, Essex

A. Perhaps you could adapt a method used by the

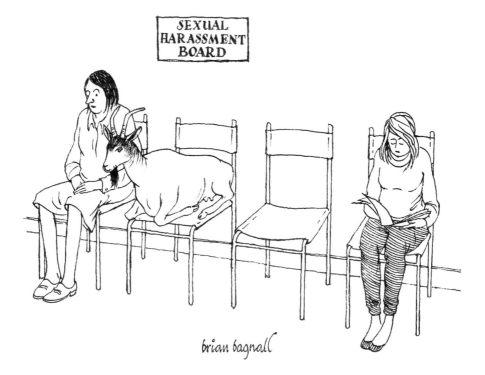

fashionable art dealer, Mr Gerry Farrell, who, distressed by certain pages of the *Daily Mail*, has asked his newsagent to deliver only the Dempster page with its convenient television guide on the verso. It would be an even easier matter for your newsagent to snip out the offending 'Dear Mary' section from the back page before delivering *The Spectator* to your door, and I am sure that in the current recession he would be only too happy to co-operate.

22 February 1992

DIARY

Keith Waterhouse

I have gone through life believing, and telling anyone who cared to listen, that I was born in a condemned hovel, one of the notorious back-to-back terrace slums in which the inner city urchins of Leeds slept three to a bed. We were shipped to a council estate when I was two and a half, and I have always been hazy as to whether this was because the house was pulled down or fell down about our ears, or whether we were rehoused because of overcrowding. To clear up the point, in the course of research for a book on growing up in Leeds which I am about to embark upon, I wrote to one of my brothers. So it comes about that I have just learned, at the age of 63, that far from being a slum my first home was a substantial double-fronted house with a walled garden, the former residence of a doctor, and that far from our being overcrowded there were rooms to spare, in which my mother installed electric meters with the idea of taking in boarders. None came, and so we had the run of the house, and the surgery was our playroom. The only reason we had to move, apparently, was because the council planned to pull the house down for a road-widening scheme. Thus no longer can I claim to have been a scabby-kneed slum-dweller – instead, I seem almost to have stepped out of the pages of E. Nesbit. Suddenly I feel underprivileged.

29 February 1992

OPERATION BENT SPOKE

Robert Gore-Langton

Bicycle thieves in Brixton are, as Frankie Howerd would say, about as subtle as a Roman orgy. Not only do they steal your bicycle but you are quite likely to see them shamelessly 'hotting' it around the neighbourhood. Car theft is now so brazen that reports are filtering through of vehicles being stolen with their owners still inside them. Lambeth police, presumably fully employed in filling in stolen car forms, have come to regard mere bicycle theft as not so much an offence, more a way of urban life. The only recourse against the bicycle rustlers is, as I discovered, to deal with them personally.

In my case the crime was invited: I had dropped in on my local off-licence, stupidly leaving my new bike unlocked outside. In a matter of seconds I reappeared to find the thing had vanished. The cluster of teenagers on the nearby wall had apparently seen nothing. I decided the only thing to do was to offer a ransom. My insurers would take a dim view of a second claim within a week. (My previous bike had been taken from a locked shed by three ten-year-olds in the middle of the night. I know, because my neighbour saw them run off with it.) So I duly handed out my phone number to any youth I could see with mention of a £50 reward for the return of my bicycle. £50, I hoped, was probably as much or more than the local fence would pay.

A call came through next day quaintly asking for 'the man of the house'. 'I've got a friend who knows who's got your bike. Except he wants 70 quid,' a voice muttered. I reiterated my original offer and angrily told him to get stuffed. 'I'll see what I can do,' said my unchastened contact. 'Meet me in half an hour where it was lifted from.'

It was at this point that I decided to ring the police for a little moral support. On hearing my plan, the desk sergeant audibly drew breath like a builder being asked for an estimate. 'You've given them your phone number. Big mistake, sir!' he said gleefully. 'Never hand out that sort of information – they could trace your address and things could get nasty.' (Actually, it's extremely difficult to trace an address from a number.) As an idle afterthought, he suggested that I might take a camera and try to get a picture of them. Great idea, I thought to myself. I'll take my tripod along and ask them to say cheese. 'If you do go,' he finally said, 'we'll send a car round, but you'll have to report the bike stolen first.'

I declined the offer. The police-car would, of course, blow the whole deal and I would certainly never see my bike again. This was strictly a plain-clothes operation. I persuaded my neighbour to accompany me, giving him instructions to look mean and dangerous, an easy job, I thought, for a permanently unemployed musical director. We soon stood like a pair of fools, waiting on the kerb by the shop. Two small black schoolboys walked past and asked if we were detectives. Unconvinced by our reply, one then asked, 'D'you like cops, then?' We said that we didn't know any. They sneered and walked off, swinging their satchels.

It was getting on now, and my neighbour decided to leave me to it; something about a rehearsal I knew he didn't have. Within a few minutes, two likely lads sidled up and asked me if I was 'the bike man'. 'It's still 70 quid,' said the tall one. I started to walk away. 'Okay then, he says he'll take 50,' came the hasty response. 'Give us the money and we'll get your bike.' Wising up, I demanded to see the 'merchandise' first. Not for nothing have I seen The French Connection twice.

Soon my beloved bike appeared around the corner, pushed by a gang that looked as if it had stepped out of a multi-racial Ealing comedy. There were a dozen of them. It is a persistent myth that under-age crime in Brixton is committed by blacks. Around here, the gangs that do all the thieving consist of a mix of every racial group that the census has ever dreamt of. In my district, street crime, Lambeth town hall will be pleased to know, is a fully multi-cultural, equal-opportunities activity.

It was now time for the swap. I insisted I got on the bike before the money was handed over. But any thoughts of doing a nifty bunk were soon quashed. We were in an alley of sorts and the bigger chaps (they were looking bigger every second) had blocked my only exit. Each of them had a hand on the frame. There was nothing for it. I gingerly produced the money from a top pocket and handed it over to the teenage Mr Big.

By now I was most certainly not enjoying myself. As the money left my hand, I started to push off. 'Uh uh,' came the communal grunt, meaning I wasn't going anywhere. But to my relief, I had simply forgotten the ritual counting of the tenners. The tall one soon gave me the all-clear, and they let me go with a few triumphant jeers and whoops. Pedalling home, I was elated. I don't know why: after all, I had just paid good money for the return of my own bicycle. Anyway, the feeling didn't last long. I soon noticed that the lock was missing. It cost £30 and, as I had both keys, the thing was useless to anyone except me. It quite ruined my mood.

Later that evening, I met another neighbour, Charlie, an unemployed Irish surveyor. I told him how I was intensely annoyed that I had been robbed and then cheated out of my lock. Don't get mad, get even, was his motto. His idea was to mount a frontal raid on the estate, in a van filled with burly Irish plasterer chums fuelled up on Guinness that I would supply. I admired his plan very much but decided it would perhaps be wiser and cheaper to negotiate. Together we walked back to the estate.

All the lads we had dealt with spied us from afar. One key player, a pizza-faced Scottish lout, emerged with a manky alsatian called Reefer. The gang by now started to coalesce into a loose pack. But far more terrifying was their reserve force. Bustling up behind, threatening everything in sight, came a cohort of mothers. One huge, sour-faced woman emerged in carpet slippers with her muscly arms folded. She looked as though she could have sucked the corners off a house-brick.

Our enquiries were absurdly polite. 'Could anyone perhaps, er, possibly by chance, have seen a lock that might possibly have got lost?' I muttered to this wall of flesh. One boy said the lock had

been thrown away. His mother roundly abused him for interrupting. Realising we were not police, she walked away, deeply unimpressed by us. In retreat, I lamely said to anyone listening that there would be an extra fiver for the return of the lock. We would be in the local pub.

Before we had walked over the threshold, a ten-year-old boy came sprinting over, the item in hand. I would have given him a Dock-Greenish on-your-way-now-laddie thwack on the ear, but I remembered his mother. I paid up. Over drinks, I counted up the cost of Operation Bent Spoke. My pride was, admittedly, a complete write-off, but the bike had been retrieved intact and with no loss of life for £55. Best of all, I didn't have to argue a futile case with my insurers. There's one other bonus. I am looking forward to telling that desk sergeant that I have knowingly taken possession of stolen goods, while withholding my name and number, as he previously advised.

29 February 1992

LONG LIFE

EARLY BLOOMERS

Nigel Nicolson

The most humiliating occasions occur in youth, not because the elderly are any less liable to miscalculate, but because we are more experienced at covering up, and mind humiliation less. These three incidents all happened during my brief career as a subaltern – not even a subaltern, but an ensign with one pip.

I was ordered to join my regiment at Windsor in February 1940, straight from Sandhurst. In the officers' mess nobody spoke to me. Silence, implying disapproval, was part of the indoctrination. The mess-sergeant called us in to dinner. I had no idea where to sit, so I took the chair at the very bottom of the table. Unfortunately it was not the bottom but the top. The commanding officer took the seat next to me, glancing at me with surprise, but uttering no word of admonition or welcome.

The sergeant's next duty was to enquire what the officers would like to drink, and as I was sitting in the place of honour he asked me first. I glanced down that long table, at the silver statuettes of guardsmen in heroic attitudes, at the sparkling wine-glasses, at the flags stiff with embroidered battle honours, at the two rows of my brother officers not one of whom I knew, exquisitely tailored, all valiant. I had seen such scenes in the movies. Did not *The Four Feathers* start like this? There could be only one possible answer. 'I'll have half a bottle of champagne, please.'

'Certainly, sir.' As the sergeant made his way down the line of backs, I overheard the first few responses: 'Half a pint of beer'; 'Have we got any cider tonight?'; 'Just mineral water, please'. There was no countermanding my champagne. It was brought to my chair and detonated. Everyone looked up. But such is the courtesy of the Brigade of Guards that nobody guffawed. They just looked away. The colonel still said nothing.

That was bad, but the next incident was worse. It was the period of the phoney war. I had been transferred from Windsor to Wellington Barracks. One day I received an order to take a detachment of 40 men to France as reinforcements to one of our battalions. It was my first independent command and I was exceedingly proud. I marched them from the barracks to Waterloo station, where they were to entrain for Portsmouth. A few bystanders cheered. 'Good old Blighty!' they shouted, incongruously. We crossed Westminster Bridge with heads high and a single drummer tapping out the step. At the far end of the bridge, I called out the command, 'Left wheel!', indicating the cavernous entrance to the station. But it was not the station. It was the entrance to the LCC's vast courtyard, from which there was no escape at the other end. I shuffled my men to a halt, attempted an about-turn, but then the lance-corporal led the column, not the sergeant-major, and we had to run ignominiously around. The typists leant out of the windows and tittered.

The third bloomer of my military career was unforgettable in its dreadfulness. By now it was the week of Dunkirk. I was still at Wellington Barracks. I came down to breakfast one morning well-rested, well-groomed, brilliantly polished, and helped myself to a large plate of kedgeree. All the talk was of the evacuation. I repeated, quite loud, something I had heard the night before. 'The infantry', I said with all the authority of my recent command, 'are behaving excellently. It's the odds and sods, the engineers and truck-drivers, who are panicking and fouling up the whole thing.' I wondered at the silence that greeted this remark. Opposite were sitting two officers haggard with exhaustion, their uniforms sodden with salt water. One was a colonel in the Royal

Engineers, the other a major in the Royal Army Service Corps. 'I don't think', said the colonel eventually, 'that this young officer can have been there.'

29 February 1992

BUT DO THEY BELIEVE IN GOD?

Damian Thompson

'He's very reluctant to discuss these things in public,' says his colleague Chris.

'It wasn't the sort of thing we talked about much at home,' says his brother Terry.

'We tended to keep off the subject. I knew it wasn't one of his great interests,' says his best man Clive.

'Funny thing, but the subject has never cropped up,' says his friend Jeffrey.

Religion is rarely, if ever, an issue in British politics. In America, no election is complete without the spectacle of hard-bitten candidates shamelessly invoking the deity at 'prayer breakfasts'. But in this country politicians, and particularly prime ministers, shy away from appealing to religious morality to justify their policies, or from raising the subject of their own beliefs. If they go to church, it is for the photo-opportunity. One thinks of a *Private Eye* cover from the 1979 election, showing James Callaghan coming out of the Chequers church with two angelic granddaughters. 'I didn't know Grandad believed in God,' says one. 'He does once every five years,' says the other.

The secular tone of British politics is not a recent development. 'Things have come to a pretty pass when religion is allowed to invade the sphere of private life,' said Lord Melbourne. Few of his recent successors would put it so boldly, but most of them have appeared to think that it should not invade the sphere of public life. The exception, of course, was Margaret Thatcher. More than any prime minister since Gladstone, she wanted her policies to be legitimised by religious leaders. If the Church of England would not do it, then the Church of Scotland might, if not the Kirk, then the Chief Rabbi.

Indeed, her insistence that her ideology was rooted in biblical morality goes a long way to explain the anger she aroused.

Mrs Thatcher demonstrated that a prime minister's religious outlook is not merely a matter of academic interest, but can have an interesting effect on the tone, if not the policies, of an administration. It is no coincidence that many of her policy advisers were evangelical Christians inspired by the Protestant work ethic; they are central to any understanding of Thatcherism. Indeed, their current absence from Downing Street may well turn out to be central to an understanding of the Major administration.

The contrast between the Thatcher and Major approaches to religion has attracted little comment in political circles, but it has not gone unnoticed in the Church of England. There has undoubtedly been an easing of tension between the Church and Downing Street, though not necessarily because the two have reached a new understanding. 'Frankly, he just doesn't seem interested in us,' a bishop told me at last week's Synod. 'None of us has a clue what he actually believes.'

The bishop's lament has a familiar ring to it. What does John Major believe?

Friends who have known the Prime Minister for years profess ignorance on the point. Major himself is strongly disinclined to talk about the subject. Gus O'Donnell, his press officer, told me he was unlikely to grant an interview on the subject because 'he likes to keep these things private'. Chris Patten was equally discouraging, explaining that Major was 'very reluctant to talk about these things in public'.

And in private, it seems. For the most part, the Prime Minister's friends and colleagues have never heard the subject broached. His best man, Clive Jones, a close friend during the Sixties and early Seventies, says Major was 'more of a nominal Anglican than a practising one at the time, though I've no doubt he believes in God'. Terry Major-Ball, his older brother, told me his parents were religious but not churchgoers: he wasn't sure whether John had been confirmed, but was 'pretty sure he believed in God'.

Major's past throws up few clues. He once told his biographer Bruce Anderson that he was 'high rather than low' and it is true that as a young man in Brixton he was friendly with the Revd J. Franklin Cheyne, Vicar of St James's, Knatchbull Road, a high churchman and active Tory. But there is no evidence of Major going out of his way to attend high-church services. On the contrary: in his early years in Huntingdon, he occasionally attended the family service at his local church in Hemingford Grey, an evangelical establishment verging on the happy-clappy.

*'Remember, don't let following traffic worry
you too much.'*

On the one occasion when Major was asked about his religious beliefs, he ducked the question. During the leadership contest, Radio 4's *Sunday* programme asked him about the importance of his religious faith. 'As I interpret faith it incorporates instincts and values,' he replied. 'If you lose faith in your own belief that you're living by the instincts and values that you think are important, then you should stop doing what you're doing, for you'll have no pleasure in it and I doubt you will do it well. So I think the answer to the question is that it is very important.'

But 'instincts and values' are not the same thing as faith, though they are often invoked by people who are unwilling to discuss their belief, or lack of it, in the doctrines of Christianity. It may be, of course, that Major has a strong faith which he regards as too private to expose to the public gaze, but even his friends doubt it. A devoutly Christian member of the Cabinet told me he thought the Prime Minister might qualify as an agnostic – 'though not in the sense that he doesn't care about these things'. The implication was that Major might be an agnostic, but he wasn't totally godless; not like Neil Kinnock.

Kinnock does not exactly advertise the fact, but if elected he would be the first British prime minister who is a professed agnostic. He has had 'difficulty' in believing in God since he was a teenager, he told

Adam Raphael of the *Observer*. 'The more I thought about it the more I realised that you had to take a leap of faith ... In my case, I find the subjective evidence is against making it, so I have never been able to do it.'

Note the apologetic tone. Kinnock is not like Michael Foot, proudly trumpeting his freedom from superstition. In his *Spectator* diary last month, Ludovic Kennedy made the point that many unbelievers regard it as bad form to admit to being an atheist. In what is supposed to be a post-Christian age, in a country whose people have always found it embarrassing to talk openly about God, there is still an atavistic reluctance to deny the existence of God. But people can identify with a politician who talks regretfully about his personal failure to make a 'leap of faith'. In any case, Kinnock is too shrewd an operator to leave it at that. His values, he says, have been strongly influenced by the passage in St Matthew's Gospel in which Christ tells his disciples:

> I was hungry and you fed me, I was naked and you clothed me, I was in prison and you visited me; in as much as you do it to the least of my brethren you do it to me.

'As an article of social faith,' concluded Kinnock, 'as an objective for the conduct of life, I think it is very difficult to better that.'

On the basis of this, Kinnock seems to be saying, like innumerable public figures put on the spot about their beliefs, that although he has difficulty with the supernatural elements in Christianity, he follows the ethical teachings of Christ. But on closer inspection, this isn't what he is saying. In another interview, Kinnock singled out 'the absolute requirement of forgiveness' as a Christian precept he could not accept. At other times, too, he has hinted that his own beliefs are far removed from the Christian ethic. Was he a good hater? Raphael asked him. No, he replied thoughtfully, he tried to keep his hate in check because 'hate, like love, is something to be applied in measured quantities, otherwise it starts to lose its purpose'. Whatever this is, it is not Christianity; but in the light of his other statements, it is not entirely incoherent.

The same cannot be said of Paddy Ashdown's ventures into this field. Asked whether he was religious, he said 'yes and no': he did believe in a Christian God, but not one who 'conformed to the rigidities of any particular portion of the Christian church'.

'To be precise,' he went on, 'I pray at nights and that's an important anchor in my life and it's very odd recently, particularly recently, when I've been in contact with George Carey – he was my bishop – and others, particularly a priest in my constituency, my own church, I felt a very strong pull of the formalised Christian church and I suppose rather like [Francis] Thompson's the Hound of Heaven chasing down the nights and down the days and down the avenues of the years and eventually catch [sic] up.' It is extraordinary how questions about religion can turn the most confident performer into Dan Quayle.

But does it matter? Who cares if a party leader is a Calvinist, or a Scientologist, or doesn't know what he believes? Potential bishops do for a start: although the Prime Minister's role in Church patronage is often over-estimated, it does extend to vetoing a particular candidate.

A party's supporters, too, can take a surprising interest in these things, as Mr Ashdown is in the process of finding out. He recently gave an interview to William Leith of the *Independent* in which he outlined 'the Ashdown theory in full'. This turned out to be surprisingly exotic. Mankind, explained Ashdown, was on the verge of a 'fundamental millennial shift' after which society would become 'flatter' and less hierarchical. In future, the most influential group in society would be the 'inner-directeds', people who valued co-operation rather than consensus. 'Sort of New Age?' asked Leith shrewdly. 'That's not a bad way of putting it,' mused Ashdown.

In fact, many of Ashdown's supporters thought it was a *very* bad way of putting it. For the evangelical Christians in the Liberal Democrats – and they are a surprisingly important lobby, led by Clive Calver of the Evangelical Alliance – the New Age movement is evil, maybe even the false religion that will herald the apocalypse. Ashdown's fluency in New Age jargon like 'inner-directed' has revived doubts raised by his attendance at a seance a few years ago. 'I don't know whether he knew what he was saying, but it gave us the creeps,' says one prominent Liberal Democrat. 'Clive was chewing the carpet.'

Arguably, Ashdown would be well advised to take this problem seriously. Calver's organisation now has a million members, and is increasingly concentrating on a political agenda. This election will be the first in which it has really flexed its muscles, relentlessly prodding candidates on a 'Christian' portfolio of issues including euthanasia, foreign aid, abortion and Sunday trading.

The Movement for Christian Democracy, a Catholic/Evangelical pressure group whose founders include the Liberal Democrat MP David Alton, has given every candidate an A, B, C or D rating based on their response to questions about these issues. None of the party leaders has responded, earning them an automatic D – even if they had, none of them would have rated higher than a C. This may not worry the established churches, some of whose representatives are as evasive and apologetic as any politician when asked precisely what they believe. But a new, more aggressive breed of Christian will have registered it with alarm.

This will be the first general election in British history in which none of the party leaders is a publicly committed Christian. It is only a footnote, perhaps, in the history of the decline of organised religion in this country, but worth noting all the same.

7 March 1992

LET MY PEOPLE STAY

Clive James

Grizzled Aussie expatriates who thought they were safely holed up in this country have been shaken to their foundation garments by the explosion of interest in the subject of Australian republicanism. There was no dodging the issue. Some said it was the first eruption of a long-simmering volcano. Others thought a squib had gone off. The initial evidence supported the latter theory. Meeting the Queen during her tour of Australia, the Australian Prime Minister's wife had several times failed to curtsy, while the Prime Minister himself, on at least one occasion, had physically touched the Monarch.

For a while it was not established whether these were deliberate acts of *lèse majesté* or examples of disarming Australian casualness. But the prominent British art critic, Brian Sewell, was already certain. The *Evening Standard* ran a full-page article from him recommending that all Australian expatriates in Britain should be deported back to their inherently treasonable country.

My own name was high on the list, with a full description. I reacted with some alarm. Though Auberon Waugh once made the same suggestion, he had been talking about voluntary repatriation, like Enoch Powell. Brian Sewell's tone was less kindly. I had always thought he sounded like a decorative attack dog, a sort of pit bull poodle, but this time he was really barking. Those British cultural journalists of the second rank who enjoy baiting Australians as a form of licensed racism had previously worn muzzles. Brian Sewell gave you a taste of what it must have been like to be Jewish in occupied Paris when Brasillach was writing for *Je suis partout*. First the denunciation, then they wake you up during the night.

Sleeping that night with my passport in my pyjamas pocket, I was woken early by a telephone call from the *Evening Standard*. Quelling the urge to answer in a disguised voice and exit backwards through the bedroom window, I bravely asked them what they wanted. It turned out that Prime Minister Keating, responding in Parliament to a taunt about his behaviour *vis-à-vis* the Monarch, had condemned Britain's shameless indifference to Australia's fate during the Second World War. Would I care to comment? I told them to ask Brian Sewell.

There was no getting out of it that easily. Over the next few days, *Newsnight*, *The World At One* and most of the newspapers were all on the trail. Everyone wanted my expert opinion on the Australian constitutional issue. Did I *look* like an expert on the Australian constitutional issue? I tried on a false beard, but it made me look like Tom Keneally, who *is* an expert on the Australian constitutional issue. He is in favour of an Australian republic. I'm not, but I'm not sure why. To get out of having to dodge any more questions, however, let me give the few answers in my possession.

Paul Keating is a man of conspicuous virtues. He has a nice line in invective which could have made him a successful debt collector in another life. When the moment came to pull the lever which dropped Mr Hawke through the trapdoor to the waiting crocodiles, Mr Keating did not pretend to share their tears. His boldness is proved by the unblushing confidence with which he now proposes to rebuild a national economy that all Australians, including possibly himself, are well aware he destroyed in the first place. He will probably make a good, long-serving Prime Minister in the not impossible event that the opposition remains so short of credible leadership that it can't beat even him.

But he knows nothing about the modern history of Australia or anywhere else. He left school early and has too readily excused himself from making up his educational deficiencies late at night. Instead of reading English books, he collects French clocks, which can tell him nothing except the time. Compared to most of his predecessors as leader of the Labor Party, he is an ignoramus. Dr H. V. Evatt might be said to have been privileged, because he went to Sydney University and had a dazzling academic record; and Bob Hawke was even more privileged, because he went to Oxford University and drank beer; but Ben Chiffley, though his school was the footplate of a locomotive, found out about the world by asking. Paul Keating doesn't ask. He can't be instructed because he is always instructing. Tempted out of his field, which is bare-knuckle politics, he finds himself compelled to relay, as a substitute for what he has found out from experience, stuff he has got out of the air. What is of interest is not his belligerence but how the stuff got into the air.

As Alistair Horne made clear, when the posh papers wheeled him into the argument, the idea that Britain deliberately did less than it could to save Malaya, Singapore, and finally Australia, has no basis in fact. It shouldn't have needed Mr Horne to point this out. Republican-minded Australian revisionist historians have been able to float the notion only by blinding themselves to the obvious. The Malaya campaign was a bungle which cost Britain dear, and if there were any plans by Britain to abandon Australia, they were scarcely more sweeping than Australian plans to do the same. Planning against the worst is a military necessity. When the Australians counted up their resources they had to face the possibility that if the Japanese got ashore the only defensible perimeter would be the eastern seaboard: 'the Brisbane line'. This proposal, which was drawn up in some detail, is no reason for the inhabitants of Adelaide and Perth to now demand a separate country of their own. Luckily the American navy fought a crucial draw with the Japanese navy at the Battle of the Coral Sea and the Australian army stymied the Japanese army in New Guinea, so the prospect of abandoning Australia ceased to loom. But it might have happened, because it might have had to.

The Australians showed more resentment for the Americans who came to their rescue than for the British who had been so ineffective in defending the Empire. The idea that Australians *should* have borne ill-will towards Britain was hatched subsequently by revisionist historians with an interest in republicanism. It is a legitimate interest, especially in view of Britain's undoubted indifference to the sensitivities of Australia and New Zealand at the time of its belated entry into the Common Market. But to play fast and loose with the truth in order to further a political interest is not legitimate, and nothing is more likely to make Australia go on seeming provincial than this propensity on the part of its artists and intellectuals to tinker with ideology. You can understand it from the Murdoch press. Its proprietor favours Australia's cutting itself off from Britain because he has cut himself off from both countries, in pursuit of some dreary post-capitalist Utopia in which the hunger to acquire is exalted as a spiritual value, and the amount of debt magically testifies to financial acumen. But there is no good reason why some of Australia's most creative people should share his bleak vision.

And yet they do. In Australia the conspiracy theory of history wins in a walk and the cock-up theory comes nowhere. At the Dardanelles, three times as many British troops were uselessly thrown into the same boiler as the Australians, but the fact doesn't get a mention in the Australian-made film *Gallipoli* because its writer, David Williamson, favours a republic. Williamson is a gifted man who must know the truth. But he has an end in view. The conspiracy theory that Britain cynically exploited Antipodean cannon-fodder in both wars is seen to further this end.

I wonder if it will. Ordinary Australian people, less bound by the requirements to write a neat article or a clear-cut screenplay, are more likely to favour the cock-up theory, especially if they are old enough actually to remember what the war in the Pacific was like. Indeed, some of them might be inclined to extend that theory to a full-blown view of the world's contingencies, one of them being that if the British had done everything right in Malaya, they might still have lost.

It is racism of a particularly insidious kind to imagine that the Japanese were able to advance only because we retreated. General Percival, commanding for Britain, was certainly no genius, but even if he had been Montgomery and Slim rolled into one he would have had trouble with General Yamashita, a strategic prodigy in command of an army which comported itself brilliantly all the way down to platoon level. After the fall of Singapore, a jealous Tojo banished Yamashita to Mongolia, but with the war almost lost he was brought back to stop the rot on Luzon, where the Americans, by then wielding limitless resources, found to their horror that his troops had to be cooked out of their holes, and came out shooting even when they were burning.

Mr Keating's assumption that a modernised, Asia-minded Australia needs to be a republic might be greeted with some puzzlement by present-day Japan, whose economic clout dominates the region and whose Emperor, at his coronation, spent a night in the embrace of the Sun Goddess. Mr Keating's real problem, however, is with my mother. Though fiercely proud to be Australian, she has made a point of seeing with her own eyes all the officially visiting members of the Royal Family since the present Queen Mother, then the Duchess of York. When the present Queen first visited Sydney in 1954, my mother came in by train to wave. She was there again for the Queen's visit this year. The two women are very like each other, sharing the same past, if not the same income. My mother did not, and does not now, regard my father's death as a pointless sacrifice on behalf of British interests. She believes that he was defending civilisation. Though Mr Menzies took care to keep her war widow's pension small so as to encourage thrift, she voted for the Liberal Party as often as for Labor, and always according to her assessment of which party had the firmer grip on reality. She has personally elected every Australian prime minister for the last 60 years and if Mr Keating thinks he can do without her vote, it might be his turn on the trapdoor.

Nor should he put too much faith in the argument – much touted by the Murdoch press and slyly put forward as fact by the Australian broadcaster Mike Carlton in his entertaining article in the *Sunday Times* – that as Australia's demography alters to put people of Anglo background in the minority, the majority are bound to prefer going it alone. Whether from Europe two generations ago or from Asia in the last generation, many of Australia's migrants were refugees from political instability, and won't necessarily favour any proposal that encourages more of it in their chosen home. Their progeny might be persuaded, but let it be by reasonable argument, on a basis of truth. Meanwhile for Australians like myself, resident in Britain but still holding on loyally to their Australian passports, caught between Mr Sewell and Mr Keating, queuing in the 'Other Passports' channel while ex-SS tank commanders are given the quick welcome reserved for the EEC, there is nothing to do but wait, and screen all incoming calls.

7 March 1992

DIARY

Keith Waterhouse

It was with a wince that I read that L. S. Lowry's 'VE Day', which has gone missing from the Kelvingrove municipal art gallery in Glasgow, was valued at £150,000. I never learn the current price of one of his paintings without being reminded that years ago, after a prolonged lunch, I gave a Lowry away to a lady I was briefly in love with. At least it was not one of the much-prized busy Salford street scenes but a small, isolated study of an old woman with a shopping bag, so it would now be worth no more than – I hope – a mere four figures. I bought it, for £100 I think, at a Lowry exhibition at the Crane Kalman Gallery in which these single, solitary characters, rather than his more familiar crowded canvases, predominated – among them, I remember, that very famous one of the chap lying on a wall with umbrella and briefcase. The critics made much of this change of tack, which they interpreted as Lowry finally homing in on the 'essential loneliness' of his superficially gregarious matchstick figures. I got the true explanation from the eccentric artist himself, when I went round to collect my picture immediately before that fateful (though highly enjoyable) lunch, and found Mr Lowry enjoying a cup of tea with Andras Kalman. 'Well, y'see,' said Lowry, 'I knew I had this exhibition coming up and I'd promised Andras here some new paintings for it, but I was very busy doing a six by three for Merthyr Tydfil corporation, d'y'see, so I thought what I'd better do, I'll knock off some of what I call my ones.' Thus it was that one of Lowry's 'ones', expressing the essential loneliness of an old woman with a shopping bag, came to grace the drawing-room of a certain flat in Bayswater. I never saw his six by three. I do wonder if Merthyr Tydfil corporation ever fell in love.

What is the policy of *Spectator* readers on removing the names of the

*'I once got a picture of Liz Taylor not wearing a
wedding dress.'*

deceased from their address books? Looking up a telephone number last week, I found it nestling between two entries, one an old friend, the other a business acquaintance, who have been dead these many moons. I chanced to be holding a red Pentel, the ideal instrument for making excisions. Before I knew what I was doing I had firmly struck out the two now superfluous names and their accompanying addresses and phone numbers. Immediately I was seized by feelings of melancholy and guilt. I felt like a vandal in a cemetery, flitting through the tombstones with a spray-can. I thought seriously about restoring the two defaced entries on a new page, but then dismissed the notion as mawkishly sentimental. But certainly I will expunge no more of the late lamented, and there must be enough of them to fill a small graveyard, from my address book. When it grows too dog-eared for use and I have to compile it afresh, I suppose I will prune their names along with those baffling Smiths and Joneses one has never heard of who somehow manage to infiltrate one's address book. Until then, RIP.

14 March 1992

THE END OF GEOGRAPHY

Noel Malcolm

Now that 'PC' (Political Correctness) is part of the language, perhaps it's time to introduce the concept of 'GC' – Geographical Correctness. There is a lot of it about. Most of the quality daily papers in this country now refer blithely to 'Moldova' instead of Moldavia, 'Ukraine' instead of 'the Ukraine', and 'Belarus' or 'Bielarus' instead of Byelorussia. And what used to be Kirghizia or Kirghizstan has now turned into the answer to a demented Scrabble-player's prayers: 'Kyrgyzstan'.

While I was thinking about this, and wondering whether it could really be necessary to explain to readers of *The Spectator* why this journal will continue to use 'the Ukraine', 'Byelorussia' and the rest, a letter arrived – from an English subscriber living in Rumania:

> Sir: I am sure that your readers in Romania are delighted to hear of your initiative for free copies of *The Spectator* for them, if somewhat bemused by your gratuitous mis-spelling of their country's name.

To which the only possible reply is that 'Rumania' would indeed be a mis-spelling if *The Spectator* were written in Rumanian – which, fortunately for all but a hundred or so of our readers, it is not.

The basic point at issue here is so hoarily familiar that one hesitates before trotting it out yet again: commonly used place names are part of our language, not the exclusive property of the local inhabitants; we say Finland (not Suomi), Albania (not Shqiperi or Shqiperia), and North Korea (not Choso Minjujuui Inmin Kinghwaguk). Why should anyone think that the traditional English spellings of 'Rumania' or 'Roumania' – which, as it happens, match the traditional English pronunciation – are incorrect just because Rumanians spell it 'Romania'? Would he also like us to pronounce it 'correctly'? For English eyes and ears, the spelling of the authentic pronunciation would be something like 'Rommernear' – so perhaps that should be the ultimately 'correct' way to spell it in England.

The psychology of Geographical Correctness is a complex of complexes. There is a craving for authority on the one hand, and a yearning for absolute, unalterable, objective certainty on the other. This ideal of certainty involves thinking of each place name as a verifiable scientific fact, equally valid in all languages, just as the atomic structure of caesium, say, is the same in all parts of the world. But the atomic structure of caesium is not changed every half-century or so by government decree; here the demands of objectivity and authority are in open conflict.

Some defenders of GC try to reconcile these two principles by appealing to the example of personal names: if Theodore Brown changes his name by deed poll to Theophilus Smith, then that becomes the objectively correct name, and it does so by his own personal authority. But the names of people are not like the names of countries. 'Theodore Brown' was not part of the English language, brimming with historical resonances in the way that 'Vienna' and 'Siberia' and 'the Ukraine' do. And in matters of language, neither authority nor objectivity can be our ultimate guide. The only final arbiter is usage; the only ultimate test is whether something sounds correct or incorrect to a competent user of the language.

People who do not understand this simple principle always try to reduce the criterion of correct usage to something else: they appeal to etymology, historical accuracy, logical consistency, or whatever. All they do thereby is to set up false standards which they themselves cannot meet. Consistency is not the most obvious virtue of people who write 'Bielarus' and 'Moldova' but 'Ukraine' instead of 'Ukraina', and 'Kiev' instead of 'Kyiv'.

As for etymology and historical correctness, most of these names are mares' nests of ancient controversy; to suppose that one has to understand all the issues involved before one can use the English language correctly is absurd, and to imply that choosing the correct English usage involves taking sides in those controversies is preposterous. Take 'the Ukraine', for example. For years, the Ukrainian émigré nationalists based in Canada have been campaigning to call it 'Ukraine' *tout court*; the main reason for this is their feeling that 'the Ukraine' makes it sound like a region of something else, rather than a country in its own right. (And in any case, 'Ukraine' comes naturally to them, since there is no definite article in Ukrainian.) In most Slav languages, 'Ukraina' simply means 'borderland' or 'frontier-territory'. The nearest English equivalent would be 'the Marches' – hence, historically, our use of the definite article. Ukrainians prefer a slightly different explanation of the early meaning of 'Ukraina'; but this is a matter for philologists and historians to worry about, not for ordinary users of English.

If Scotland had always been called 'the Highlands', and if it became independent tomorrow, we would continue to call it 'the Highlands', and no one would seriously imagine that we were thereby claiming it was still part of the United Kingdom. Today, whenever I hear a newscaster talk about 'events in Ukraine', I can't help wondering momentarily whether he is using one of those northern English dialects in which people say 'I've put 'teapot on 'table.'

Historical sensitivities are ultra-tender in Eastern Europe, and the only safe procedure for English language users is to ignore them altogether. 'Romania' is a classic example, signifying as it does the determination of modern Rumanians to claim that they are descended from Trajan's Roman legionaries – and hence, of course, that they bagged Transylvania before the Hungarians. Under a Soviet-inspired spelling reform, the 'a' with a circumflex in the middle of Romania was changed (as it was in all other words) into an 'i' with a circumflex; but the Rumanians objected so strongly to the idea that they were descended from ancient Romins that this one exception was eventually permitted.

As for Moldova, this is simply the word in the local language (which is Rumanian) for what we call Moldavia. The north-eastern region of Rumania is also called 'Moldova' in Rumanian; but all users of English, even the Geographically Correct, continue to call it Moldavia. In time, it might be rather useful if a distinction were to evolve between the two, just as 'Britain' and 'Brittany' evolved out of 'Bretagne' in English. But the simplest solution would be to call the new country Bessarabia, which is what that region always used to be.

Byelorussia means 'White Russia' (in German it is Weissrussland); as

'Belorus' or 'Belaya Rus', it was the area of the ancient Slav territory of 'Rus' which escaped Tartar domination. The term 'Rus' evolved into 'Rossiya', which all of us (even the Geographically Correct) call Russia. It's easy to see why modern Byelorussians should want to remind themselves of ancient 'Rus', thus asserting a kind of priority; but those arguments are their concern, not ours. Byelorussia (pronounced as in 'yellow', not as in 'good-bye') is the English for 'Belarus', just as Prussia is the English for 'Preussen'.

Sometimes, however, traditional usage is no help. What are we to call the thing that calls itself the Commonwealth of Independent States? Not the CIS, surely; they're the people I insure my bicycle with, the Cooperative Insurance Society. When the first agreement between Russia, Byelorussia and the Ukraine was signed in Minsk, I wondered if they might call it 'the Empire of All the Russias', since those were the three territories originally implied by that phrase: Russia, White Russia, and Little Russia – a Tsarist name for the Ukraine. A few other candidates spring to mind: 'Absurdistan', perhaps, or 'Eurasia' (with apologies to George Orwell). What about the Unco-ordinated System of Semi-Soviet Republics, or USSR for short?

Which brings me, finally, to that other great artificial creation of our times. Every time I refer in this journal to the Strasbourg Assembly, a saintly man who is the London representative of that body writes in to correct me. I call him saintly because his patience in this matter is inexhaustible, even though he must have worked out by now that I am only doing it to annoy him. He never tires of pointing out that some piece of legislation or other has described the Strasbourg Assembly as the European Parliament. But names are established by usage, not fixed by legislation. That is why I can call our proper Parliament 'Westminster', or the French Foreign Office 'the Quai d'Orsay', regardless of how they are described in treaties or statutes.

In the eyes of the man from the Strasbourg Assembly, however, names are made by law. Yet the last time he wrote to me, he enclosed a helpful booklet about the Assembly, the first sentence of which referred to something called 'the European Community' – a thing which, in legal terms, does not exist. There are three Communities (EEC, Coal and Steel, and Atomic Energy); although their administrations were merged in 1967, their legal identities remained distinct, and official documents still refer to 'the European Communities'. Only when the Maastricht Treaty comes into force will there begin to be a legal entity called 'the European Community'. Meanwhile, millions of people have what they think of (incorrectly) as 'European passports', with the words 'European Community' printed on the front. Never underestimate the power of names; if war is too important to be left to the generals, then names are far too important to be entrusted to the legislators.

14 March 1992

ANOTHER VOICE

TU ES PETRUS ET IN HOC PETRO AEDIFICABO ECCLESIAM MEAM

Auberon Waugh

'This is an historic occasion,' said Canon David Goldie at the dedication of the first purpose-built ecumenical city church in Britain – the new £5 million church of St Christ the Cornerstone, Milton Keynes – last week. And so, of course, it was. Canon Goldie may not be able to compete with Peter Simple's Reverend Eric Shrike, Vicar of the Church of Christ the Non-Smoker, Turgis Hill, in the single-mindedness of his mission. Mr Shrike, on Sunday, called for a 'supreme effort' to extirpate 'this last and greatest of all evils, this primal sin which, to speak in allegory, may have begun when Adam and Eve smoked their first cigarettes in the Garden, and thus brought death into the world and all our woe'.

But then one could scarcely expect Canon Goldie to compete with Peter Simple in anything. The time is long since past when the Church could reckon to attract the brightest and best – men of intelligence and promise like More, Wolsey, Erasmus, Richelieu, Mazarin – as the most obvious ladder for their ambitions. The group that gathered in Milton Keynes on Friday included the Archbishop of Canterbury, Cardinal Hume, the leaders of Methodist, Baptist and United Reformed groups and the Queen, suitably clad in a pontifical red coat over a Paisley dress. It must have been one of the gloomiest gatherings in England which heard Cardinal Hume, on behalf of Christ the Cornerstone, say: 'May this church in Milton Keynes be a pledge of our common commitment, a signpost to an increasingly shared future and a beacon of hope for the whole community.'

The gloom which attended this historic occasion would not necessarily have been caused by scepticism about the workings of the Holy
Ghost, in concert with Christ the Cornerstone, to bring the Christian
churches together again. It would have been caused by the enforced
optimism at an event which, in fact, marks an admission of failure
by all the participants. In the same way Dr Peter Carnley, when laying
his hands on ten Australian women recently in the hope that it would
somehow ordain them priests to do so, announced: 'Today we ordain
ten but liberate tens of thousands.'

Once again, we should feel nothing but pleasure at the thought of
those tens of thousands of liberated sheilas bouncing around in Western
Australia, if Dr Carnley honestly thinks he has liberated them. But a
suspicion arises from the fact that the great sheila liberation movement
coincides with a catastrophic shortage of priests. Is he really concerned
to liberate women, or simply to fill the vacant situations, and how long
will it be before advanced theology, in tune with the green movement,
starts ordaining and liberating all the kangaroos of Western Australia
in their tens of thousands?

This may seem a cynical attitude to take, but there is plenty of
other evidence that the new indifferentism – once condemned as the
mother of all modern heresies – springs from desperation rather than
from a sudden vision of alternative truth. Necessity was always the
mother of invention, of course, but need it also mother quite so much
enthusiasm?

'A very special characteristic of this church is that it has been planned
and built with the whole Christian community in mind,' said Cardinal
Hume. Yes, yes. We got the message. Looking at its design – by no means
as disgusting as Paddy's Wigwam in Liverpool, or the atrocious Roman
Catholic cathedral in Clifton – it crosses my mind that a lantern on top
of the dome might yet double up as a minaret, from which the muezzin
can call the Islamic faithful of Milton Keynes to prayer on a Friday, even
as the rabbis move in on Saturday and Christian anti-smoking counsellors stand by for their Cornerstone Coffee Sessions on Sunday.

If people say that we are far removed from the jump to any wider
ecumenism, I can only draw attention to Dr Carey's break with a
150-year-old tradition in refusing to become patron of the Missionary
Society, the Church's ministry among Jews. His reason for this, plainly
stated, is that he now thinks it wrong to convert Jews to Christianity.
Never mind about the Christian's charitable obligation to bring all to
the Way, the Truth and the Light. It was up to Dr Carey to 'do all in
my power to encourage trust and friendship between the different faith
communities in our land'.

It goes without saying that the Jewish religious establishment is delighted by this development. Neither of the other great monotheistic religios – Judaism or Islam – has quite reached our own semi-collapsed state.

There may be inexorable historical reasons for the collapse of Marxism as an economic creed, but I can think of no reason for the collapse of Christianity *vis-à-vis* the other great world religions unless it is something to do with the falling sperm count.

Even those who thought Carey was putting up some sort of Last Stand for orthodoxy against homosexual takeover when he succeeded in banning the SPCK manual, *Daring to Speak Love's Name*, should look again at what he actually said.

One could easily suppose, from the bare fact of Carey's having threatened to resign the presidency of SPCK if it went ahead with the book, that he disapproved of homosexuality. He might even, in an awkward moment, have remembered the various biblical references to it as an abomination, crying out to Heaven for vengeance. However, this was not, apparently, the basis of his objection. He found it 'regrettable' that prayers for people with Aids should appear alongside liturgies for people 'coming out'.

'Surely this will only foster the myth that HIV and Aids are confined to the homosexual community. I find it difficult to regard this book as the contribution to the educational process for which the bishops called.'

Anglicans in this day and age have simply got to accept that Aids has absolutely nothing to do with anal intercourse. If they are not prepared to make that one little act of faith, they will be refused coffee in Nerdley's new Pantheistic Temple of Christ the Left-Hander . . .

It becomes easier and easier to imagine that Peter Simple – or at any rate Michael Wharton, his creator – is God: not just writing the history of our times, but in the particular sense of continuous creation, that we all exist only as reflections of his benign imagination.

This year, to the relief of all, he wrote on Sunday, there was no 'unseemly protest at the Tomb of the Unknown Non-Smoker over the implication, regarded by some as heretical, that it is possible to die from a cause other than smoking. There is a small, growing sect of mystical non-smokers who hold that non-smoking can actually ensure immortality . . .'

I can think of no religious need in the modern world which would not be met by quiet weekly readings from Simple's 'Way of the World' in the *Sunday Telegraph*.

21 March 1992

BOOKS

SOMETHING FISHY ABOUT
THE SEX

Julie Burchill

CRIMSON
by Shirley Conran
Sidgwick, £14.99, pp. 600

Conran is, of course, a brand name. But even something as solid as a brand name may, these days, melt into air and drift downmarket. Thus Conran, once a byword for chic, has become a synonym for tat, as in Habitat. Proof that the name has lost its glamour comes on the back jacket bio of this truly appalling book, where once just mentioning her marriage to Sir Tel would have sufficed, Shirley now drags in 'fashion designer Georgina Godley, her daughter-in-law', giving the term 'relative values' a whole new meaning.

Like the last piece of Habitat furniture I bought, this book is perfunctory, uninspired and falling apart at the seams, which is a shame, because the blockbuster genre as a whole is far from worthless. The works of Jacqueline Susann, Molly Parkin and Jackie Collins tell us more, and tell us more skilfully and amusingly, about life in a certain semi-trashy fast lane in the Sixties, Seventies and Eighties than any number of 'serious' books on the same subject by Norman Mailer, Martin Amis and Brett Easton Ellis. With the exception of Susann's seminal *Valley of the Dolls*, the form probably reached its peak with Collins' 1977 masterpiece, *Lovers and Gamblers*; not only was it the most deadly accurate portrait of the music business ever painted but it contained, in the person of the hero's nerdy son, the most convincingly grungy depiction of adolescence since Holden Caulfield. Now, however, only Pat Booth writes with anything approaching the sass and savvy of the senior sorority. For the rest, the blockbuster scene is a barren wasteland. And it has been rendered so by Shirley Conran, Celia Brayfield and Jilly Cooper, all of whom seem suicidally intent on proving repeatedly what we've always known; that the English middle class is Not Good At Sex.

Susann, Collins, Parkin and Booth all came from showbiz or working-class backgrounds; Brayfield, Conran and Cooper are public schoolgirls

Which means they can't help but be conscious that they are *writing down*. Blockbusters are great when they're lowdown, dirty and honest – 'Eat my meat, junkie bitch!' (J. Burchill, *Ambition*, 1989) – but when they go in for 'fine' writing ('The perpetually green forest of the hinterland, which still provided shelter for wild boar, rabbits and birds') they are risible. Like calling a napkin a serviette, or pornography 'erotica'.

In such language does Conran relate the sorry tale of dying old biddy, Elinor, author of 22 – count 'em! – romantic novels, whose fortune is desired by her three granddaughters – the model, the tycoon and the socialite with the social conscience. Set in London, Los Angeles and the Med, but most of all set in the Sixties, the book has a remarkable lack of period grasp; the men, as in Cartland's Regency romps, have 'firm-hewn features' and the women have 'fey, elusive charm'. Whereas anyone looking at pictures of the age's icons, like Julie Christie and Brian Jones, knows that it was the other way around.

Such zeitgeistian figures as William Holden and Simone Signoret make cameo appearances at 'right rave-ups': the gracelessness of the writing is hard to communicate without quoting verbatim.

> 'What's so terrible about escapist literature?' Annabel demanded. 'Most women read it – and why not?' 'Gran's books sell by the million,' Miranda said. 'So obviously a great many people enjoy them.'

This sort of chippy defensiveness goes on for pages, and makes it very clear that what is wrong with *this* 'escapist literature' in particular is not only that it is not literature, but that it is not even escapist. It is the sound of one hand clapping, of one voice cheer-leading, of one middle-aged, middle-class, middle-brow woman reassuring herself that she is not wasting her education by writing trash. But it is not just her background which makes Conran so unfit for the task; it is her opinion of sex. Does she actually *like* it? Ninety per cent of the sex here is dismal for the women involved, and I always thought the *Lace* goldfish was a dead giveaway. I know that some people have strange tastes, and find attractive that which is not apparently so – dwarves, amputees, Gentile men – but there can be no sexually aware person who wants to shag a shubunkin. (Conran's got a thing about fish – 'She had thrashed around like a freshly caught trout on a grassy bank.' That's the most unappetising description of an orgasm I've ever encountered, unless you're an angler.)

On every page I found something which jarred on my nerves and spelling standards, which is the opposite effect to the one escapist literature is meant to have. Conran keeps comparing the smell of men to the smell of horses; interestingly, the Jew smells like a 'sweaty' horse while the WASP smells like a clean one. She spells jewellery 'jewelry', which I know is an option, but it seems to me typical of Conran's lack of feeling for the fitness of things.

Blockbusters depend most of all on their energy; the work of Susann, Collins, Parkin and now Booth fairly crackles with it, like sparks of static out of a cheapo carpet. The books speed towards their dénouements and destinations like whippets on crystal meth. *Crimson*, contrarily, seems utterly enervated, hobbling along like a sloth on its way to the dentist for extensive root canal work. Conran just obviously *doesn't want to be doing this*; she should write her Margaret Drabble novel and have done with it.

'Crimson is the colour of passion, the colour of rage, the colour of blood,' pants the blurb. It's also the colour of embarrassment, and all concerned in this book's production should turn it. If you're interested, Conran's also launching a scent of the same name, though I don't know why she bothers. She's already selling something that stinks.

21 March 1992

GOING ON

John Mole

Scotch and water, warm,
Medicinal, two tablets
On a little tray, his *Times*
Tucked underarm, a dignified
But frail ascent, prolonged
Undressing measured out
By heavy footsteps, coughing
Gently not to worry us, as if
A mere polite reminder, then
The silence of the grave.

And why must I recall this now
As half-way up the stairs
I hear my grown son calling
Going on, then, Dad?
An early night? Sleep well.

21 March 1992

A NASTY AND MENACING
ELECTION

John Simpson

'There you are, bright-eyed and bushy-tailed,' said the bouncy man in grey, rather bushy-tailed himself. He clasped his hands together like an American preacher about to pounce, and beamed at the audience. They were sitting in a large circle around him, as though they were at a high-tech circus and he were the ring-master. 'I can always tell a Conservative at a hundred yards,' he confided. 'Who on earth is this?' I asked someone from Conservative Central Office, as we waited for John Major to make his big entrance. 'Bill Roache from *Coronation Street*,' he answered, and there was a wariness in his voice. The one who successfully sued some newspaper for calling him the most boring man in the world, I asked? 'I'm sure you'll report that fully,' said the party figure nastily, and moved away. At that moment music blared out, and the prime ministerial face began appearing on several enormous screens at once. But the way the official had spoken remained in my mind. Where had I heard that tone before? It was only when John and Norma Major made their big entrance, and Purcell broke out like an electronic coronation anthem, that I remembered. It was precisely the way Dr Sa'ad used to speak to me.

Dr Sa'ad was the television censor in Baghdad: my least favourite government official there, which is saying something. 'Always you are putting in unpleasant things, Mr John,' he would say. 'I know you, and I know your ways.' The big problem with Dr Sa'ad was that he also thought he knew what we were really doing. If we showed a general view of Baghdad – known in the trade as a 'g.v.' – he would cut it out on the grounds that we were trying to send pictures of potential targets to allied intelligence. If we used a pleasant, colourful shot of an old man with a donkey, he would cut that out too: 'You are trying to imply that Iraq is a poor, undeveloped country.' My words on the sound-track were minutely examined for signs of hidden malice. 'You said "the President's palace", because you are trying to imply that he owns it himself,' Dr Sa'ad once declared in triumph, as though he had caught me out at last; 'you should say "the presidential palace", because it belongs to Iraq.' Useless to argue that the point was ludicrously far-fetched, that no British audience would spot such a distinction: Dr Sa'ad, looking dreadfully pleased with himself, cut it all out. 'This report was subject to Iraqi censorship,' intoned the newsreader in London that night; she didn't know the half of it.

It is extremely wearing to have to deal with people who think you have a hidden agenda, and that they know what it is. In travelling round the country with John Major's campaign, it is no part of my job to be snide or destructive: the fact that the warm-up man had been accused of being boring (and won damages when the court disagreed) was irrelevant to the Conservative campaign, so I did not report it that night. What was not irrelevant was to point out that in its early stages many people thought the campaign itself was dull and lifeless. The result of my saying that was distinctly Sa'ad-like. A Conservative Party official was on the phone to London in no time, contesting the words I had used and wanting changes.

The various television organisations are becoming wearily used to these calls, which are known to them as 'heavy breathing'. The Conservatives are certainly not the only party to go in for this tactic: the Labour Party and the Liberal Democrats vie with them in the scope, frequency and intensity of their own heavy breathing: no doubt by the end of the campaign there will have been a rough parity between them, all trying to intimidate the broadcasters into toning down the negative comments, toning up the positive ones, and giving greater prominence to their candidates and their campaign.

This is a nastier and more menacing election for the broadcasters than that of 1987, when I covered Mrs Thatcher's campaign. Hers was just as flat as John Major's, and some of the preparation was even worse. No one, however, slipped into the seat beside you on the Conservative campaign bus and told you where you had gone wrong and what you ought to report next time. They do now. No one, either, let you know which were the important parts of that night's speech, with the faint suggestion hanging in the air that if you chose other parts of the speech to report on questions might be asked about it later. They do now. The term 'spin-doctors' is imported from America; but there is an important difference between the American and British practice. In the United States the parties try, as they do here, to ensure that the coverage will be as favourable as possible to them; but if it is not they change their own approach. They do not attack the broadcasters nor hint at their possible dissolution. 'Spin-doctors': the expression has a pleasant, sporting sound to it. In reality the function they perform has nothing to do with cricket. It is Sa'adism.

If Mrs Thatcher tripped over or said something silly, her people were perfectly phlegmatic about it when the pictures hit the news programmes. Much more thick-skinned than Mr Major, she never seemed to know what one had said about her, nor to care. This time, though, the politicians have convinced themselves that a single slip in their campaign will lose them the election. As a result, there is immense nervousness in the two main political camps. In the Conservative one it may have something to do with experience: the oldest member of the campaign team is said to be 35, and most of the others seem to be in their twenties. On the Labour side the position is different, but the sensitivity is the same. A senior figure in Neil Kinnock's campaign went out of her way to tell me she would be watching my reporting on John Major 'with great interest'. That didn't mean she was a fan: merely that she would be on the telephone at any sign that I might be unfairly favouring him.

The tension among some of Mr Major's officials is especially noticeable, however: they all know what happened on Wobbly Thursday last time, and they know that it is perfectly possible for Mr Major to win the election yet lose the campaign, with all that this would mean for them in terms of lost reputations and lost job opportunities. To an outsider, it seems that the one centre of calm and reflection in Mr Major's entourage – apart from Mrs Major, who has kept remarkably cool – is Sir Norman Fowler, his personal adviser. Sir Norman has a safe seat and a Committee post which keeps him interested and occupied; he does not make you feel he is nervous about his personal future. The advice he gives John Major seems likely, therefore, to be both disinterested and considered.

'This whole bloody business has been got up with your cameras in mind,' a splenetic journalist hissed at me as we stood in a vast, barren, do-it-yourself supermarket in Bradford. The store had marked down everything by 20 per cent for the day in order to attract more customers, but business was still deplorably slack. The television crews and photographers shuffled backwards in the path of John and Norma Major as they tried to look interested in the shelves of gloss paint and the displays of plastic knick-knacks. Customers were thrust forcibly aside, wares smashed to the ground. 'If I'd known it was going to be like this,' said the manager afterwards, 'I'd never have invited you all here.'

My sentiments exactly. Who is it that plans these things, that brings the Prime Minister to Yorkshire, one of the national centres of manufacture, and takes him round a supermarket in preference to a factory? Who is it that thinks this makes good television? Most television editors will do anything to avoid these stagy occasions if they can. A Channel 4 programme last week told us that by lifting up a calf in the 1979 campaign Mrs Thatcher inaugurated a new era in television's coverage of elections. Not so. These photo-opportunities, so beloved of the party managers, are done in order to get pride of place on the front pages of the next day's newspapers. They are single shots, planned with stills cameras in mind, and they date back to the 1950s: the time when television interviewers still asked prime ministers if they had a word for the nation.

What television wants is what, by sheer accident, the Major campaign twice provided in the first week of the campaign: the chance to see how a politician behaves when faced with ordinary people. In spite of themselves, Mr Major's team felt afterwards that the brief, noisy confrontation in Bolton had been a success for them. And when an unemployed Liberal Democrat tangled with Mr Major in the gentrified Corn Market turned shopping mall in Leeds, it was the Nineties' version of the good old 1950s' election meeting in the school hall. This is the kind of thing that makes the best television, because it shows in close-up and at length how a candidate for the prime ministership of the country behaves when his or her views are challenged. There is no need to edit it or to add a commentary: the viewers can judge for themselves.

Perhaps for this reason, the party managers are deeply nervous about such moments, believing as they do that a single slip could cause

'And we'd have someone to grope!'

their man's downfall. But it is what television is there to find and make the most of if it can. Margaret Thatcher loved these things, and wanted more of them than her handlers provided; I remember seeing her in some desolate place in 1987, eyes alight, having to be restrained almost physically by her security men from charging across and telling a group of chanting anarchists what was what. That spirit seems to have gone.

An embattled campaign team quickly identifies objectivity with opposition. Looking on as an outsider, it seems to me that neither of the main parties (I have no experience of the Liberal Democrats) appears to have any great understanding of, or sympathy for, the notion of independent reporting. The Conservative Party has grown used to the journalist as court flatterer; with the result, you feel, that they think this is how reporters should behave. 'Big Yes for Tory Tax Cuts,' yelled one *Daily Express* headline last week, in defiance of everything that seemed to be happening in the polls at the time. The idea that broadcasters are, by statute, not permitted to be part of this claque seems to have passed the Conservatives by. In similar fashion the Labour Party, used to the idea that most of the nation's press is against them, seems to swing between believing that the broadcasters are part of the grand anti-Labour conspiracy, and trying to force them to counterbalance the excesses of the Conservative press. In 1987 there was far more heavy breathing from Labour than from the Conservatives. In 1992 the Conservatives have caught up.

The Home Secretary last month gave an interview to the *Observer* in which he did some heavy breathing of his own. Kenneth Baker was quoted as saying, 'The BBC has got to be very careful indeed over the next eight to ten weeks. The country expects the BBC to be absolutely impartial as it is the state-funded body.' The extraordinary fact that the politician with overall charge of broadcasting seemed to be under the mistaken impression that his government funded the BBC, and therefore, perhaps, owned it went unnoticed. In reality, of course, it is the ordinary television viewers of the United Kingdom who pay for the BBC, not the state. The man in charge of Labour's campaign, David Hill, has also been making threatening noises. The BBC, he said, could not necessarily expect that Labour would be sympathetic to it if it did not report on the Labour Party in the way the Labour Party liked. 'If the BBC believes it can operate like this because the Conservatives hate it but Labour has a sentimental attachment to it, it had better think again. If it goes on like this and Labour wins, there won't be as much sentiment around for the BBC as it believes.' Whichever party wins will presumably dictate the BBC's new Charter, and therefore its future after 1996. So far, it is hard to avoid the suspicion that both Labour and the Conservatives are using this fact to try to frighten the BBC for their own party advantage: as though the BBC belongs to them and their parties, rather than to the nation as a whole. Life will not be easy for the broadcasters after the election if the politicians do not like the coverage they have received, but it will be even harder if the viewers and listeners – the real shareholders – believe the broadcasters have not been independent-minded.

So far, this has not been a good campaign for independent-mindedness. When the campaign managers say they want impartial reporting, they seem to mean reporting which either favours them or which at least does not point out their shortcomings; at the same time, they hope for actively hostile reporting of the other parties. All this may be a political ploy, but it is also their right in a democratic society. Once the election is over, though, are politicians (on the evidence they have so far shown us) really going to be the right people to judge the objectivity of the broadcasters? The main distinction between Dr Sa'ad and the British political party media manipulators is that a democratic society does not allow them the same kind of scope or the same kind of control as Saddam Hussein allowed him. We hope.

28 March 1992

BOADICEA FOR THE MODERN WORLD

Francis Wheen

Most weeks, the classified section of the *Paddington Mercury* carries about a hundred advertisements under the heading 'Massage'. The purveyors of these rub-downs usually give their first names only – or, rather, the pseudonyms that they hope will justify the adjective 'exotic' in their advert: Adriana, Amber, Anina, Britta, Corina. But two advertisers print surnames as well. There is 'affectionate, caring, educated Sara Dale', Norman Lamont's former lodger, who offers 'sensual massage to discerning clients'. And there is 'Rent-a-Fantasy. Call Lindi St Clair.'

I called Lindi St Clair. The phone was answered by her maid. 'Madame

specialises in kinky sex and bondage,' she said briskly: '£50 for a f—
and a suck, £40 for dressing up, and £100 an hour for a kinky mixture
– that's a bit of everything.' She added: 'The more you spend, the more
you get.' It is a truth which neither Norman Lamont nor John Smith
would deny.

Any politician who grumbles about long hours should study Lindi's
routine: from 11 a.m. to 7 p.m. every day of the week, including
Sundays, she thrashes and fondles clients in her basement flat near
the Earls Court exhibition centre; in spare moments she writes her
autobiography; and she leads a political party.

Lindi St Clair is – has – a striking figure – 'a Boadicea for the Modern
World', one of her leaflets modestly suggests – and the programme of
her Corrective Party is both succinct and radical. After a trudge through
the other parties' interminable manifestos, the Corrective 'statement
of policies' is as bracing as a gin-and-lime: 'Equalise the age of consent
for homosexuals and heterosexuals . . . Permit Sunday trading . . . Tax
the monarch's private wealth and profits . . . Legalise cannabis . . .
Proportional Representation . . . Better burial rights, e.g. at sea, or
on private land . . . More scientific research into obesity, calories and
metabolism.' There is some self-interest in this last policy: speaking
'as a fat person', St Clair points out that smokers and alcoholics can
get help from their doctors 'but alas, poor fatties are told "you must
have will-power" and are left to their own devices'.

When I first spoke to the new Boadicea, at the beginning of March,
she told me that Corrective candidates would 'definitely' be standing in
at least 50 constituencies, entitling the party to a five-minute election
broadcast. Ken Russell had volunteered to direct it, but his budget of
£45,000 was rather more than the Corrective Party could afford. 'So
we're going to go the cheap route and get this chap round the corner
who does wedding videos,' she told me with a raucous laugh. 'He
charges £700 a day and can get it all done for about £3,000. It's going
to be filmed down my brothel with my girls. I'm going to show the
nice side of prostitution which no one ever talks about. We pay tax,
yet we're criminalised at the same time.'

For someone who had just been socked by the Inland Revenue with
a tax demand for £68,000, the Correctives' leader seemed remarkably
cheerful. But when next I telephoned her, at the beginning of the
election campaign, she was in a foul mood. 'I don't want to speak to
the press,' she snarled. '*The Spectator*? That's Labour trash, isn't it?'
She then put the phone down on me.

After I had mollified her with a flattering fax, she rang back. 'Sorry
about that,' she said. 'It's just that we're fed up with the media

trivialising us.' What most irks her is that newspapers always refer to her occupation and her nickname. 'I've not called myself Miss Whiplash for three years. The *Sun* made up that name for me in the 1980s. The days of Miss Whiplash and prostitutes and brothels are over now. I've had two apologies from the *Western Mail* and the *Guardian* for the way they've written about me. I'm not going to put up with it any more.' Henceforth, she announced, the Corrective Party would have nothing to do with journalists. Nor, for that matter, would it be holding meetings, or canvassing, or hiring poster sites. 'We're putting all our energy into doing our party broadcast. The BBC reckon it'll get the same viewing figures as that documentary about the Queen.'

She sent me the script. I was puzzled to notice that, in spite of St Clair's unwillingness to have her name associated with prostitution, at least a third of the film was to be about the oldest profession. Still, it sounded a good deal more stimulating than the ghastly B-movies served up by Hugh Hudson and John Schlesinger on behalf of Messrs Kinnock and Major.

Regrettably, however, we shan't have the chance to see it: last week, harried by the Inland Revenue, Lindi St Clair decided that the Corrective Party could not afford to contest 50 seats after all. Although some newspapers reported that she might still stand herself – against Chris Patten, in Bath – last Sunday night she told me that she would probably not bother. Instead, she is exhorting her fans, clients and sex-slaves ('these submissives – they do as I tell them') to switch their votes to the Liberal Democrats.

Paddy Ashdown seems a poor substitute for the Spanker of SW5. Asked for the Liberal policy on burials at sea and research into obesity, a spokeswoman at Cowley Street told me: 'I'm sorry, I haven't the first clue.' After a brief consultation with a colleague, she returned with an official Liberal statement: 'I understand from our Director of Policy that we have never made any comment on either of those.'

Meanwhile, Lindi is hoping for a hung parliament and another election in the autumn, by which time she ought to have raised the £25,000 necessary for 50 deposits. She boasts that she has 'gone back on the game' with new zeal, charging £300 for an evening and £1,000 for a whole night in her company. (It seems no worse as a fund-raising wheeze than the Labour Party's £500-a-head dinners at the Park Lane Hotel.) If Lindi St Clair can find 25 men who want to pay a grand for the privilege of waking up next to a dominatrix, the Corrective Party may hold the balance of power before the year is out.

28 March 1992

LOW LIFE

SURVIVAL OF THE UNFITTEST

Jeffrey Bernard

I don't think I would have had the operation had I known beforehand just what it would entail. Before I went into hospital I was given the impression that it would be a straightforward 30-minute job during a 24-hour stay inside. I knew that they were worried about my ability to withstand a general anaesthetic but I didn't realise they were that worried until the second day of tests on my lungs, liver and heart.

In the event I was out for just over four hours. Anxiety is infectious and the cysts grew in my mind if not on my head, although the consultant anaesthetist, a charming but formidable woman, somewhat jocularly asked me for a tip for the Grand National shortly before the operation. When I woke up in a darkened side ward I was in some pain and it increased considerably during the following three hours. Eventually they decided it was being caused by a build-up of pressure of the blood inside the wound and so they inserted a tube in my head to drain it away. After a while I tried to sit up in bed and by so doing accidentally tore the tube out. The result was nothing if not spectacular. A fountain of blood, later estimated at a pint, shot over the bed and on to the floor and completely soaked the gown I was wearing. I was only surprised and thought it would stop if I held the wound.

And then the angel of mercy, Belinda, an expert nursing sister, arrived to stem the flow. She stood by my side for no less than two hours pressing swabs on the reopened wound, exerting great pressure, and still the river ran. During that time (it happened at 1 a.m.) the surgical team was aroused: the surgeon, two anaesthetists, a registrar and another doctor. While they examined the flow I thought it was a nuisance and even reflected that blood is a very pretty if not spectacular colour. I asked Belinda if I could keep the gown as a souvenir to throw in the face later of any editor likely to accuse me of malingering.

But then I saw that awful look of anxiety come over their faces again. They decided on an emergency operation there and then and I suddenly realised that they were wondering whether the bag of bones with two holes in the head could withstand two general anaesthetics within 12 hours.

'I'm feeling a little peaky.'

As I went under for the second time the would-be lady Grand National punter later told me I asked her, 'Why aren't I panicking?' Why not indeed. I came to in the intensive care unit with an oxygen mask over my face and a catheter in my bladder, a new experience for me. I am glad I didn't suffer the insertion of that while conscious.

It took three days to metabolise the toxic effects of the anaesthetics but my throat is still sore and swollen because of the tube for gas they stick in it once you go under. I was then anaemic due to the loss of blood. The nurses helped me out to the landing outside the ward when I wanted to smoke a cigarette and it is always on the landings by the lifts in hospitals where patients congregate to chat and smoke. Anti-smoking lobbyists should have the grace to realise that smoking is occupational therapy. I discovered I was surrounded by people suffering from that dread illness pancreatitis. Until then I thought I was almost the only man in the world who had suffered from it. One day I said to a man out there, 'I suppose you've got pancreatitis too?' He said, 'As a matter of fact, I've got cancer of the pancreas.' And he said it in a matter-of-fact way too. He shrugged his shoulders at what is almost certainly a death sentence.

But after all the blood, pain and anxiety what I remember best and with great affection is my heroine, Belinda. I don't know what would have happened without her. Waterloo without Wellington? The chocolates I gave her when I left were miserably inadequate. A good and kind woman.

28 March 1992

LONG LIFE

AN ACT OF UNSELFISHNESS

Nigel Nicolson

On every 28 March I think of Virginia Woolf, why she drowned herself in the Sussex Ouse on that day in 1941 and why she chose that horrifying method. Imagine her half-mile walk from her house to the river and how she stuffed a big stone into the pocket of her overcoat, laid her walking-stick on the bank (as a marker, I suppose), threw herself into the cold water, struggled not to swim, and sank. All this time she had at home the lethal dose of morphia which Leonard had provided for both of them in case the Germans landed at Newhaven, only three miles away.

As I edited the last volume of her letters and read what she had written almost gaily to her friends, planning future meetings to mislead them, all the while knowing what she intended, having indeed tried unsuccessfully to drown herself in a dyke ten days before her actual suicide, I wondered whether the coroner's explanation that she was insane could be true. Her letters and diary (but there is no diary entry later than 24 March), the handwriting of her three suicide notes, all seem normal. The war distressed her, of course, but its drama had excited her to unwonted patriotism. It is true that she was not content with her last novel, *Between the Acts*, telling John Lehmann that she intended to revise it drastically, and that Leonard had noticed that her mental condition was more ominous than it had been at any time since 1913. But mad? She was not mad when she died. She *feared* madness. She was beginning once again to hear voices. In the middle of the war she would impose an intolerable burden on Leonard if, as a sort of Mrs Rochester, she was confined to a bedroom at Rodmell, unable to write, perhaps unable to move. Death was preferable. She had always been preoccupied with death. It was a sort of magnet, drawing her towards the river. That was the best explanation I could manage in 1980.

Since then, I have read accounts of Virginia's suicide which put the blame on Leonard. He should never have left her alone. Some writers have accused him of insensitiveness towards her genius, weakening her resolve to live and work, even of conniving at her death. Could these authors have seen them, just once, together, as I often did, they would have realised the absurdity of the charge. The Woolfs' marriage was of course unconventional. They slept always under the same roof but not since the earliest years under the same ceiling. They respected each other's independence and guarded it against outsiders. But it was always to Leonard that Virginia would first show her books in typescript and await his judgment with trust and dread. It was a relationship of mutual love, encouragement and support.

Once when I was on a visit to Rodmell as a boy and they were discussing women's disadvantages, Virginia grew so animated that Leonard, watching her, suddenly rose and touched her on the shoulder. Without a word of protest or enquiry she followed him upstairs, where they remained for some ten minutes. When they returned, nobody referred to their absence. Everyone except me knew that Leonard had seen in her excitement the warning signals of insanity.

I shall always remember that gesture. It was almost biblical in its tenderness. She by her response expressed all the trust she had in him. In her last letter to her sister Vanessa she wrote, 'L. has been so astonishingly good, every day, always'; and to him, 'I don't think that two people could have been happier than we have been . . . I know that I shall never get over this, and I am wasting your life'. So when I think of her walking across those sodden meadows to her death, I know that her suicide was as much an act of unselfishness as a symbol of despair. As Olivier Bell has written, 'It had a certain valiancy'.

28 March 1992

'IT WAS WHAT WE BELIEVED'

Simon Heffer

There is one respect in which the election campaign has changed hearts and minds. In their hearts and minds, many who wrote off Mrs Thatcher as the woman who could not win the Tories the election, and who wanted her kept as far away from the campaign as possible, now suspect they have made a mistake.

This week Mrs Thatcher went to Essex. She spent most of her day in the more rural part, well away from the heartland of that brash Thatcherite invention, Essex Man. Only a few press, mainly photographers, awaited her. They had been deterred by her apparent lack of bile towards Mr Major, and her infuriating insistence that she wants him to win.

'Today,' a party activist told me when I arrived at Maldon on a filthy, raining morning, 'you will see our people meet the woman they still regard as their true leader.' That is not to say that dear, nice Mr Major is held in low esteem in these parts; not a bit of it. 'If he came here, I think you'd find he was quite popular,' a genteel lady said, defensively, in response to the inevitable comparison. Yet, if Tory leaders are regarded by the troops as royalty, Mrs Thatcher is the Queen Mother to Mr Major's Princess Margaret. A few days earlier, a Minister said to me: 'Do you know, in the last election the ladies stuffing envelopes would be talking all the time about Mrs Thatcher. She really inspired them. I don't think I've heard them mention Major once.'

Mrs Thatcher's pain at the departure from fiscal rectitude by the Government she once led is no secret. She is, though, passionate for a Tory victory, optimistic that things may yet be put right and still filled with hate at the prospect of socialism. Those waiting for her to (as they say in Essex) go nuclear about the Tories' retreat from Thatcherism will need to wait until after 9 April. As she will have been abroad for the week before polling day, she promises to say nothing until she has gauged the mood of the party and the country. Beyond that there are no promises. On the day of the Dissolution of Parliament an admirer expressed the hope to her that she would not fade away in the Lords. 'I shall be a real irritant,' she replied, fiercely.

She moves serenely among her loyal subjects. She knows that had it been up to them in November 1990 she would not now be the leader of the internal opposition. In Essex, which (until the recession) had benefited spectacularly from Thatcherism, her legend is rampant. Mr Major happens to be Prime Minister. She, however, is Britain's most famous politician.

'Are you sorry to be going to America on Wednesday?' the press barked as soon as they could get at her. 'I'm a born campaigner. But I have to keep my commitments. We Tories always keep our commitments.'

'Do you really believe there is not enough oomph in the campaign?' came the next bark. 'That's what I'm doing, dear. I'm putting the oomph in it.' Mrs Thatcher's real view of the campaign is obvious. Conservative Central Office run their campaign completely unlike the way she runs hers. As it happens, she doesn't think Central Office is right.

Her day had begun in an electronics factory, where she motored around busily asking questions about circuit diagrams and being charming to the typists. Despite having visited hundreds if not thousands of such factories across the world, she still manages to seem enthusiastic about them. However, you could tell she was dying to get out and impart the message.

So she went to Maldon High Street, among bemused shoppers and children dragged from their lessons to witness this moment in the history of Maldon. People of both genders, whom she has never met before, have an extraordinary habit of telling her they love her. They beg for her autograph, and she (to the consternation of her party minders, but with the active assistance of her Special Branch detectives) stops to sign them.

Laden with flowers, she lectured bewildered passers-by about the iniquities of socialism. She quickly made it clear that the Liberals are socialists too. 'They kept the socialists in power until 1979. They allowed the socialists to have a top tax rate of 98 per cent!' It was the first sign of her convictions; and the rest of the day was to be more stuffed with convictions than the Old Bailey.

The conviction thing frightens the new unconvicted Tory party. Even in private, Mrs Thatcher said nothing in Essex in direct criticism of the Prime Minister and his policies; but every castigation of the socialists for their craven attitude towards Europe and their promiscuous view of public spending was a two-edged weapon, a code to conceal her real feelings. She damned the socialists for policies already discharged by this Government. She feels acute distress at the spectacle of a Tory Public Sector Borrowing Requirement of £28 billions.

I was asked to a private lunch given for her by the Maldon constituency at a rainswept golf club. I was, though, firmly told that her speech would be entirely off the record, 'just in case'. This depressed me, for there was some strong stuff in it. It was therefore most helpful that, an hour later at another golf club in Chelmsford, she delivered an expanded and undiluted version of the same speech, on the record, to a rally there.

As at the private lunch, the sense of expectation and excitement among her audience was debilitating. The Chairman of the Chelmsford Association, fighting to restrain his emotions, proclaimed that 'there is no one else in the world I would be prouder to introduce today than you'. The faithful roared with adulation; at last there was someone great to motivate them. 'The utmost pride,' continued the Chairman, still – just – containing himself. 'I've only been Chairman for three weeks. After this it's downhill all the way.'

Mrs Thatcher's opening demolition of the socialist case was followed by a plea for a government that 'does not follow, but leads'. This call for the unavailable came in a crescendo designed for applause, but no one clapped. It was not apathy; the faithful were simply too overwhelmed by this militant, vigorous and angry spectre, so unlike anything else seen these last three weeks.

'Come on, clap!' she cried. 'Aren't you pleased about that?'

Once they had clapped, she carried on. Socialists were bad because they spent too much money. 'Your money!' she roared, in that tone that does not brook contradiction. The code broke out again. 'You just have to learn to say no!' she seethed, that £28 billion (and rising) deficit in her sights. 'To coin a phrase, you have to say no, no, no!

'There are too many people who interpret democracy as keeping your seat by promising all sorts of things other taxpayers have to pay for. They think all they have to do is say yes, and the money appears.'

There were signs of mild agitation at this point among the one or two Major loyalists present, not least the Social Security Secretary, Mr Tony Newton, who is standing in the adjoining constituency, and just happened to be passing by.

'We had sound financial policies! We held down our public expenditure!' It was all becoming rather pointed. 'Our finances were so sound we did not have to borrow a penny piece for four years. We brought taxes down. And we had a surplus that we could use to repay our debts. That was sound Conservative government!' We waited with interest for examples to be given of an unsound one.

The nods of agreement and approbation among the true believers who had packed the golf club dining-room almost to the point of causing it structural damage showed quite clearly where their opinions lay.

'It was a matter of principle with us. It was what we believed,' she banged on. Note the careful use of the past tense.

Nothing gets the faithful going more rabidly than Europe, and Mrs Thatcher was, as always, ready with her answer. She had rid this country of socialist evils, 'and we do not want them coming back now in the guise of a socialist charter from the socialist Delors and the unelected European Commission. We have different ways of doing things.' This was the great unexplored issue of the campaign. One suspects that, were she in charge still, the talk these last few weeks would have been of little else.

Mrs Thatcher's vivid language, her direct appeal to the emotions, her confrontationalism, are exactly what the Conservative Party needed in an election where its own lack of conviction has allowed it too easily to be forced on to the defensive. Her language is of a type it is hard to imagine any current minister using. There is her rampant patriotism and nationalism ('Britain defeated half of Europe and rescued the other half'), and memories of the glory days of the Falklands and the miners' strike: 'We had to fight because we believed what we were doing was right. We had the guts to see it through.'

Her words were as remarkable for what was not said as for what was. The record she praised was her record, the record of the eleven-and-a-half years. Mr Major was mentioned only in a recherché reference to his superiority to the other two party leaders when being interviewed on television; the Government's policies of the last 16 months not at all. Now she is in America, not to return until half-an-hour before the polls close. She has done her best, and can say (if the worst happens) that she had no part in a Tory defeat.

4 April 1992

THE HEREDITARY PRINCIPLE

Rebecca Nicolson

In July 1963, some months after the death of his father, the second Lord Milford attended the House of Lords to make his maiden speech.

The occasion was the second reading of the Peerage Bill, a measure sparked by attempts of the former Anthony Wedgwood Benn to cast off the unwanted burden of an inherited peerage. Not surprisingly, the Bill had stirred many of their Lordships to strenuous defence of their parliamentary privileges and position. Wogan Milford, educated at Eton and Magdalen College, Oxford, was welcomed by his old friends and contemporaries into the warm folds of their Lordships' House.

He proceeded to betray them. His speech urged the immediate abolition of the House, 'an undemocratic anachronism, composed of the inheritors of wealth and privilege and bent on their protection, and an indefensible obstacle to progressive legislation and the forward march of world socialism'. The House of Lords, he declared, was anathema to his party. (Several Lords: 'Which party is that?') Britain's only Communist member of Parliament had hoisted the red flag in the Upper Chamber, and the sight proved most unwelcome.

Now 90, and living in a modest flat in Hampstead, Milford remembers the appalled reaction. 'They were friends from Eton and Oxford, you see, and so they regarded this as a class betrayal. When I left the House, there was a tense silence,' he explains.

It fell to Earl Attlee to offer customary congratulations. 'There are many anomalies in this country,' said Attlee. 'One curious one is that the voice of the Communist Party can only be heard in this House. That, of course, is an advantage of the hereditary principle.'

Still a believer ('Even though the Communist Party no longer exists, I am still a communist,' he announced on his 90th birthday last month), married for 38 years to the widow of a former editor of the *Daily Worker*, Wogan Milford is one of the last survivors of that generation of upper-class Englishmen (and women: Lady Mosley is another) whose lives reflected the eccentricities and misconceptions of the first half of this century.

His father, who was made a baron in 1939, came from an old but impoverished family: the sons of a rural clergyman, he and two of his brothers made huge fortunes through shipping and insurance before and during the first world war, and were duly ennobled. In the early 1920s, Milford (then Wogan Philipps) graced the London débutante scene and worked in the family shipping business. His life first changed direction when in 1928 he married the novelist Rosamond Lehmann (then married to the heir to another family shipping fortune), whose first book, *Dusty Answer*, had brought her fame. 'Through her I got on the fringe of the Bloomsbury world. I met intelligence for the first time. It knocked away all the things I'd been brought up to value, the values, or lack of values, of the snobbish upper classes.'

At least on the fringe, the 'Bloomsbury world' was less austere and intellectually rigorous than it is sometimes portrayed. Milford's good looks (commented on by all his contemporaries) and high spirits endeared him to his new circle.

In the early 1930s, he and Rosamond went on holiday to Spain with their Bloomsbury friends Ralph and Frances Partridge. Milford fell in love with the country. In 1936, early in the Civil War, following his friend Julian Bell, he and Stephen Spender drove out to join the International Brigade.

It was not a political decision. 'When I set out, I wasn't a political animal at all.' The light in his eyes as he remembers those days makes it clear that the whole thing was an adventure, a lark, rather as driving buses through picket lines in the General Strike had been for the same generation. For the English upper classes, political conviction – if it comes at all – follows on the heels of romantic enthusiasm. Once in Spain, Milford's life changed again. 'I met a whole new set of people, the unemployed working classes. It was a new world for me.'

He was badly wounded when a shell hit his ambulance, returned to England, and then returned to Spain. Unable to serve in the front line, he took advantage of his family connections, no thanks to any co-operation from his father, to organize shipping to break Franco's blockade.

'It was a very exciting time. My family, of course, wanted me to come back, but I stayed until Franco had won. Then I had the job of getting refugees out of Spain. I found an old ship, the *Mecca*, which took thousands of refugees, packed like sardines, to Mexico. They were mostly children – I don't know what happened to them.'

As one war ended in 1939, the next began. Milford failed on medical grounds to get into the Merchant Navy, and spent the second world war, in true Orwellian spirit, working as an agricultural labourer on a large government farm in Gloucestershire.

His marriage to Rosamond Lehmann had not survived his departure for Spain. In 1944 Milford married Cristina, Countess of Huntingdon, a staunch communist whom he had met in the Civil War. (Cristina, daughter of the legendary hostess, the Marchesa Malu Casati, died in 1953.) 'We read a lot of Marxism together. We found we agreed on it.' After the war, he too became a member of the Party. 'My father wrote to me and said, "Any child of mine who joins the Communist Party will not get a penny." I never really spoke to my father after that.' On the first Lord Milford's death in 1962, his son was indeed left nothing.

The decades after the war were spent farming ('I introduced artificial insemination to Gloucestershire'), painting and spreading the word. Milford's entry in *Who's Who* summarises his political career:

Former member of Henley on Thames RDC; Communist Councillor, Cirencester RDC, 1946–49; has taken active part in building up National Union of Agricultural Workers in Gloucestershire and served on its county committee. Prospective Party candidate (Labour), Henley on Thames, 1938–39; contested (Con) Cirencester and Tewkesbury, 1950.

'I lost my deposit – oh God, yes!' He polled 423 votes, less than 1 per cent of the votes cast, in the constituency later represented by Nicholas Ridley.

Ridley is Milford's godson. Woodrow Wyatt was his stepson-in-law, although Wyatt's early socialist commitments were rather more short-lived than those of his single-minded stepfather-in-law. Family lore has it that when Nicholas Ridley was standing for parliament in Cirencester and Tewkesbury, Ridley's agent rang him to say that his godfather,

'Luckily a building society uses an old song of mine about smashing the system on a telly ad'

Wogan Milford, was standing against him in the Communist interest. 'Oh good, that'll split the Labour vote,' was Ridley's response. When eventually Ridley asked Milford if this really was the case, Milford said, 'I'll stand if you lend me the £150 deposit.'

His former son-in-law, P. J. Kavanagh, recalls how at political meetings Milford would be 'chased by agricultural students, who would suddenly haul up and say, "Hang on chaps, he's a gentleman!" And during the war his telephone was bugged, and he would occasionally get so fed up he would say, "Oh come on, constable, get off the line," to which the constable would reply, "Sorry, sir."'

Kavanagh also describes how occasionally delegations from the Soviet Union would come down to the farm at weekends to shoot with the communist peer. 'They would all stand round a rabbit hole. As Wogan said, if a rabbit had ever appeared, the comrades would all have shot each other.'

Less charmingly English are the passions which this most courteous and well-mannered man seems to arouse in his political opponents. After his maiden speech, Milford was largely ostracised in the House of Lords, even though for many years he spoke for his party at least twice a week ('on Vietnam, on Nicaragua, on the abolition of the House of Lords'). On the Rural District Council, feelings ran even higher. 'They were all Tories except me, and in the meetings notes were passed round about me, things like "Doesn't he stink!" They were all very rude – I was rather proud of fighting them.' He lost his seat in 1949 by 14 votes. 'The Tories mobilised every vote they could. They didn't just get people out of hospital, they organised a smear campaign. "We'll never allow Colesbourne to become another Hungary," they said.'

The extraordinary thing is that his opponents were so blinded by his communist label that they failed to see that Lord Milford would never have allowed it either. He is much too English, too much a product of his own background, for anything like that. Stalin 'became an enemy when the truth emerged'.

His two visits to the Soviet Union left him 'very disappointed. I went to look at their farming. It was very bad. No one knew about agriculture.' These days he feels keenly that communism as put into practice has failed. 'The problem is ethnic.' Their Lordships need not have worried about the Red in their midst: at the end of the day, as the agricultural students of Cirencester realised, a gentleman is a gentleman. That, of course, is an advantage of the hereditary principle.

4 April 1992

FEAR OF TRYING

James Michie

Suddenly, in my late forties, I resolved to do the three things which had always filled me with special fear. They were: to attend one of those Californian-style, personality-expanding, inhibition-lessening group encounters, to parachute, and to answer a sex advertisement in person.

I was frightened of the first because I'm only at ease with individuals or very small groups. Crowds, even demonstrations I'm part of, give me the jimjams. Nevertheless, I signed on and paid for a course of 12 evenings in St John's Wood and arrived punctually, equipped, as ever, with cigars and hip-flask. I accepted their immediate confiscation, but I struggled a bit when I was asked to remove my shoes. I was then led into a room in which over a dozen people were sitting in a circle, shoeless and cross-legged. Perversely, I adopted some different posture, but it was soon adjusted to the norm by an assistant therapist. I smiled in what I thought was an all-embracing way and looked round – not a single face that one would be drawn towards at a party, let alone one that, *faute de mieux*, one might pick out if a train stopped in a tunnel for three hours.

During that evening, between coffee-breaks, we publicly confessed our woes and inadequacies, we did little solo dances to express our unexpressed aggression, we pretended to be animals (I thought I did well as a jerboa, but had to be histrionically captured and devoured by wee Kevin, who had chosen the role of desert wolf), we wrestled (I was 'too rough'), we played 'truth games' (in which I was much the best liar), and we each had to have a cross-legged, eyeball-to-eyeball personal confrontation with the Leader, a girl from the mid-West who was built like a buffalo but had just been impersonating a vole. At last I was on home ground, one to one. 'Why don't you like me?' she led off. 'Why are you frightened of me?' 'But I do like you,' I lied. 'If I'm nervous, it's only because I feel there may be a current of sexual attraction between us. Do you like me?' 'No. Isn't it obvious I don't?' We got no deeper or further.

I left a few minutes before the end, reclaiming my shoes and life-support equipment. Glancing back into the room, I saw that wee Kevin, egged on by the rest of the group, was beating an elderly Viennese lady on the bottom with a sort of bladder which caused thunderous repercussions but apparently no pain. I had 11 more sessions ahead of me. You can guess the rest.

Most people are scared of parachuting, but I was extra scared because I had lost my head for heights – I had recently had to be talked round a section of the Tower of Pisa on hands and knees, a jelly of nerves. (I remember kissing the earth when I got down.) Feeling the need of company for this exploit, I engaged to do a jump with my young brother-in-law, a pilot, and four of his friends. Off we went to the Metropolitan Police training centre in Hertfordshire for two weekends' instruction. My notion of parachuting was based on old war films: I imagined you simply fell, almost willy-nilly, through a hole in the plane's floor, pulled the ripcord and hoped for the best, and I reckoned I might just be able to do that. I was now shaken to learn that although the ripcord was going to be pulled automatically (not really reassuring, I would rather have done it myself) I should have to climb out of the cockpit onto a platform the size of a very occasional table, grip the wing-tip with both hands and throw myself backwards into the sky in the 'seagull' position, shouting, as I fell, the ritual chant, 'One thousand, two thousand, three thousand . . .' etc. With black-humoured relish the instructor added advice for emergencies, such as when the automatic ripcord-pulling device failed or your descent entangled you in high-tension wires ('Not much hope then, mate').

The day came. Waking with a hangover, I felt like Tweedledum – 'I'm very brave generally, only today I happen to have a headache.' We drove down to a small aerodrome in Kent on a nippy November day. Our plane was not there, due to engine trouble. After two hours of hanging about, it arrived – mended, we only half hoped. Although my lightly gloved hands felt too cold to grip anything, it had to be done, and it was. My companions all went down like parcels and duly landed near the drop zone. I made the mistake of trying to be clever. In training I had been encouraged to use some strings for steering called 'toggles', and these I tugged like mad, hoping to score a bull's-eye landing. The result was that I went a mile adrift, came down in a marsh and had to be recovered by a special van. I was quite proud of my mud-spattered self, until I was greeted back at the aerodrome by my small son, Jake, with 'What a rotten jump that was, Dad!' Still, I remained grateful to the Metropolitan Police, for they had given us all a Parachute Club sticker for our cars, which made illegal parking almost safe for years.

My fear of answering the advertisement is harder to explain. I suppose I was alarmed by the thought of, yet curious about, commercial or arranged sex, which I had never experienced. I wasn't at all sure whether I wanted to experience it or not. Accordingly, late one autumn afternoon, I travelled to a remote-sounding address – something like 237B Majuba Road – in north London, in response to what read like a simple invitation. As I walked down the long road under a light drizzle, I imagined significant glances from passers-by or men tinkering with their cars. I rang the bell. The door was opened by no Madame La Zonga but a mousy, average-looking girl who led me upstairs to a bookless but magazine-filled sitting-room, furnished with an electric fire, nothing comfortable to sit on, and several lurid pictures, including a bare-breasted negress I'd often seen on the walls of East End pubs.

We made conversation about the weather, buses, the news in the *Evening Standard*. Her husband, she mentioned, was a photographer. To my surprise, he now entered left on cue and offered me a cup of cocoa with such nervous solicitude that I guessed at once that he was hoping, on or off stage, to play a part in any possible scene. I made up my mind to leave as soon as I politely could. Immediately after that decision I felt more at home, and we chatted for 20 minutes. Don and Sandra were a pleasant, sad couple. They loved each other, she said, but couldn't have children and weren't any good in bed together. They'd previously lived in Slough and attended some wife-swapping parties, but it hadn't worked and they didn't like 'the type of person' involved.

So I was a writer? . . . Great! They enjoyed reading too, and ice-skating. Seeing that I was in imminent danger of passing their suitability test with flying colours, I made my excuses and promised I would ring them again soon and visit them. They waved me goodbye from the doorstep. I think of them still; I'm certain they never think of me.

4 April 1992

ART

TYCOON'S BUZZ

Giles Auty

Why is Mr Charles Saatchi apparently an obsessive collector of modern art?

I am afraid that why many people behave as they do must remain one of life's more unnerving mysteries. Indeed, why a very large audience of outwardly intelligent people sat through the whole of the Walter Neurath Memorial Lecture delivered at Senate House very recently by famous feminist art historian Griselda Pollock is a puzzle which will go on haunting me for the rest of my life.

As I wandered the whited acres of Mr Saatchi's shrine to new art, a brilliantly converted paint factory at 98A Boundary Road, NW8, last week, surveying his latest acquisitions (*Young British Artists*), no obvious answer presented itself to explain his actions. Someone suggested to me once that it must be the power to choose which talentless artist to elevate to heights of modish fame that appeals to him. To possess a godlike power to make random interventions into human affairs may well have some attraction but I do not think this is the answer. Looking about me at mounds of mouldering blowflies and such, the pleasure of ownership, in any ordinary sense, seems a fairly unlikely explanation also. Nor is any consistent taste, other than for novelty, perhaps, readily discernible in Mr Saatchi's vast range of purchases. Some regard him as a shrewd businessman whose sheer weight of spending has influenced the market. Others see him more kindly as our sole American-style patron who shows concern for an avant-garde which is neglected cruelly otherwise by the beastly British. Since I know Mr Saatchi slightly, though largely as a tennis player, the easiest solution might be to ask him the nature of the buzz he gets from buying entire exhibitions of modern art simply by telephoning him. But as he is reputedly shy and ill at ease with the press – on this particular subject, at least – to do so could seem an unjustified intrusion.

Travelling home from Mr Saatchi's remarkable gallery, replete with its latest example of ichthyolatry – a tiger shark in a tank – and other putrefying phenomena, my eye lit by chance on the main story in the *Evening Standard*. Although its subject was the Duchess of York, the insight it provided may well account not just for Mr Saatchi's idiosyncratic-seeming behaviour but for that of many of the artists he collects. The *Evening Standard*'s story was of the apparent rift between the Duchess and advisers to royalty within Buckingham Palace, the cause being the former's feckless-seeming behaviour. Oddly, instead of exhorting the Duchess to act more circumspectly, the Palace had preferred to plump for a public relations palliative. In short, image, rather than duty, was perceived as the crux of the problem. Indeed, no matter how indifferently the Duchess might behave, the trick was to persuade the rest of us to believe otherwise.

Those with memories of any length will recall that Mr Saatchi's own background – and the basis of his fortune and princely levels of artistic patronage – is the wonderful world of publicity, wherein if a product or service can be presented plausibly enough the pounds and pfennigs will positively leap from our pockets. Much of Mr Saatchi's business fame rests on his erstwhile company's successful presentation of the Conservative Party. But would not his company and all the skilled minds it employs have been just as happy selling political parties of some other hue, provided only that the colour of their money was essentially correct? Publicity is a realm in which skills are for hire and wherein personal beliefs of any kind can prove inconvenient impediments. How many covert socialists were obliged to work on the Conservative Party account? Publicity is a force which not only makes some things happen – increased sales of baked beans or hairspray – but makes others appear to happen: an amelioration in the Duchess of York's sense of responsibility, for instance. If the good journalist's world is one of fact, the good advertising man's is one of fancy. The latter's aim is to elide reality and illusion to an extent where they gradually become indistinguishable in the mind of the consumer. This kind of mental manipulation does not happen only in consumer societies, of course. It is also the standard practice of propagandists in every type of totalitarian régime: one has only to think of the poor citizens of the USSR who seldom got the chance to consume anything. But all the countless thousands of lies printed in the pages of *Pravda* could never really affect the truth of what happened one iota. As the Soviet communist régime has crumbled away, the truth of its cruelty, corruption and inefficiency stands exposed like a reef at low tide. The true grimness of the Soviet régime was known for all the years of its existence, of course, to all the people who suffered under it. We may pride ourselves on our freedoms in democratic countries, yet yield unwittingly to such intellectual tyrannies as modernism, feminism or political correctness which rely for their influence similarly on methods of mass persuasion rather than on reasoned argument.

Mr Saatchi seems happy enough to play the role of an inspired collector of avant-garde art. Many believe him to be an enigmatic encourager of genius in others because they have read this frequently in the papers. Regrettably, I feel the distinctions between real and apparent may no longer be entirely clear even to Mr Saatchi himself. I blame this on his former profession. Of the tests I would apply to establish a wealthy connoisseur, Mr Saatchi qualifies only in wealth and willingness, for I cannot discern any consistency, pattern or particular inspiration in his buying. More to the point, as the sole mover now in forming the collection that bears his name he seems unable and unwilling to explain his aims, leaving this task to the doubtful competence of others. Few do a plausible or even intelligible job. Langlands and Bell, exhibitors in the collection's current show, attract the following language in a reprint handed me by the collection's publicity department:

> This repetition involves what henceforth shall be called the logic of the again and anew. Marking out a co-presence which is never a simple presence. Not simple because, as will be suggested, the origin is diremptive: anoriginally diremptive. . . .

In flight from such language I turned to a text by the ever-articulate Andrew Graham-Dixon, art critic of the *Independent*, describing work by another of the current show's youthful exhibitors:

> The fact that the Shark appears to move contributes to its considerable power as an object of contemplation. It is a paradox made solid, this creature, at once frighteningly dynamic and completely still. It is, of course, a vanitas, albeit of an unusual kind: a work of art that prompts reflections on death, its inevitability and our habit of avoiding that most unsavoury and basic fact of our existence. . . .

Those who saw only a slowly decomposing shark in a tank of formaldehyde need not rush either to their opticians or psychiatrists, since Mr Graham-Dixon is merely describing a personal reaction. I must confess that neither the shark in the tank, which is not a work of art, nor another of this particular young man's creations, 'One Thousand Years' (blowflies, maggots, cow's head, insectocutor etc.), which is not a work of art either, prompted any thought of death in me, unless it be by boredom. Nor are rows of cabinets full of discarded pills and potions, by the same artist, works of art, though they may cause other critics than I to contemplate anything from haemorrhoids to hot flushes. One of the major purposes of what was once considered a sound education is that it dissipates the attractions exercised by superficial thinking and writing: its recipient is encouraged to learn how to think clearly. Calmness and clarity of thought are the most potent weapons for cutting through inflated claims of any kind, whether they are found in advertising copy, art reviews or feminist oratory. A basic interest in and instinct for the truth arms us against hustling of all kinds. A person so armed may never be particularly popular or powerful and would probably prefer to end up on the side of angels rather than of Engels. Such a person is never a member of a modish mob.

The current exhibition at the Saatchi Collection purports to introduce the brightest of young British hopefuls to an admiring audience.
The first time I was told about the most publicity-conscious of their
number, I understood his name to be Damien Hearse. As possessor of
what Andrew Graham-Dixon describes as a 'single-minded morbidity',
Mr Hirst should at least consider my recommendation for a new surname. The college at which he studied – Goldsmith's – trains its young
artists in the manipulation of publicity. Clearly Mr Hirst has absorbed
his lessons very well and is already a minor star of the avant-garde
firmament in consequence. Mr Saatchi, like Graham-Dixon, cannot
but see more in Mr Hirst's festering displays than I do. Possibly both
hope to discover the meaning of life from contemplation of foetid
fish or fly-blown skulls. I should admit here that if I were seeking a
philosophical guru, I doubt I would be scouring the ranks of immature
former art students – but then my tastes in art seem different from
theirs, too.

What of the other exhibitors? John Greenwood also seeks to say
something significant, but through surrealist similes. His complex,
organic constructions are drawn and painted carefully and may well be
autobiographical: metaphors for romantic mishaps in bedsit land. Alex
Landrum, by contrast, paints single-colour canvases which conceal,
quite cleverly, the names given by the manufacturers to the household
paints he uses. The process used resembles simple blind-embossing but
moves the critic Sarah Kent, who has written the exhibition catalogue,
to ecstasies of philosophising: 'The proportions of his canvases are
derived from old master paintings so as, subliminally, to affirm their
status as artworks . . .'

Why do Mr Saatchi's exhibitions encourage even semi-respectable
art critics to gush like geysers? There is so little satisfaction or sense
to be extracted from so many of the works on view that it seems to
me an attempt is made to obscure their shortcomings in clouds of
verbal steam. Mr Saatchi is a shrewd and successful man with apparent
ambitions to be remembered as something more. For my part, I hope he
will emerge one day from his veil of vapours and swarm of sycophants
to create an achievement of real rather than simulated substance.

4 April 1992

THREE TIMES A CANDIDATE

Nigel Nicolson

How I longed for elections when I was a candidate, and loathed them when I was an MP. I fought four elections in all, lost two, won two, and was therefore three times the candidate, once the sitting Member. As a candidate I welcomed the election because it might signal my political beginning, and as a Member loathed it because it might mean my political end. Also because I knew that I would be obliged to act out of character.

It may not have been a very fine character, but at least it was my own. In normal times the MP does not need to dissimulate very much. At elections he dissimulates all the time. He must never be seen to agree with his opponents, when he agrees with them 80 per cent, since the rivals are expected to bump off each other like dodgem-cars. He finds himself using combative expressions wholly alien to him. He toes the official line even when he doubts it, and in his election address simply ladles out to the electorate a bowl of soup from the party tureen. He must solicit votes from total strangers, a process insulting to them and humiliating to himself. At public meetings, if he still holds them, he addresses only a handful of the faithful. (Candidates might try attending each other's meetings – there's no rule against it.) He makes no converts, because people do not like being deprived of their prejudices and grievances, but by his manner or his ignorance he can deflect support. By once failing to recognise a local councillor I lost the allegiance of half his ward, and the most effective question I was ever asked at an election meeting was, 'Will the candidate tell us how much half a pound of butter costs?' I had no idea. Remembering Dick Crossman's advice that you can only say 'I don't know' once in the course of an election, I said it, but as I had to say it again later, it was one of the elections I lost.

The trouble is that we have never made up our minds what sort of politicians we want. If the electioneering of candidates is unedifying, so is the ambivalent attitude of the electors, creating what Simon Heffer described in *The Spectator* last week as 'mutual loathing', the candidates sucking up to the electors and the electors treating them as muck. In my political days I tried the sweet reasonableness approach, finding merit in all parties but slightly more merit in mine. It was considered kid-glove, feeble stuff, and I had rapidly to change my tune, becoming aggressive, simulating fire and indignation, and hating myself for doing so.

At the highest level this is also John Major's problem. In him you might think you had every ingredient necessary to attract popular acclaim. He is young, courteous, bright, articulate, sexy, unintellectual, humbly born and unsnobbish, because you cannot be a snob if you are the person people are snobbish about. Yet he is found wanting even by his closest supporters. An elderly lady with a pedigree as long as a sofa said to me last week that she liked John Major, 'but he hasn't got . . .' She paused. 'Class?' I suggested helpfully. 'No, not that.' 'Culture?' (because she is very musical). 'No, no.' 'What then?' 'Spunk,' she eventually replied. I did not suspect that she even knew the word.

Spunk. The capacity to startle, shock, challenge, insult, abuse, the opposite qualities to those which won John Major his arguments at Maastricht. Yet when we see them displayed by Neil Kinnock at his most explosive, we dislike them equally. Politics is without question the most difficult of the performing arts. If I had my time

again, I'd choose a nice, safe, rural-cum-maritime constituency, or a cathedral town, somewhere like Truro, where controversy is rusticated, diminished by being spread through a hundred villages, and everyone knows how much half a pound of butter costs because they make it.

4 April 1992

LORD LANE AND I

Ludovic Kennedy

Next Wednesday morning in the Law Courts, Bench and Bar will assemble to take farewell of Geoffrey Lane, the outgoing Lord Chief Justice. They will pay tribute to him, as is customary on these occasions, for qualities which some see as having marked his term of office: courtesy in court and encouragement to young advocates; the informality which has often characterised his conducting of proceedings and determination not to see time wasted in getting through the business of the day; helpful guidelines to fellow judges in the application of the law; and his uncomplaining mastery of the heavy (and many think unnecessary) workload which is the lot of all Lord Chief Justices. What we shall not hear is any mention of what others see as his failings: impatience with those who fail to meet his high standards; a belief that only judges are qualified to pronounce on sentencing; and, above all, a blindness in rejecting appeals which allege corruption by the police.

It was when he was representing the police at the Brabin inquiry into the case of Timothy Evans (10 Rillington Place) that our paths first crossed. One afternoon after the lunch interval he began his cross-examination of me by asking in a tone of undisguised hostility, 'Mr Kennedy, have you been talking to your counsel during the adjournment?' I said I had, it never having occurred to me not to. Later I was told that in criminal trials counsel are not permitted to talk to their witnesses during adjournments. Yet this was not a criminal trial but a public inquiry. It seemed to me that Lane was attempting to intimidate me so that I should not be too critical of the police, and in this he partly succeeded.

I next ran across him some ten years ago when he was the chief guest and I had some minor role to play at the Scottish Lawyers' annual conference at Aviemore. On the Saturday morning he made an excellent, witty speech, after which we went our separate ways before meeting for a hula-hula cocktail party (lei and Bermuda shorts) in the evening. My wife and I went off in the car to Mr Campbell's famous tweed shop in Beauly, and Geoffrey Lane and others drove to Grantown-on-Spey for a round of golf. At the hula-hula party Lane asked me how I had enjoyed my round. I said I hadn't been playing. He looked unbelieving and said, 'But don't you remember, when we were going down the ninth, you were coming up the eighth and I waved, your wife waved back and then you waved?' I said I had spent the afternoon in Beauly. He said, 'That's extraordinary! *I could have sworn* it was you.' Too late I thought of adding, 'On oath, my lord?', for I have never seen a more striking example of what the law calls 'fleeting identification', and this from a witness to whom I was not a total stranger and who himself, as counsel and judge, had had some experience of judging the worth of ID evidence in court. (It is perhaps worth noting that in 1962 he had helped to prosecute James Hanratty, whose dubious conviction had also rested on a fleeting identification.)

For a year or two after this, we became friends and, as I was then living in Edinburgh and he had a cottage near Dunbar (outside his own jurisdiction), we played the odd round of golf at Luffness (I had recently been blackballed for membership at nearby Muirfield by the Scottish legal establishment for questioning the verdict in the Meehan case) and met on several social occasions. I can now disclose that once, over tea at Luffness, I quizzed him about the Luton post office murder case in which two innocent men had been framed on a murder charge by a corrupt Scotland Yard detective and sentenced to life imprisonment. I had written a book on the case to which Lord Devlin had also contributed, as a result of which Willie Whitelaw, then Home Secretary, ordered the men's immediate and unconditional release. Later, meeting Willie on holiday, I asked why he had not recommended them for a free pardon. 'I wanted to,' he said, 'but Geoffrey Lane objected. When I asked Geoffrey why he objected, he looked embarrassed and muttered something about special considerations.' I had no doubt then, nor have I now, that the special considerations were no more than deep reluctance on his part to have to admit to a wrongful conviction followed by ten years of Appeal Court hearings in which, on no fewer than five occasions, judges like Lawton and Roskill were quite unable to recognise that the men were innocent. I found this closing of establishment ranks deeply shocking. Willie should have ignored Geoffrey's protests and Geoffrey should never have made them. As a result the two framed men are today, many years after their release, still branded as convicted murderers.

Although by this time I had come to know Geoffrey Lane a little and to enjoy his company, I felt that both to the press and public at large he was a somewhat shadowy figure. I therefore floated an invitation to him to dine in a private room in a London club to meet a few senior journalists such as Robin Day, Peregrine Worsthorne and Anthony Howard, etc. The occasion would be off the record, but by a free exchange of views at least some of the press would be enabled to form an idea of the personality and attitudes of the Lord Chief Justice. Disappointingly, he turned the invitation down saying that he had no views worth hearing. A truer explanation, I felt, was that he was a subscriber to Lord Kilmuir's notorious dictum of 1955: 'So long as a judge keeps silent, his reputation for wisdom and impartiality remains unassailable', a view which might be thought to be pushing things a bit and happily not one supported by the present Lord Chancellor.

Time marched on. After 14 years inside, the Guildford Four lodged a further appeal and as the prosecution didn't contest it, Lane quashed the convictions and ordered their release. (But for the blindness of Roskill and his colleagues their convictions would have been quashed at their first appeal 12 years earlier.) For Lane and his fellow judges to have offered an apology to the appellants for what they had suffered would have been a graceful gesture, but it was not in their nature to do so.

A little later, and as a result of some assiduous research by the solicitor Gareth Peirce, the case of the Birmingham Six pub bombings came up on appeal. It lasted six weeks and was heard by Lane and Lord Justices Stephen Brown and O'Connor. They dismissed the appeal with these words: 'As with many cases referred by the Home Secretary to the Court of Appeal, the longer this case has gone on, the more this court has been convinced that the verdict of the jury was correct.'

At this time I knew little of the case of the Birmingham Six, although I remembered a conversation I had had with Douglas Hurd when he was Home Secretary. He was worried about the Guildford Four, he said, but he didn't think there was anything of substance in the case of the Birmingham Six. Against this, I had worked with Gareth Peirce on the Luton post office murder case, and if he believed that the Birmingham Six were innocent, then there must be something in it.

Two years later I was invited by the Sunday Times to conduct my own investigation into the case, and having read the transcript of the appeal hearing as well as Chris Mullin's book, Error of Judgement, interviewed some of the Six, their wives, counsel and several witnesses and visited the locus of the explosions and the police station where the Six were held and allegedly beaten up after arrest, I had not the slightest doubt that they were innocent; and for the three judges to assert that the convictions were *safe and satisfactory* (the stipulated criterion for proof) was not only perverse but an abuse of the English language. The Six's claims that their 'confessions' had been beaten out of them by the police were supported by witnesses who had either seen them being beaten up or had observed the results of it. The 'confessions' themselves of how and where they had planted the bombs were clearly false and contradicted by police evidence; none of which prevented Mr Justice Bridge (now Lord Bridge of Harwich) from rubbishing most of the defence's witnesses and more or less urging the jury to convict. One scientific witness for the prosecution had said that it was *possible* that one of the defendants had traces of nitroglycerine on his hand. In their judgment Lane and his colleagues said that this was *proof* that he had.

Three years after the 1988 appeal and as a result of Esda (Electro-static document analysis) tests on the notebooks of the investigating officers and fresh technical evidence about nitroglycerine, the case returned to the Appeal Court for a third time. Unlike the successful appeal of the Guildford Four, it was contested by the prosecution; but the new evidence was overwhelming and after 16 years inside the Six walked out of the Old Bailey free men. I do not recall any apology being made to them on this occasion.

The crassness of the judgments of Lane, Stephen Brown and O'Connor in the previous appeal being now evident to all, it was expected that Lane at least would have lost no time in retiring. Indeed an editorial in *The Times* urged him to, and some 140 MPs signed a Commons motion to that effect. Had he heeded their advice, he would, I believe, have departed with dignity and honour. But those who wield power are always reluctant to forgo it, and he stayed stubbornly where he was, no doubt hoping that things would soon blow over. And they well might have done had not the case of the Tottenham Three once again raised its ugly head. These three had been convicted of the horrific murder of PC Keith Blakelock in the course of the riots in Broadwater Farm, and sentenced to life imprisonment. A year later their case came up on appeal and despite the unreliability of the evidence leading to their convictions, Lord Lane refused leave to appeal.

Now (1991), as a result of fresh evidence, the case returned to the Appeal Court, the convictions were quashed and the men released. And for the first time to my knowledge the law was prepared to admit its culpability. 'In allowing these appeals,' said Lord Justice Farquharson of the appellants, 'we wish to express our profound regret that they have suffered as a result of the shortcomings of the criminal process.' This was a kind of breakthrough and one hopes that when future miscarriages are corrected such expressions of regret will be considered routine.

Inevitably there were further calls for Lane's resignation, but although by now a wholly discredited figure, he still stayed his hand. Apologists for him said that he would go in his own time, that he was determined not to be pressurised. I have seldom heard a more wretched excuse for staying put. To have condemned nine men who should never have been convicted in the first place to several further years of wrongful imprisonment was an error of the first magnitude. If the managing director of some professional or business concern had made a similar sort of cock-up, and *not once but twice*, he would have been dismissed or obliged to retire without delay. But then the Bench have always believed that they inhabit a rarefied world where normal professional and ethical practices do not apply; a view detrimental to themselves, to society and to justice.

It wasn't until some six weeks ago that Lane, no doubt prodded by the Lord Chancellor, finally threw in the towel. 'Lane's exit,' ran the *Times* headline, 'a relief to friend and foe alike.' It was a sad way for a man of such accomplishments to go. His Achilles' heel, like that of so many of his brethren, was a deep reluctance ever to recognise, let alone admit, that police officers in their misguided zeal to see justice done can and do fix the evidence to secure a conviction and can and do tell lies in the witness box every bit as venal as those of other witnesses. If Geoffrey Lane's going results in a change of attitude by the Bench in this respect, then, quite unintentionally, he will have achieved a much needed reform.

11 April 1992

DIARY

Dominic Lawson

There were some unhappy faces at the election night party held at the Savoy by our proprietor, Mr Conrad Black. They were owned by the champagne socialists – or *gauche caviare*, as the French have it. Although I was sure that the *g.c.* had showed up in anticipation of witnessing the public humiliation of the cream of British conservatism, I still felt some pity as I saw them dejectedly ordering yet another consoling glass of champagne, yet another comforting plateful of lobster. I wanted to say something to cheer them up, but I could find few crumbs of comfort other than those surrounding the goujons of Dover sole. It was at 4.30 in the morning, as I went up to my suite on the fourth floor, that I had an *esprit d'escalier*. The champagne socialists could yet triumph over Conservative greed and self-centredness! All they have to do is to work out the extra tax and national insurance they would have paid under Labour's redistributive policy, and donate it to the Treasury. That is what Labour would have done. Or, if they wanted to be more specific, they could send the money, as regularly as PAYE, to their local NHS hospital or Education Authority. I wish, I wish, I had thought of that while the election results were pouring in: I am sure the suggestion would have brought smiles back to the faces of the Savoy socialists, and the party would have gone with even more of a swing.

18 April 1992

THERE IS A CHOICE: GOOD OR EVIL

John Patten

I believe in God. I worry about Him. I think that He probably worries about me. But to most Christians in this country He now exists not as the omnipresent God of daily life, but only as the God of adversity. Standing in the queue in the House of Commons tea-room on the morning Parliament dissolved, I was given a definition of this God of Adversity by Mr Speaker's Chaplain, the Reverend Donald Grey. 'Yes,' he said, 'it's what I call Funk-Hole Religion.' The bumpy plane ride, the bomb scare at the railway station, and it is, 'Dear God, please get me home.' Pope Pius XII put it another way. '"Help",' he said, 'is a prayer.' Adversity apart, baptisms, marriages and funerals are the only occasions when most of us, in this secular age, display our faith. This demotion of God signals loss of belief in the fundamentals – redemption and damnation – and loss of two of the key drives in the way we behave in our daily lives.

My own bumpy plane ride, which triggered these thoughts, was from London to Cornwall. I flew along the liturgical ley-line that links some of our greatest cathedrals and ends with Pearson's rock-solid Truro edifice. The faith that raised Salisbury, Exeter and Wells was, broadly, sustained through all the succeeding centuries until the present one. It provided a bedrock for civil behaviour. Civility led to eternal life, badness to eternal damnation.

This growth in secularisation, so evident since the Second World War, has had profound effects on how we are now. Death, the gateway to eternal life, has become Death the unthinkable. Health and safety at work regulations replace tough readings from the Gospels, and even tougher ones from the Old Testament. The invention of these absurd groups of Thirtysomethings, Fortysomethings and Fiftysomethings erects morale-boosting barriers against ageing and the ultimate unknown. Science, which has helped so much to prolong the quantity of our years, has had a deep effect on the quality of our faith. Scientific thinking means that all things must be proved before they are. Faith is irrational because it is unprovable. Doubting Thomases have been elevated from the pitiable to the theologically correct. Secularisation is summed up by advertising, pedalling our 'right' to happiness. It also submerges the quaint and old-fashioned idea that in the end happiness comes not from cars, colour televisions and consumables but from within ourselves.

Dwindling belief in redemption and damnation has led to loss of fear of the eternal consequences of goodness and badness. It has had a profound effect on personal morality – especially on criminality. Loss of faith is hard to measure. The best gauge of secularisation available to us statistically is church attendance. This is falling steadily throughout the United Kingdom. In a few areas church attendance remains relatively high, such as in Northern Ireland and parts of Scotland. While peace and personal happiness are not necessarily evident in those places, there does seem some link with lower levels of crime and better education results. The few churches where attendance is rising seem to be those which have allowed much abused fundamentalism to creep in again. In such churches, redemption and damnation are preached as they have been for the thousand years of Christianity in this country.

I expect that a statistician studying the records of post-war Britain could produce some interesting inverse correlations between the decrease of church attendance and the increase in marital breakdown, divorce, abortion and other measures of personal morality. I expect, too, there would be a clear decline in the inclination of the leaders of our Churches to suggest anyone could be bad – governments and institutions, certainly, but individuals, no. A couple of years ago on BBC Radio 4's *Today* programme, when questioned about the causes of crime, I suggested one cause might be that people had chosen to be bad. Brian Redhead's beard quivered in disbelief. So too did Mr Hattersley's jowls during the general election campaign when, on the same programme, he said the idea that crime had anything to do with people being bad was 'patently preposterous'.

It is, to me, self-evident that we are born with a sense of good and evil. It is also self-evident that as we grow up each individual chooses whether to be good or bad. Fear of eternal damnation was a message reinforced through attendance at church every week. The loss of that fear has meant a critical motive has been lost to young people when they decide whether to try to be good citizens or to be criminals.

A decline in church attendance is not, of course, the only reason why crime has gone up all over the Western world in the last 20 or 30 years. Increasing affluence means many more consumer goods lying around to be stolen. There is a standing temptation to break the seventh commandment, particularly when doors and windows are left open (as happens in about a third of all cases of burglary in Greater London).

There have always been people who have chosen to be bad rather than good. Therefore, there has always been crime, and variations in the degree of 'badness' of crime. It is hard to analyse crime historically, as figures do not exist before the 19th century. However, there does seem a clear relationship between the growth of 'Victorian values', church attendance and low crime figures.

In mid-Victorian England, overall reported and recorded crime was lower than now. This was perhaps because there was less to steal. On the other hand, people felt much less restrained about killing each other. 'The use of a revolver by burglars was somewhat frequent,' declared the Report of the Commissioner of the Police of the Metropolis for 1882. The 1880s was a decade that saw constables only carrying out night patrols with the security of large numbers. They also carried guns in the more vulnerable parts of the capital. London, 100 years ago, was a dangerous place. The great Trafalgar Square riots, not of 1986 but of 1886, were described as 'one of the occasions that a crowd managed to get the upper hand of a large body of Police Constables'.

Deterrent punishment alone was not the solution. There were numerous executions in Victorian times, but one detailed study shows that, typically, homicide levels dropped for only a fortnight after a well publicised hanging.

The now derided Victorian 'values' of godfearingness and hope of redemption developed towards the end of the 19th century. They rose, with church attendance, to their apogee in Edwardian times. Despite unemployment at its highest levels, crime fell to its lowest precisely in that near-mythical age when no one bothered to lock his door and the world was a village.

Since the Second World War, crime has risen. So has secularisation. What is to be done? I conducted a small and not at all random survey of clerical opinion. I asked Father Tolkien, J. R. R.'s eldest son and our parish priest, the question, 'Does anyone believe that badness exists any more?' 'Yes, of course,' Father Tolkien said, 'I do.' He took three paces towards the sacristy, swung round, took three paces back again and continued, 'But, of course, there's good in everyone and you have to start there.'

He is right. The very young are the problem, though looking for the good and stopping the bad can seem a Sisyphean task. Go to my local jail in Oxford, hard by the Norman motte and bailey, and you will find that 70 out of every 100 inmates have been in prison before. They are not deterred by incarceration any more than were their forebears by penal servitude or even the lash, the recipients of which showed an alarming propensity to come back for more (particularly pimps). Today a tiny minority of people are responsible each year for the great majority of crimes. And they start very young. Glib talk of 'grubbing up the roots of criminality' means searching for the green shoots in the 10-, 11- and 12-year-olds. While each of these children ultimately has to make his (it is rarely her) own choice between good and bad, he can be helped in that choice by family, school and Church – the forgotten norm of the pre-1950s.

Enough has been written about the decline in family authority and values, and the way in which some have debauched their own authority, being kind, ultimately, to be cruel. Delinquent parents need to feel the contemporary lash if they won't persuade their children to behave, and that is what the Criminal Justice Act allows. Parents will have to be in court with their children, pay their fines, and may be bound over against a hefty sum to stop their delinquent children doing it again. The other side of the coin is to mobilise some schools to be surrogate parents. Who knows, religious teaching may even come back into fashion, too. Communities and voluntary organisations can help persuade those children identified as at risk to grow up straight rather than crooked.

But above all the self-confident voice of the Church should be paramount. It must encourage parents and exhort children. It must recognise that evil exists, not endemically in the corridors of power, but individually in the sinews of society. It must proclaim, too, that responsibilities are as important as rights; that there are no excuses for crime; that the victim comes first; that there is good in everyone; and that even those who have turned out to be bad can be helped to be good.

In this, as in so many areas, the Church's guiding hand could and should be felt in turning the tide of secularisation, in improving church attendance, in beginning the long march back to personal morality.

First, there is the Church Visible, with churches, chapels and its infrastructure of synods, deaneries and dioceses. Second, there is the priesthood. Some very clever, very nice and very holy people need to be turned from internal debates on the relative clap-happiness of church services or the sexual inclinations of the clergy or whether to write letters to the papers campaigning for this or that party in general elections. They need to be turned towards teaching the fundamental lessons of redemption and damnation, right and wrong, good and bad. Third, and most powerfully, there is the Church Invisible, the deep and instinctive gift of faith that turns many an Anglican agnostic or lapsed Catholic to call to God, even if only in adversity.

This belief that, deep down, people still want God, want redemption and want faith, leads me to think, in a politically wind-blown Holy Week, that the message of hope this coming Sunday is still worth a Mass. And, as Jesus promises, the Christian Church will survive and 'the gates of Hell shall not prevail against it'.

The author is Secretary of State for Education and Science.

18 April 1992

BOOKS

FINAL VICTORY TO THE SILK DRESSING-GOWN

John Osborne

NOËL COWARD
by Clive Fisher
Weidenfeld, £17.99, pp. 289

There is a quotation in this book which, quite literally, stopped my breath with dread identification. It is from a letter, written in 1935 from Noël Coward's loyal secretary, Lorn Loraine, to his mother:

> We have got to go very, very easy on money and economise rigidly wherever it is possible. Mind you, I am pretty sure the shortage is only temporary and would never have arisen if it were not for the fact that all Noël's personal earnings have to go into a special tax account as soon as they are received. Still, the fact remains that money is definitely tight and has been for some months. Both bank accounts have overdrafts and there is very little coming in just now.

'There is very little coming in.' How often have I myself been subjected to this gleeful accountant's verdict. The author of this dull and artless biography adds his own jeering stricture:

> Unfortunately, these reversals in prosperity [the poor devil was as good as broke] coincided with a lean period of creativity. There was no drop in the quantity of work Coward produced in the middle and late Thirties, but there is a fall in its level of invention.

A familiar tone of voice, and one that was addressed to me directly the other day when a man at lunch asked me what I did for a living. Usually, I say 'writer'. 'Playwright' sounds rather presumptuous, like calling yourself a poet. Then he asked my name. Perhaps I should have equivocated and said Noël Coward or David Hare, but I owned up. 'Oh yes,' he said, with all the dislike and distrust my odd profession inspires. 'You've just had a *come-back*, haven't you?'

Coward was a working-dog of his calling as actor and writer all his life. By the end of a retrieved career in cabaret he was also, in the unkind words of an American tabloid, 'the highest paid British tulip ever imported into the United States'. It may seem that he had achieved the most enviable life, doing all the things he wanted with minimal effort, hopping on and off steamships as he pleased. But behind it all there lay prodigious effort and the rewards often seem rather meagre. After a lifetime of what young men today would regard as masochistic drudgery, he was still unable to earn enough to appease the Inland Revenue and assure himself of some reward and comfort in a rather cruelly induced old age.

The reminder of the master of self-invention, limping finally off to a forwarding address in Switzerland with the consolation of a last-minute knighthood, confirms the impression of a rather inelegant exit from the world's stage of his own creation. No wonder he was perhaps over-effusive in his gratitude to America:

> My own dear land which for years has robbed me of
> most of my earnings, withheld all official honours from
> me and . . . frequently, made me very unhappy.

The predominantly lower-middle-class English Press could never restrain their spite against someone who must surely be of their own kind (from Twickenham, for God's sake), who had sustained a legend about himself and whatever such hacks think are the rewards of fame – ill-imagined debauchery, I suppose. But Coward's physical appetites were constrained by a thirst for work. He lived on chocolate and cigarettes. No gluttony there. As for sex, Mr Fisher's book promises revelations which simply don't exist, and for very good reason. Old Noël, whatever his protestations about 'being no good at love', was too busy and self-preoccupied to *be* any good at it.

There simply isn't much left to be said about Coward, as this slovenly and pointless re-hash confirms. (Although I did learn that he wanted to play Madam Arcati himself and that the Blithe Spirit of Elvira was named after Binkie Beaumont's housekeeper, the one who denounced my social promotion so roundly when it was suggested I might move to Lord North Street, with the words, 'No 'e's not ready for it yet'. She was right.)

I had thought that Fisher or someone might come up with some insights about the nature of homosexual deceit and dissembling, but that now seems too much to expect. Coward's spirit of evasion is, at the last, impenetrable. Concealment was first nature to him and, most of all, he lacked any sense of awe, except at the prospect of his own next achievement. 'It's my best, it has "smash hit" written all over it', he wrote to Beaumont, his treacherous ally. Such a statement, on any terms, seems incomprehensible, no, meaningless.

As to my own feelings about him, I find that they have changed. For a long time I thought I had perhaps behaved churlishly and with not much lustre or imagination in the face of his own generosity to me. Then last year I came upon the telegram he sent to me from Switzerland: 'I LOVE YOU – NOEL'. What may have prompted it, I can't remember, but I was strangely astonished by its very lack of either implication or obligation.

We had many things in common: social backgrounds, more or less; professional progress; even the same slugging out with the Lord Chamberlain. The insulting assessments on his plays from that office almost defy belief. But I still feel that the Master did irreparable damage to my profession and all those in it. No one has yet managed to dispel the aura with which he surrounded the very word 'theatre', an abiding synonym

'Don't put yourself down, Ben.'

for superficiality and deception. Intelligent people who read new novels if they can afford them and study the form carefully in their film-going remain wary about setting foot in the perfidious playhouse. I see only too well what they mean.

I once said that it was impossible to imagine Coward at prayer, let alone on his knees. That may not be a fault, after all. Pride has never seemed to me to be a great sin, unlike avarice or envy. But I do believe he gave theatricality a bad name for good. The term 'kitchen sink' was a lead weight from the outset. The silk dressing-gown won the day, as the present applause for *The Chalk Garden* revival makes plain.

Finally, one of the recurring tediums of the chafingly off-hand *Sunday Times/Independent* know-all, imagine-nothing style in which this book is written, is the author's repeated reference to Coward's lack of education. He is not the first to seize upon it. Binkie used to relish saying, to myself of all people, 'Well, of course, you know – Noël's quite uneducated.' Mr Fisher went to Oxford. It is clear enough from this sneering and inept stab at diminishing a talent which informed and altered the century, that slickness will get you anywhere these days, and with pretty paltry effort.

It is also plain that Noël Coward could put a sentence together better than any cocky little detractor from Academe or wherever. Perhaps those who seem obsessed with what they call 'racism' or 'sexism' might now turn their attention to this bizarre 'educationism'.

2 May 1992

LOW LIFE

HACK OFF

Jeffrey Bernard

It came as no great shock to me to be fired by the *Sunday Mirror* last week. I was only surprised that the editor, Bridget Rowe, bothered to let me know. It was the first and only occasion in all her time at the helm of that ship on which she has bothered to communicate with me. Even Eve Pollard once took me to lunch. For all I know it might have been Ms Rowe who told Robert Maxwell to go take a running jump. It was a black day for me and many others when that man kicked Mike Molloy upstairs. So, goodbye Mirror Group Newspapers after 27 years of on-and-off hacking. I must say that in the last four years or so I never wrote a single column that came anywhere near pleasing me although I received three proposals of marriage from so many demented female readers, one free ride in a taxi from a driver who recognised me and a five-pound note from a reader who wrote to say that I sounded like a man in need of a drink. Cheers to that.

From time to time I would moan about the difficulty of writing for the *Sunday Mirror* and I always had the horrible feeling that I must write down to its readers as opposed to *Spectator* readers. I confided the fact to Keith Waterhouse one day and he said, 'A juggler doesn't change his act because he changes his venue.' How very right and true. But with Mike Molloy it was different and not quite so like defecating in public. In his time I never once faxed a column or dictated one to a copy-taker because it was always a pleasure to go to the office and deliver it personally. He always had the time to read it after telling me to help myself to a drink and he always had something encouraging to say – a pat on the head, so to speak, for this little boy, who I am ashamed to say still needs one from time to time. But an editor who is always too busy to give you the time of day isn't on top of his or her job.

I first worked for Molloy in 1969 when he was the editor of the *Daily Mirror Magazine*. Jolly days they were too. Incidentally, Eve Pollard was the fashion editor and I worked alongside Bill Hagerty, Scarth Flett, Russell Miller and Colin Bell when I wasn't downing oysters in Wheeler's in Old Compton Street. When the magazine finally folded Colin Bell hit the nail on the head when he said, 'Gravy train derailed'. I think it must have been then when I took to drink.

The next job on what was then IPC was a twice-weekly column for the *Sporting Life*. That wasn't exactly a gravy train but it kept a pack of wolves from the door while ruining my pancreas. The letter of dismissal from the editor said my behaviour was unpardonable. And now, last week, it was called unforgivable. I would say it was unfortunate. I should never have taken time off and away from this awful machine, Monica, to go to Australia. It has resulted in a double kicking of sorts, since what I wrote for the *Sunday Express* who arranged the trip out there was postponed. Bridget Rowe's secretary told me I was forbidden to write for the *Sunday Express*, but why not? I was never ever under contract to the *Sunday Mirror* and Ms Rowe wouldn't have subsidised a trip to Notting Hill Gate.

But never mind all that; the bad news is that my daughter has just shaved a patch of her lovely hair and she was to sit for her portrait to be painted by Michael Corkrey in two weeks' time. And I have just heard that his portrait of me is to be exhibited in the National Portrait Gallery soon. I am delighted for him and Guy Hart who commissioned the painting. Perhaps Mirror Group Newspapers may buy it. Or slash it? From where I am sitting everything, but everything, is quite absurd.

2 May 1992

POLES APART

Radek Sikorski

Dwór Chobielin, Poland

It was a Friday afternoon. I was, as it happened, on the roof of Chobielin, the old manor house I'm restoring, checking the tiles. They are old and must be laid in an old-fashioned way; the workmen don't always get it right. This time they did, and I was just about to pronounce myself satisfied when one of them ran up, panting, from the keeper's lodge. There was a telephone call, he said, all the way from Warsaw.

I ran back to get it. The line was faint – the last mile of telephone cable leading to Chobielin is of pre-war vintage, the wind rocks the wires and creates an echo – but I made out the voice of Jan Parys, Poland's first civilian, non-communist Minister of Defence. I knew him slightly. We belonged to the same political clubs in Warsaw; his wife, Poland's Madame de Staël, runs one of the city's best-known salons. He had worked on negotiating the withdrawal of Soviet troops from Poland, and had a reputation for toughness.

A few years ago I wrote a book about Afghanistan, and had consequently brushed up against the British and American military establishments. Minister Parys is a staunch Atlanticist, interested in developing better links with those countries. Now, over the crackling telephone wire, Parys asked whether I would become his deputy, responsible for security policy and foreign relations. It meant giving up my job, taking a salary of $266 per month, slowing down work on the house, and living in polluted Warsaw. I rang my fiancée; within the hour I rang back the minister and accepted.

But those telephone calls were our first mistake. They were bugged, and the listening ears of military intelligence were not friendly. While the old Polish security police had been purged two years earlier, military intelligence and counter-intelligence, known in Polish as WSI, were untouched. They did not like my appointment. I had travelled in Afghanistan on the side of the mujahedeen, and in Angola with Savimbi. My sympathies were unlikely to lie with a corrupt, disloyal, unreformed communist secret service.

So as soon as they heard my name, they knew exactly what to do. By Sunday morning – meaning that they submitted the information, already laundered through several hands, between Friday night and Saturday noon – the London *Observer* ran a short, slanted little story about me in its gossip column. That article did what it was meant to do, causing a furore in Poland ('why are our ministers known to the British press and not to us?') and calling the appointment to the attention of President Lech Walesa.

It is a time-honoured method. In provincial societies, people presume foreigners to be right. When the communists wanted to broadcast something widely, they bounced the information off foreign sources, even if it had to be the *Morning Star*. Nowadays, when President Walesa wants to have flattering things said about himself, he gets the television news presenters to quote the *New York Times*, never the Polish press. The hack at the *Observer* who gave his name to the story patted himself on the back for his 'scoop' the following week; I later confirmed that the WSI (more on them later) had been the ultimate source of the story.

I won't dwell on the media campaign which followed. In practice, Poland has no libel laws: you can sue, but it takes years and the court usually awards negligible damages. So I could do nothing when the press hinted that British intelligence paid my university fees (I had a standard ILEA grant), and insinuated a 'friendship' with Minister Parys, whatever that meant. I could not object when I was pilloried for 'disloyally' choosing to take a British passport when, in 1987, I thought I would never be allowed to return to Poland again. 'Radek Sikorski really ought to be in gaol,' wrote one charming woman, 'for travelling armed in Afghanistan in 1986 without the permission of Poland's [then communist] government.'

Even *Gazeta Wyborcza*, a Polish newspaper which prides itself on its cosmopolitanism, hit positively Stalinist chords and called me 'an agent of foreign capital'. My crime was to have worked for a British company trying to secure investments in Poland. A friend rang up, laughing, to say that, according to Warsaw gossip, I had never been an undergraduate at Oxford at all. The word was out: I had invented my entire curriculum vitae. Throughout my 100 days in office not once did a Polish journalist ring me to check a story.

But my worst offence by far was to be too pro-Western, too pro-Nato. Those who attacked me and Jan Parys the most viciously were either former communists or old dissidents, members of the former opposition whose sympathies also lie on the Left. There is virtually no newspaper, magazine, or radio station which one of these groups does not control. They fully supported the old Polish defence establishment, which had committed itself if not to remaining in the Warsaw Pact, then at least to approaching the West at a snail's pace. I had not anticipated the sheer malice of the attacks. But then I had not expected that the man spearheading this drive away from the West, back towards the East, would be President Walesa.

My ministerial office was in a small villa across the street from the presidential palace. On the other side, the Soviet Embassy – a building much bigger than the presidential palace – towered above me. Inside, fake leather armchairs and brown wallpaper testified to the tastes of previous occupants. General Jaruzelski was said to have recorded the television speech announcing the imposition of martial law there in December 1981. It felt odd to sit in an armchair from which orders for arrests and internments were once barked.

I didn't bother to have the villa swept for bugs. If our neighbours across the garden wanted to listen, a directional microphone would have done the trick. Fortunately, the villa stood near Lazienki, Warsaw's St James's Park. Over the next few weeks I became good friends with the ducks in the pond, and I ordered a move to a different location as soon as possible.

My first day in office, I asked for a telephone connection to Brussels. 'Three hours wait, two with luck, Minister' came the reply. Ordinary Warsaw phones now connect within a couple of tries. But using the antiquated Defence Ministry exchange I could not dial direct to anywhere outside Warsaw. Those trying to reach me were often connected to the teachers' common room of a primary school in another part of town. Yet I was responsible for the foreign relations of a 220,000-man army. I thought with admiration of my predecessor. How did he manage to do his job without talking to Washington, Moscow or London several times a day? I threatened a couple of generals with early retirement, and a satellite line was installed.

True, an official, ministerial telephone stood by the side of my desk. It was a large chest covered with inscrutable dials and buttons, just like a time machine from a 1930s science-fiction movie. I told the staff to take it away and give me an ordinary Panasonic.

They were surprised: 'But, Minister, you are entitled to a telephone as large as this.' Apparently the size of one's telephone used to be a phallic symbol, a sign of political potency. But of all my office appliances only the shredder worked tolerably. How did the communists manage to run anything at all?

A Polish eagle with a crown, our pre- and post-communist state symbol, hung on the wall. On the reverse side was an old cardboard portrait of Lenin. You could change from Lenin to the eagle, and back again, with just a flick of the wrist.

I soon learned that, although I was a minister, there was virtually no ministry for me to run. I had an office, the Defence Minister had an office, and the other Deputy Minister had an office – and that was it. There was no policy department, no strategic think-tanks, and the first independent Polish operational plans were written on Parys's orders.

In the past, plans had simply been made in Moscow and delivered in sealed envelopes. We received intelligence assessments which still spoke of German revanchism raising its ugly head, and warned of menacing Nato aircraft encroaching on Polish airspace. Minister Parys said that these comments might be slightly misplaced; within a week, the reports described Soviet revanchism raising its ugly head and menacing Russian aircraft. Promotions had always been given for political obedience rather than excellence of analysis. Old habits die hard.

The chief of my secretariat was a slow-witted, dull-eyed, sycophantic former communist. While you cannot rid the Polish army of all its former Communist Party members (membership was required for promotion) you can try to distinguish between those who joined for pragmatic reasons – most of whom were excellent soldiers and very good officers – and those who were the active agents of Soviet control.

This is not as hard as you might imagine. There is a communist way of thinking, and a communist way of behaviour. Rather than taking a problem and finding a solution, someone trained in dialectical materialism will find an excuse for why the problem cannot be solved. Such a person will never give you a straight answer, he won't look you in the eye. Rather than saying what he believes is true or right, he tells you what he thinks you want to hear. I fired my chief of secretariat within the week. He has just recently been rehired and given a promotion.

Minister Parys was also busy with personnel matters. At the first meeting of the Military Council, he asked for the resignation of those generals who felt they could not support the idea of Poland moving closer to Nato. Soviet spies were also given seven days to come forward with impunity. Several did. We bade them farewell with Georgian champagne, toasts and gifts of garish landscape paintings. It was the most civilised purge ever conducted.

But while generals could be fired and my staff were under my control, the WSI – for now we must return to them – were not. When we arrived, they were the last, functioning communist organisation which could have taken control of the country should a chillier wind begin to blow from the East once again. And until well after the August coup in the Soviet Union, the WSI leadership in Poland still thought that their time might come.

Remember: this was no ordinary military reconnaissance organisation. After martial law, General Wojciech Jaruzelski, himself a former Defence Minister, had relied upon the WSI to run the army and the country. Current and past WSI officers owned flats and foreign bank accounts, they ran gun-running and smuggling operations, they had their own sources of income and their own contacts in the East and the West. In the last few months of communism, they had sold their secrets to anybody who would pay. They were rich men, virtually self-governing, and they were far from unique in post-communist Europe. They have Russian counterparts – also under unclear political control, if any – and I know of Rumanian ones as well. We will hear more of them in the years to come.

After Jaruzelski's fall, the WSI began looking around for a new patron. Just about the same time, Lech Walesa, Poland's newly elected president, was also looking around for a new power base. Walesa had already alienated most of his former associates – first the old dissidents, then the new Right, who had helped him become president. He saw a weak parliament, an impotent government administration. He saw squabbling politicians, and petty bureaucrats. No one seemed to have any real power – except the old guard. Instead of trying to build a new consensus Walesa took the easy route. It seemed to me that they would help him maintain power, supplying him with information on ministers and potential challengers. He would keep their organisation intact. There is no grand conspiracy – it was all perfectly sensible.

It still seems unbelievable, even to me who watched it at close quarters. How Lech Walesa, the symbol of the anti-communist revolutions of 1980 and 1989, ultimately came to co-operate with the very people he had deposed – and why no one predicted such an outcome –

deserves a longer explanation. There is no room for that here. Perhaps it is sufficient to quote *The Spectator* of 24 November 1990, when I tried to explain the Walesa phenomenon. I described him as 'uncouth, unpredictable, irresponsible, dictatorial, vain and manipulative', yet still hoped that 'he will find himself institutionally tamed ... he will set a straightforward agenda and pursue it with his customary determination'. But the moral authority of the Polish presidency was not good enough for him. Like the peasant he is at heart, Walesa likes the physical exercise of power, he likes to issue decrees, to order people about, to hire and fire prime ministers at will. Instead of pursuing a straightforward agenda, Walesa pursues power for its own sake. No one understood this better than the old communists, and no one was better prepared to help him. We had to purge the WSI, both for internal and external reasons. Before Poland could be a credible partner for the West, the service had to stop leaking. And before our democracy could be secure, one branch of government could not be permitted to spy on another.

We, the nominal bosses, had to capture the institution in a sudden swoop. We lured its chief – Admiral Wawrzyniak – out of his office on a pretext: an armed team stood by to capture the archives in case of resistance. I was there. I wouldn't have missed watching the death of Poland's last communist institution. But that was also the day that the political battle between the president and the government of Prime Minister Jan Olszewski escalated beyond repair. Walesa had been deprived of his private spy network, and he was livid.

The next skirmishes were over policy. In a communist country, all government departments were ultimately run by the Politburo and the Central Committee. In a post-communist country, it is as if you have removed the brain from the nervous system. Government departments behave like unco-ordinated limbs, acting in opposition to one another and to the body itself. It is confusing even if all the various branches have the same policy. It becomes a total muddle when, for example, the Defence Ministry and the prime minister want to bring the country closer to Nato, and the president does not.

There were amusing incidents. I was in Brussels, pestering Nato officials, hoping for broader contacts – things like help in teaching foreign languages to our officers – and trying to persuade them that Poland should be considered part of the West and should lie within the Nato security perimeter. Unknown to me, Walesa was in Germany on the same day, advocating the formation of a new organisation, comprising all post-communist and post-Soviet countries, which he called 'Nato-bis'. Surprised, I rang his chancery to find out what this meant. None of his staff knew. But it sounded a lot like the old Warsaw Pact. I wonder what our Western partners imagined our policy to be.

Later I was at a diplomatic party in Warsaw, chatting, as it happened, to the local KGB station chief. 'Don't you know?' he asked, surprised. 'The Polish–Russian treaty has been finalised.' I didn't know. Neither did the prime minister. Walesa, it emerged, was running his own foreign policy behind the government's back.

Now we did not object to the idea of a treaty – a similar one was signed with Germany – but we did object to some of the clauses, or rather, one clause in particular. The Russians had agreed, at last, to withdraw their troops from Poland. But they wanted to maintain financial and intelligence assets in the country. Their military bases – which include airfields, barracks, and shooting ranges – lie, *de facto*, outside Polish control. They are already used to evade customs and excise taxes and to smuggle goods between Russia and Western Europe. They are huge money-making operations for the old Soviet military establishment. If anyone wanted to smuggle nuclear material out of Russia, they would have made the perfect route.

We wanted them closed. The Russians wanted to turn some of them into 'joint ventures', legalising their presence forever. Walesa wanted to go to Moscow and sign a treaty with his new friend, Boris Yeltsin, and he was prepared to let the Russians have their way. It was only the prime minister's veto – he sent a cipher to Moscow, categorically telling the president he did not agree to the clause – and the threat of a major scandal which forced the president to stand up to the Russians at the last minute. A new text was improvised and written out in longhand ten minutes before the signing ceremony.

It was our last success. Not long afterwards, Parys was forced to resign. The prime minister hoped that his absence might induce the president to calm down. My resignation followed. A few days later, the entire government fell. Now, President Walesa has appointed Waldemar Pawlak, a 32-year-old farmers' party leader, as the new prime minister. Pawlak, a leader of the former United Peasants' Party, was a loyal ally of the Communist Party in Poland's old puppet parliament. He negotiated on the communist side during the round-table negotiations that brought down the old régime in 1989. At last Walesa can work with a man he feels comfortable with: a prime minister who comes directly from the old communist camp, and will not mind who he chooses for friends. So ended our battle.

Were we really so controversial? When I came to the job, I was excited by the prospect of helping transform a Warsaw Pact army, trained and equipped by the former Soviet Union – whose officers had sworn their loyalty to the Soviet Union – into a modern Polish army, loyal to Poland only. I had hoped we could make our army into a realistic partner for the West, and for Nato. It seemed, a few months ago, that we had a chance.

We were criticised for firing people. But while I am sorry about bringing so many illustrious communist careers to an end, we couldn't talk about joining Nato at the political level while our Moscow-trained operatives were getting caught conducting inept intelligence operations in Western capitals, while some of our Moscow-trained generals kept in touch with their old chums in Russia and while our military hardware remained incompatible with that of the West. Changes had to be made. And while we were not trying to antagonise Russia, we did need to disentangle our security apparatus from theirs. We came into conflict with the president, but that was not the point. Our real fight was not against Walesa himself but against the network of communist élites who plague the reform process, not only in Poland but all over the old Eastern bloc.

I fear that Europe is in danger of dividing again. The fault line will not follow the Iron Curtain and it will no longer separate the free world from its totalitarian neighbours. Instead, it will separate enthusiastically pro-Western, pro-capitalist states from those who have not made a clean break with the past.

On this reckoning, Hungary already lies on the Western side, while Bulgaria, Rumania and the former Soviet Union look set to remain in the East. Czechoslovakia is already dividing, with Bohemia joining the West and Slovakia, with its new ex-communist leadership, looking as if it will slide east too.

Poland, whose confused political culture puts it right in the middle, could still go either way. If my 100 days mattered – and I'd like to think that they did – it was because they coincided with the few months when Poland's leaders were trying to uproot the country's old communist élites for good, trying to bring Poland back into the Western camp. We lost this round, but there will be another.

27 June 1992